SHAKESPEARE'S
ROMAN PLAYS

SHAKE-SPEARE'S ROMAN PLAYS

The Function of Imagery in the Drama

By MAURICE CHARNEY

Harvard University Press, Cambridge

Third printing, 1968

Distributed in Great Britain by Oxford University Press, London

Publication of this book has been aided by a grant
from the Ford Foundation

Typography by Burton J. Jones

Library of Congress Catalog Card Number 61–8838

Printed in the United States of America

for
G. E. BENTLEY
magister ludi

ACKNOWLEDGMENTS

I am deeply indebted to the following persons who read the manuscript in various stages of composition and who offered painstaking and valuable suggestions: G. E. Bentley, Alan Downer, Francis Fergusson, Wilson Follett, Edward Hubler, S. F. Johnson, and Harry Levin. The indebtedness to G. E. Bentley is further acknowledged in the dedication, which is still only a token of a profound appreciation. I owe much, in a general and personal way, to the humane and critical values of Harry Levin and the late F. O. Matthiessen. To my wife, alas, I cannot inscribe my gratitude for typing the manuscript, but there still remains something to be said for abundant wit, a marvelous eye for *bêtises*, and an elaborate and unacknowledged collaboration. It is difficult to register my debt to my parents, whose fidelity and devotion are at the same time uncanny and overwhelming.

I wish to thank the Editors of *ELH* and *Studies in Philology* and the Director of Rutgers University Press (*Essays in Literary History*, ed. Rudolf Kirk and C. F. Main) for granting permission to use material which first appeared in their publications in a rather different form. Many kindly librarians at Princeton and Rutgers universities, as well as at the New York Public Library, have been of great help to me. I am also indebted to the Research Council of Rutgers University for a grant during the summer of 1958.

A final word must be added for the diligence, charm, and whimsicality of three booksellers: Sam Colton, Peter Lader, and Irving Binkin.

New Brunswick, New Jersey
October 1960   M. C.

CONTENTS

SHAKESPEARE'S
ROMAN PLAYS

Chapter I

INTRODUCTION:
THE FUNCTION OF
IMAGERY IN THE DRAMA

ACCORDING to a customary and rather inaccurate analogy, a play is like a musical score: both are "realized" only in performance. In this realization the play as literature or as poem may seem to disappear and what remains be merely "good theater." To the literate public the theater smacks of popular entertainment, and "good theater" refers, paradoxically, to a play not worthy of serious literary interest. The Broadway production of *Anastasia* in 1954–55, for example, created a sense of guilt in some viewers at being moved by an obviously contrived seventeen-minute recognition scene; the power of the actors seemed to prevail over the better judgment of the audience. Or plays that are primarily vehicles for a star to show off his brilliance — as the cadenzas in a concerto display the virtuoso's powers — also support the feeling that the play as read is quite different from the play as performed. We recall that the Elizabethans spoke of acting as "feigning," a sort of histrionic legerdemain by which something attractive and entertaining — "good theater" — can be made out of patently worthless materials. I have perhaps exaggerated the dangers of being taken in by the illusion of the play, but suspicion of the theater is a part of our literary tradition, if not of our moral tradition as well.

One reaction to the uncertainty of judgment about plays is to consider them completely outside the slippery canons of theatrical art; a Shakespearean play, for example, is basically a poetic text which ought to be studied with the same care as a difficult poem of Donne. What happens to this play in the theater is something so deceptive and so unworthy of its original that it ought not to enter into our appraisal; it is not properly part of the play at all. The strongest statement of this position was made by Charles Lamb in his essay "On the Tragedies of Shakspeare Considered with Reference to Their Fitness for Stage-Representation" (1811). The fact that Lamb saw only seriously altered and "improved" versions of Shakespeare does not seem to me to change the tenor of his argument. He believed that the theater was fundamentally inadequate to represent the greatness of Shakespeare's poetry, as in *Macbeth*:

The state of sublime emotion into which we are elevated by those images of night and horror which Macbeth is made to utter, that solemn prelude with which he entertains the time till the bell shall strike which is to call him to murder Duncan— when we no longer read it in a book, when we have given up that vantage ground of abstraction which reading possesses over seeing, and come to see a man in his bodily shape before our eyes actually preparing to commit a murder, if the acting be true and impres-

2

sive, as I have witnessed it in Mr. K.'s performance of that part, the painful anxiety about the act, the natural longing to prevent it while it yet seems unperpetrated, the too close pressing semblance of reality, give a pain and an uneasiness which totally destroy all the delight which the words in the book convey, where the deed doing never presses upon us with the painful sense of presence. . . .[1]

This leads in the next paragraph to the statement that "to see Lear acted . . . has nothing in it but what is painful and disgusting. . . . the Lear of Shakespeare cannot be acted." Lamb recoils from the emotional effects of the theater, "the too close pressing semblance of reality," and retreats into "that vantage ground of abstraction which reading possesses over seeing." He vividly describes just those powerful evocations of the theater from which he wishes to shield himself.

The sentiments of Lamb are clearly echoed in Norman Holmes Pearson's lecture at the Yale Shakespeare Festival:

If in practise I prefer to read *Antony and Cleopatra* rather than see it performed on the stage, it is because the process of understanding is simplified on the printed page. The words which I can thus see with concentration, take precedence over the action, which I can only fancy. I can linger over the printed words, delaying the action until I have absorbed the words, as I linger over the verbal counters of a poem.[2]

This statement describes quite frankly our modern predilection to "linger over the printed words" and make Shakespeare "closet drama," but the motive for simplifying the "process of understanding" is never directly indicated as in Lamb.

B. L. Joseph's book on Elizabethan acting is also, in a sense, in the tradition of Lamb; his defense of rhetoric can be construed as a defense of the integrity of the poem against the ways it may be distorted in the theater. In the final chapter, "The Poem and the Theatre," Joseph writes: "In the theatre, as in the study, the poet's words are all that count. From them alone is it possible to create his play over again." [3] And elsewhere he says: "By declaiming his lines with the action fit for every word and sentence the Elizabethan players ensured that the audience could experience the words heard in the theatre in the manner that literature is experienced from the printed page." [4] Joseph does not reject the theater as Lamb does, but he sees it chiefly as a means for the public declamation of poetry. This emphasis seems to lie behind his constant analogy between Shakespeare's plays and opera — in both, the singing or orating of the text takes precedence over the creation of character or the development of dramatic conflict.

Although Lamb, Pearson, and Joseph differ widely among themselves, they do seem to concur on one point: that Shakespeare's plays are primarily poetic texts, which may for convenience be performed in theaters, but which do not basically require such performance and may more profitably be read, either to oneself or aloud. I have set forth this argument very explicitly because I believe that most literate persons think of Shakespeare in this way. We study Shakespeare's plays in school and we continue to think of them as texts to be studied. But this point of view does not seem to me to do justice to Shakespeare. The words are, after all, only a part of the full imaginative experience of the play, and, especially for a writer so thoroughly immersed in the theater as Shakespeare, there are many nonverbal elements in a performance which work together with the poetry of the text and help to express it. We may say, then, that the

4

play an audience sees creates its own set of images and metaphors that are not merely those of the spoken lines.

It is in this third dimension of the drama that Cocteau tells us we must seek "poetry of the theater," as he develops the idea in his Preface to *Les Mariés de la Tour Eiffel*:

The action of my play is in images (*imagée*) while the text is not: I attempt to substitute a 'poetry of the theater' for 'poetry in the theater.' Poetry in the theater is a piece of lace which it is impossible to see at a distance. Poetry of the theater would be coarse lace; a lace of ropes, a ship at sea. *Les Mariés* should have the frightening look of a drop of poetry under the microscope. The *scenes* are integrated like the *words* of a poem.[5]

The poetry here is expressed in a dramatic form, and the poetic play becomes something more than either poetry or "good theater" — it has its own untranslatable and integral qualities. This concept of "poetry of the theater" has proved very attractive to modern dramatists experimenting in poetic drama. Tennessee Williams, for example, explains his *Camino Real* in these terms:

We all have in our conscious and unconscious minds a great vocabulary of images, and I think all human communication is based on these images as our dreams; and a symbol in a play has only one legitimate purpose which is to say a thing more directly and simply and beautifully than it could be said in words. . . . Sometimes it would take page after tedious page of exposition to put across an idea that can be said with an object or a gesture on the lighted stage.[6]

Unfortunately for Shakespeare, the gap in time between our age and his has removed some of the urgency of his objects and gestures on the lighted stage. Yet such dramatic effects as the intimate, personal details that precede the sudden appearance of Caesar's Ghost — Brutus takes the instru-

5

ment from his sleeping servant and opens a book to a dog-eared page; or Charmian's straightening the crown of her dead mistress; or Coriolanus' holding his mother by the hand, silent, before he pronounces the mercy that will be most fatal to him — all of these touches are the essence of dramatic poetry. The eloquence here is in the action, and the words that accompany the gestures serve to heighten and strengthen the effect.

The present study attempts to consider Shakespeare's Roman plays (*Julius Caesar, Antony and Cleopatra,* and *Coriolanus*) as poetry of the theater. The approach is chiefly through the imagery of these plays, both verbal and non-verbal, but the main purpose is a close examination of the plays themselves. I try to do justice both to the plays as read and to the plays as performed, within the limits, of course, of what we know of the Elizabethan theater and Elizabethan stagecraft. My orientation is similar to the "New Approach" to Shakespeare's imagery outlined by R. A. Foakes:

For the study of drama a new definition of imagery, one derived from drama, is needed. The general tendency to approach Shakespeare's plays as dramatic poems has led critics to stress poetic imagery, and its subject-matter especially, above all things. . . . while it is possible for a poem to be a metaphor, to exist only in an image or images, this cannot properly be said of a Shakespearian play. The poetic image in a play is set in a context not of words alone, but of words, dramatic situation, interplay of character, stage-effect, and is also placed in a time sequence.[7]

The function of imagery in the poetic drama is thus neither a question of words nor of stage effects alone, but of "the realization of the verbal image in dramatic terms. . . ."[8] How this realization is brought about can only be deter-

6

mined by a careful analysis of the dramatic contexts of the individual plays. It is quite obvious that Shakespeare did not usually create poetic imagery for its own sake on the principle of "the more the better." In some plays just the opposite seems to be true. *Julius Caesar*, for example, shows what appears to be a deliberate curbing of the verbal imagination, a "Roman" style suitable to the Roman subject matter. *Coriolanus*, too, has many examples of a sort of "depoeticizing" by which a lyric and imaginative figure of speech is used pejoratively. These examples illustrate Shakespeare's strict insistence on dramatic function and purpose as opposed to sheer poetic expression.

I use the word "image" in this study in two distinct senses, one verbal and the other nonverbal. According to the traditional definition, a verbal image must be a figure of speech, usually some form of metaphor, simile, or personification. In many modern studies, however, the concept of an image is extended to include all references to a significant subject matter, even quite casual and oblique ones that are not properly figures of speech.[9] This is the "leading" or "iterative" imagery that, by force of repetition, gives a Shakespearean play its distinctive character. The frequent talk of serpents in *Antony and Cleopatra,* or the repeated mention of blood in *Julius Caesar*, or the harping on food and eating in *Coriolanus* all serve to emphasize these themes in the mind of the audience. The figures of speech and the passing references to significant subjects work together to establish the symbolic lines of the plays.

The nonverbal or "presentational" [10] imagery, which I have already referred to as "poetry of the theater," may also have an important function in the symbolic movement of a play. I use the word "presentational" as a convenient term for the large body of images that is not part of the spoken words of the text, but directly presented in the theater. Some synonyms might be "dramatic metaphor" or "stage image" (as contrasted with "verbal" image). In *Antony and Cleopatra*, for example, it is Cleopatra's suicide by the asp which brings the serpent theme of the play to a culmination in the stage action. Throughout the play the serpent image has suggested evil and death, but the serpent that Cleopatra now uses becomes a presentational image of life, or a kind of life-in-death, as she asks triumphantly: "Dost thou not see my baby at my breast,/ That sucks the nurse asleep?" (5.2.312–13). The serpent is now an image to the audience in a very obvious and literal sense, and it will be one of the special purposes of this study to call attention to these presentational images in the Roman plays.

This type of imagery suggests certain differences between the drama and other literary forms, since it is here that the drama moves outside the reaches of a strictly verbal art. It is possible to have completely nonverbal plays, or pantomimes, or to see and enjoy a play in a foreign language we do not understand. There is obviously a significant language of gesture and stage properties which communicates meaning to us. As a matter of historical record, we know that Elizabethan companies played in English to German audiences with great success, "yet the Germans, not vnderstanding a worde they sayde, both men and women, flocked wonderfully to see theire gesture and Action, rather than heare them, speaking English which they vnderstoode not. . . ." [11] But a poem or a novel in an uncomprehended language would be incomprehensible, although we might take a certain delight in the sensuous pattern of the sound. Of course, the fact that a play can communicate meaning without words does not necessarily mean that this is a virtue, or that plays can be judged on this basis alone. Such a view would be a needless exaggeration of presentational imagery and an abandonment of the rich resources the drama shares with other verbal arts. In the present state of Shakespeare criticism, however, we need particularly to draw attention away from the verbal imagery and to show in what specific ways a play is not like a poem or a novel.

In some cases the words of a play may actually become a factor in the stage production. Shakespeare often uses verbal description for purposes that are now easily accomplished by technology. This is especially true of elaborate effects of lighting, although it is also true to a lesser extent of sound. A modern playwright would probably not indulge in such deliberate verbal scene-painting as that of the storm in *Julius Caesar* or "the mask of night" in *Romeo and Juliet*; the presentation of these effects could be entrusted to the technical staff. Whether the plays would profit from doing mechanically what Shakespeare did by words is not a relevant question. I am only trying to suggest that some of the verbal imagery in Shakespeare had a very specific dramatic function. The fact that this imagery is so intimately connected with the stage production does not, of course, diminish its aesthetic significance. Perhaps the Elizabethans were at an artistic advantage in using imagery for what we now do by machines, for the image-realizing powers of the mind are full and complex, while even a spectacular stage effect may soon seem labored, artificial, and unnecessary.

We need to insist, finally, that imagery can express the quality and intentions of a poetic play with directness, precision, and force. To use a figure, we may say that images "seed" the mind, if we understand by this a process of growth which may not be immediately visible. We may not realize that a certain image is significant until its fourth or fifth occurrence, yet when we do, our awareness is bound to be influenced by these earlier uses and to project forward to later examples. Since the play is a continuous temporal unit, this sense of the direction in which the action is moving is quite important — we cannot go back to pick up something we missed. In practical terms I do not think the ability to perceive a symbolic pattern requires great subtlety or sophistication. But in this matter the spectator has a clear advantage over the reader of a play because the symbolic themes are clarified and underscored for him by the production. Both readers and spectators, however, have this in common: they must exercise that very primitive faculty which Fergusson calls the "histrionic sensibility." [12] This is what the Prologue of *Henry V* appeals to as the "imaginary forces" (Act I, 18) of the audience, who must "Piece out our imperfections with your thoughts . . ." (Act I, 23) and "Play with your fancies . . ." (Act III, 7). In his chatty and traditional familiarity the Prologue makes some fundamental assumptions about the drama: the play is an empty illusion, a mere artifact, unless it is animated in the theater of the mind, that magical, life-giving microcosm.

STYLE IN THE ROMAN PLAYS

ALTHOUGH the Roman plays have some strong similarities as a group — their use of "Roman" costume, their favorable Roman idea of suicide, their common source in Plutarch (see Appendix) — they are stylistically quite different. The strongest contrast is between the styles of *Julius Caesar* and *Antony and Cleopatra*, which I should like to consider before going on to discuss *Coriolanus*. Actually, the Roman world in *Antony and Cleopatra* is very much like that in *Julius Caesar*, but it is "overreached" by the world of Empire and the splendors and perils of Egypt. Antony abandons the Roman style and values of Octavius Caesar — they are public, political, and objective as in *Julius Caesar* — and enters into the Egyptian style and values of Cleopatra. These two plays show the working of Shakespeare's imagination in two different moods: in *Julius Caesar* he seems to be deliberately limiting his imaginative resources, while in *Antony and Cleopatra* he appears to be trying to extend them "past the size of dreaming."

Perhaps the most characteristic example of Shakespeare's dramatic style in *Julius Caesar* is the quarrel scene (IV, iii). The verbal imagery here is fragmentary and undeveloped, while there is a brilliant presentational imagery of familiar objects and the rituals of daily life. The scene penetrates into the personal, domestic, and unheroic world of Brutus, and its disciplined use of limited means represents the "Roman" style of the play at its best.

The quarrel between Brutus and Cassius brings us closer than we have ever come to Brutus in his ordinary life. Only once before, in the scene in Brutus' "orchard" (II,i), have we seen the tragic protagonist so personally, but this was no more than a troubled glimpse. In essence, the quarrel between Brutus and Cassius is a completely external affair: an elaborate mixture of petulant accusation and lengthy self-justification. It abates with a confession of weakness and then a handshake (4.3.117), a visual sign of reconciliation (compare *Coriolanus* 5.3.182 s.d.).

We pass into a new mood when Brutus orders Lucius to bring a bowl of wine. It is a meditative mood with a strong note of sorrow, as Brutus reveals the secret he has kept hidden:

> *Cass.* I did not think you could have been so angry.
> *Bru.* O Cassius, I am sick of many griefs.
> *Cass.* Of your philosophy you make no use
> If you give place to accidental evils.
> *Bru.* No man bears sorrow better. Portia is dead.
> *Cass.* Ha! Portia?
> *Bru.* She is dead.   (4.3.143–49)

The revelation comes forcefully and unexpectedly: the soft music of "No man bears sorrow better" is suspended in a pause on the "r" of "better" — then the absolutely clear-

cut fact: "Portia is dead." The last two lines are an echo
of this rhythm, as Cassius questions and Brutus reiterates.
At this point Brutus' boy, Lucius, enters "with wine and
tapers" (4.3.157 s.d.), and the revelation is solemnized by
the drinking of wine. This is another stage ritual for reconciliation, and it recalls II, ii, where Caesar invites the conspirators to "go in and taste some wine with me . . ."
(2.2.126).

As Cassius, Titinius, and Messala are about to leave,
Brutus calls for his dressing gown, which he presumably
puts on after the others have gone (he is wearing it at
4.3.253). The investiture with the gown begins the scene
proper of Caesar's Ghost, and it is filled with a remarkable
compassion. In the acting of this scene, Brutus might remove some part of his military dress before he puts on the
gown to indicate a change in role: he is no longer the
Roman general and conspirator, but only a private citizen,
troubled in mind and weary in body and about to go to sleep.
The putting on of the gown would signify this transformation (compare the disarming of Antony in *Antony and
Cleopatra*). Brutus now appears in his personal and domestic
role, like Caesar in his "nightgown" (or dressing gown) at
the opening of II,ii.[1]

After the intense and exhausting emotion of the quarrel
with Cassius, Brutus' mind turns naturally from abstract
logic to the common concerns of life. He will not have Varro
and Claudius "stand" watch in his tent, but provides them
with cushions so that they may sleep. When Lucius dozes
off while playing, Brutus carefully takes away his instrument lest he break it. The boy falls asleep easily and in-
voluntarily, while the care-worn Brutus must go through a
long and elaborate ritual to woo sleep (compare *Henry V*

4.1.274–301). He finds a book he has been looking for in the pocket of his gown, and when he finally settles himself, he opens it to the page with the "leaf turn'd down/ Where I left reading" (4.3.273–74). All this wealth of detail — the gown, the cushions for the guards, the boy's falling asleep and his instrument taken away, the book with the dog-eared page found in the pocket of the gown — enters the consciousness of Brutus in a sudden Proustian abundance and prepares his mind for the entrance of the Ghost. In symbolic terms the Ghost of Caesar seems to "explode" into this intensely human scene. By a series of images of daily human concern, the inner consciousness of Brutus has been revealed to us, and we are not surprised to find that the spirit of the murdered Caesar has been brooding there since the quarrel with Cassius (see 4.3.19ff, 58ff, 105ff). The figure of the Ghost on stage is the external embodiment of Brutus' conscience and guilt, and the creation of a psychological atmosphere has served to identify the ghost within and the ghost without. By so doing, Shakespeare has endowed the fairly crude stage convention of the ghost with dramatic and psychological overtones, a development he will pursue further in *Hamlet*.

This scene illustrates at their best certain general features of the style of *Julius Caesar*. Most notable is the sharply limited vocabulary of the play. Only the quite short *Comedy of Errors* and *The Two Gentlemen of Verona* use a smaller stock of words.[2] Despite the fact that *Julius Caesar* was probably written just after *Henry V* and shortly before *Hamlet*,[3] its language is strikingly different, especially from that of *Hamlet*, which "contains much the largest and most expressive vocabulary" in the Shakespeare canon. Hart thinks that this peculiarity in the diction of *Julius Caesar* represents "the result of an experiment, fortunately not repeated, of curbing the author's natural exuberance of expression and restraining his fondness for metaphor and word-coining." [4]

The imagery of *Julius Caesar* is also quite limited. In Wells's count this play is twenty-sixth in volume of imagery, while *Antony and Cleopatra* is third.[5] And Spurgeon finds that *Julius Caesar* has less than a third the ratio of images to text that is present in *Antony and Cleopatra*.[6] However one may differ with the methods of classification of Wells or Spurgeon, the comparative figures are significant. In Acts IV and V of *Julius Caesar* the carefully developed themes of the first part of the play (blood, fire, storm) are almost abandoned.[7] There are also, especially in these two acts, long passages that are virtually without a conscious verbal imagery; the quarrel scene, for example, makes little use of verbal images for its effect. Typical of this almost imageless diction is the proscription scene which opens Act IV. Here the new Triumvirs decide the fate of the Roman Republic:

Ant. These many, then, shall die; their names are prick'd.
Oct. Your brother too must die. Consent you, Lepidus?
Lep. I do consent —
Oct.   Prick him down, Antony.
Lep. Upon condition Publius shall not live,
Who is your sister's son, Mark Antony.
Ant. He shall not live. Look, with a spot I damn him.   (4.1.1–6)

In these six lines human lives are bargained away and the business of the Empire is begun, but the only images are the damning "spots" that are "prick'd" down. As in *Coriolanus*, the pressure of public affairs does not permit one to luxuriate in images.

The deliberate limiting of imaginative resources in *Julius*

Caesar seems to indicate a stylistic experiment on Sha. speare's part. He appears to be attempting a special "Romaı style for the play, one that can express the clarity of though and forthrightness of action in the Roman subject matter. The "limited perfection" of this "Roman" style is perhaps best described by A. C. Bradley:

Neither thought on the one side, nor expression on the other, seems to have any tendency to outrun or contend with its fellow. We receive an impression of easy mastery and complete harmony, but not so strong an impression of inner power bursting into outer life. Shakespeare's style is perhaps nowhere else so free from defects, and yet almost every one of his subsequent plays contains writing which is greater. To speak familiarly, we feel in *Julius Caesar* that, although not even Shakespeare could better the style he has chosen, he has not let himself go.[8]

Bradley relates the style to its theme, so that the play is seen as "a deliberate endeavour after a dignified and unadorned simplicity — a Roman simplicity perhaps." [9] J. A. K. Thomson describes this style in somewhat more positive terms:

It is clear that he [Shakespeare] had formed for himself the notion of a style corresponding to the Renaissance conception of the Roman character, which in turn was influenced by the Greek conception of the Spartan character, with its martial virility and laconic speech. This is the style he uses in *Julius Caesar*. It is remarkably effective, and one does somehow feel, when Brutus or Cassius or Casca is speaking, that this is rather how a Roman would speak.[10]

This sort of writing consciously avoids the brilliance of *Antony and Cleopatra*, yet in that play, too, the Roman world is set forth in an austere imagery of hard, cold, material objects and the practical business of state; it is only the imagery of Egypt that is luxuriant. The "Roman" style is the natural speaking voice of Octavius Caesar as it is of

Coriolanus, for whom it is a mark of integrity to be "ill-school'd/ In bolted language" (3.1.321–22).

The sense of order, limitation, and control in the "Roman" style of *Julius Caesar* is expressed in the rhetorical form of close analogy, especially the simile. This form uses explicit and carefully worked-out comparisons, and there is an attempt to indicate just what specific aspects of the vehicle (image proper) are to be applied to the tenor (idea). A very clear example is Titinius' eulogy for the dead Cassius:

> O setting sun,
> As in thy red rays thou dost sink to night,
> So in his red blood Cassius' day is set!
> The sun of Rome is set. (5.3.60–63)

The formula for this image is quite simple and commonplace: the life of man is represented by the course of the sun in a single day, and death is therefore a sunset. Further, the red rays of the setting sun are like the red blood of Cassius' death wound. Not only is an analogy drawn between the individual and the cosmos, but the state is brought in as a third plane of being. The parts of the analogy are clearly identified by the "as . . . so" form of their relation, which makes the application of the analogy very specific and limited. Within this narrow imaginative framework, the image functions as a completed system, whose meanings are self-explained and self-pointed.[11] The balance and symmetry of the figure are particularly useful in a play such as *Julius Caesar*, where the dramatic action turns so significantly on the correspondences between microcosm and macrocosm: "The heavens themselves blaze forth the death of princes" (2.2.31).

By the time of *Antony and Cleopatra*, Shakespeare has

more or less abandoned the analogy form of *Julius Caesar*.
We may see this contrast in style in the very unorthodox
and dramatic way he now uses similes. In Cleopatra's final
speech, for example, the similes make a slow, rich music of
monosyllables: "As sweet as balm, as soft as air, as gentle
— " (5.2.314). There is an hypnotic sense of falling asleep,
in which it is dramatically just to leave the final figure in-
complete — Cleopatra follows the turn of her thought to
"O Antony!" (5.2.315). These similes dramatize the effect
of the asp-bite as described by Plutarch; it

causeth onely a heauines of the head, without swounding or com-
plaining, and bringeth a great desire also to sleepe, with a litle
swet in the face, and so by litle and litle taketh away the senses &
vitall powers, no liuing creature perceiuing that the patients feele
any paine. For they are so sorie when any bodie awaketh them, and
taketh them vp; as those that being taken out of a sound sleep, are
very heauie and desirous to sleepe.[12]

Antony uses a similar type of figure in his speech to Eros
in IV,xiv. The changing shapes of the clouds present a
pageant of Antony's dissolution:

> That which is now a horse, even with a thought
> The rack dislimns, and makes it indistinct
> As water is in water. (4.14.9–11)

So Antony himself is "indistinct/ As water is in water" and
"cannot hold this visible shape" (4.14.14). The strong
Roman sense of reality is slipping away from him, and the
paradoxical simile is used to emphasize the process. These
similes push beyond the ordinary limits of the analogy
form to an area of hyperbole and symbol.

The personifications in the two plays also indicate a
strong contrast in style. In *Julius Caesar* they function as a

specific allegory for their subjects, and they are highly formal and rhetorical in tone, as in Messala's address to Error after the death of Cassius:

> O hateful Error, Melancholy's child,
> Why dost thou show to the apt thoughts of men
> The things that are not? O Error, soon conceiv'd,
> Thou never com'st unto a happy birth,
> But kill'st the mother that engend'red thee! (5.3.67–71)

The use of abstract nouns as human entities is typical of Shakespeare's earlier manner, which is also suggested by the stiffness and deliberateness of the apostrophe. Conspiracy (2.1.77–85), danger (2.2.44–48), and constancy (2.4.6–7) are likewise personified.

The few personifications in *Antony and Cleopatra* have a much more vivid dramatic function, which is best exemplified by Cleopatra's dialogue with the Messenger from Antony:

> *Mess.*   Madam, he's well.
> *Cleo.*   Well said.
> *Mess.* And friends with Caesar.
> *Cleo.*   Th'art an honest man.
> *Mess.* Caesar and he are greater friends than ever.
> *Cleo.* Make thee a fortune from me!
> *Mess.*   But yet, madam —
> *Cleo.* I do not like 'but yet.' It does allay
> The good precedence. Fie upon 'but yet'!
> 'But yet' is as a jailer to bring forth
> Some monstrous malefactor. (2.5.46–53)

Cleopatra pounces on "but yet" and endows it with human attributes. These two simple conjunctions become a jailer leading forth his prisoner to be hanged. By providing an occasion for Cleopatra to personify her fears, these colorless words assume dramatic significance. Similarly, when Antony is about to depart for Rome, Cleopatra vainly searches for something to say, then bursts out: "O, my oblivion is a very Antony,/ And I am all forgotten!" (1.3.90–91). Oblivion is personified as "a very Antony," the supreme example of forgetfulness because he is leaving Cleopatra and going to Rome. Cleopatra is "forgotten" in not being able to remember what she has to say and by the departing Antony. The play on these two senses makes Antony both subject and object, and the figure fits very nicely into the dramatic action. These personifications, unlike those in *Julius Caesar*, arise very naturally out of their dramatic contexts; they are in no sense set in formal speeches.

The dramatic use of similes and personifications in *Antony and Cleopatra* is part of a larger stylistic purpose very different from the ordered perfection of *Julius Caesar*. The characteristic figure in *Antony and Cleopatra* is the hyperbole, or what Puttenham in his *Arte of English Poesie* (1589) calls "for his immoderate excesse . . . the ouer reacher" or "the loud lyer," [13] and he defines it as "by incredible comparison giuing credit." [14] In Greek "hyperbole" is *"a throwing beyond: an overshooting, superiority, excess in anything . . ."* (Lidell-Scott Dictionary). It would include the ideas of extravagance and boldness as well as exaggeration and overstatement. In essence, hyperbole is the reaching-out of the imagination for superlatives. This is I think what Coleridge means when he calls the style of *Antony and Cleopatra "feliciter audax"* — literally, "felicitously bold or audacious," but perhaps best rendered by Coleridge's phrase, "happy valiancy of style." [15]

This type of style is demanded by the spaciousness and scope of the play's themes. Perhaps the best example is Cleopatra's dream of Antony:

His face was as the heav'ns, and therein stuck
A sun and moon, which kept their course and lighted
The little O, the earth. (5.2.79–81)

The image of Antony becomes the whole cosmos, and this earth is only a "little O" in comparison — we cannot imagine in higher terms. Cleopatra continues: "His legs bestrid the ocean: his rear'd arm/ Crested the world" (5.2.82–83). This is the Marlovian strain of invidious comparison in which man is literally made the measure of all things. Cleopatra goes so far as to question the reality of her dream, as if it were beyond our mortal sense of possibility:

Think you there was or might be such a man
As this I dreamt of?
    Dol.   Gentle madam, no.
    Cleo. You lie, up to the hearing of the gods!
But, if there be or ever were one such,
It's past the size of dreaming. Nature wants stuff
To vie strange forms with fancy; yet, t'imagine
An Antony were nature's piece 'gainst fancy,
Condemning shadows quite. (5.2.93–100)

The image of Antony is "past the size of dreaming." It is unrealizable because reality ("Nature") cannot present all the forms imagination ("fancy," a kind of dreaming) can conceive. But even to think that the forms of imagination may actually exist is an argument for "Nature." We may take this statement — "Nature wants stuff/ To vie strange forms with fancy" — as a key to the character of the style. The imagination acts as hyperbole: it throws beyond, overshoots, is superior to, and in excess of nature, yet it cannot go past the size of dreaming, and therefore must remain implicit in the dramatic action and words. Where *Julius Caesar* limits and defines its figures and insists on the proper logical application of vehicle to tenor, *Antony and Cleopatra* uses a figurative language, the "strange forms" of "fancy," that tries to force itself beyond the bounds of mere "Nature."

The "hyperbolical" quality of *Antony and Cleopatra* is also seen in a special kind of superlative. When Antony tells Cleopatra, "Now for the love of Love and her soft hours . . ." (1.1.44), the doubling of the noun with "of" serves as an intensifier: it is an attempt to get at the quintessence. Antony is Cleopatra's "man of men" (1.5.72), as if only he among men could represent Man. He is also her "Lord of lords!" (4.8.16), and his sons are proclaimed "kings of kings" (3.6.13). This grammatical form echoes in the mind when we hear Antony say that Cleopatra

> Like a right gypsy hath at fast and loose
> Beguil'd me to the very heart of loss! (4.12.28–29)

No loss can be imagined greater; it is an absolute, the essence and the life of loss.

The range of diction in *Antony and Cleopatra* is very wide, and it shows an extravagant juxtaposing of latinate and colloquial words, as in Cleopatra's speech to the asp:

> Come, thou mortal wretch,
> With thy sharp teeth this knot intrinsicate
> Of life at once untie. Poor venomous fool,
> Be angry, and dispatch. (5.2.306–09)

"Intrinsicate" was considered a pedantic, "inkhorn" term in its time, a fit object for satire in Marston's *The Scourge of Villanie* (1599). When his poem "shall come into the late perfumed fist of iudiciall *Torquatus* . . . he will vouchsafe it, some of his new-minted Epithets, (as *Reall, Intrinsecate, Delphicke,*). . . ." [16] "Intrinsicate" was often used for "intricate" and meant much the same thing: "involved," "complicated," "entangled." But it also suggests a connection with "intrinsic," which refers to the essential nature of a thing. Life is the intrinsic knot — intricate, entangled, essential — which the asp, as death the lover, will at once untie. Alongside this uncommon word, "intrinsicate," are such familiar terms of endearment as "mortal wretch" and "Poor venomous fool." The use of the colloquial in Cleopatra's speech to the asp appeals to the common human emotions of tragedy, while the latinate has a heightening effect. Charmian's words on the death of her mistress also illustrate this two-fold quality:

> Now boast thee, death, in thy possession lies
> A lass unparallel'd. Downy windows, close;
> And golden Phoebus never be beheld
> Of eyes again so royal! (5.2.318–21)

The homely and familiar "lass" is placed between the long latinate words "possession" and "unparallel'd." It recalls the Cleopatra of

> No more but e'en a woman, and commanded
> By such poor passion as the maid that milks
> And does the meanest chares. (4.15.73–75)

The effect of "lass" — a common, lowly word — is immediately countered by the periphrasis of "Downy windows" for eyes and the mythological reference to "golden Phoebus." [17] The verbal context is further enriched by a covert allusion. Cleopatra, the "lass unparallel'd," now triumphs over Caesar, the "ass/ Unpolicied" (5.2.310–11) — the half-rhyme deliberately pairs these latinate-colloquial phrases.[18]

Going beyond the effects of rhetoric, we may explore the "hyperbolical" style of *Antony and Cleopatra* in a more

extended example. Cleopatra's "infinite variety" [19] is a leading hyperbole in the play, and it draws its strength as much
from the poetic language lavished on Cleopatra as from
the presented image of her character — the role demands
an "infinite variety" of gesture and stage action. The explication of this elaborate hyperbole may serve as a parallel to
the analysis of the scene of Caesar's Ghost; in both places
there is a very characteristic expression of the play's style.

The ambivalent tone of "infinite variety" is first established by Enobarbus right after his splendid speech about
Cleopatra in her barge on the Cydnus. He assures Maecenas
that Antony cannot break off from his "enchanting queen":

> Never! He will not.
> Age cannot wither her nor custom stale
> Her infinite variety. Other women cloy
> The appetites they feed, but she makes hungry
> Where most she satisfies; for vilest things
> Become themselves in her, that the holy priests
> Bless her when she is riggish.   (2.2.239–45)

Cleopatra is outside the withering toils of age and custom
and cloying appetite, for "vilest things/ Become themselves
in her," achieve their apotheosis and inner perfection. She
is even blessed when she plays the strumpet ("is riggish") —
this is the strange issue of the "holy palmers' kiss" of *Romeo
and Juliet* (1.5.102). We have been prepared for Enobarbus'
statement by many previous expressions of Cleopatra's
variousness and her capacity to exploit the range of emotions. She is Antony's

> wrangling queen!
> Whom every thing becomes — to chide, to laugh,
> To weep. . . .   (1.1.48–50)

She knows how to manipulate her sentiments and to stimulate passion by "infinite variety." As she tells the incredulous Charmian in her message to Antony:

> If you find him sad,
> Say I am dancing; if in mirth, report
> That I am sudden sick. (1.3.3–5)

This is beyond Charmian's comprehension, but Cleopatra is herself a "heavenly mingle" (1.5.59), and she knows the art to "make defect perfection" (2.2.236).

These paradoxical aspects of Cleopatra may be demonstrated in II,v, where her "infinite variety" is seen as roving desire searching for objects. We begin with the consciously poetic and languorous tone of *Twelfth Night*: "Give me some music! music, moody food/ Of us that trade in love" (2.5.1–2). The music is called for, and Mardian the Eunuch enters, but Cleopatra is no longer interested in hearing him sing: "Let it alone! Let's to billiards" (2.5.3). Now begins a series of sexual puns in the style of Shakespeare's early comedies; Cleopatra explores the witty possibilities of "play":

> *Cleo.* As well a woman with an eunuch play'd
> As with a woman. Come, you'll play with me, sir?
> *Mar.* As well as I can, madam.
> *Cleo.* And when good will is show'd, though 't come too short,
> The actor may plead pardon. (2.5.5–9)

But she quickly tires of this verbal sport and has a new whim:

> Give me mine angle! we'll to th' river. There,
> My music playing far off, I will betray
> Tawny-finn'd fishes. My bended hook shall pierce
> Their slimy jaws; and as I draw them up,
> I'll think them every one an Antony,
> And say, 'Ah, ha! y'are caught!' (2.5.10–15)

The suggestion of music at the opening of the scene is taken up again, but the mood is entirely different. The absent Antony is "caught" or "hooked" in the physically violent image of the slimy-jawed fish, which is much transmuted from the incident in Plutarch of the salt fish attached as a jest to Antony's line.

Once struck, the note of passion is intensified with the appearance of the Messenger:

> O, from Italy!
> Ram thou thy fruitful tidings in mine ears,
> That long time have been barren.   (2.5.23–25)

It is a sudden sexual fury to have Antony himself in the tidings about him. When the Messenger tells his news of Antony's marriage, he is struck down by Cleopatra (2.5.61 s.d., 62 s.d.), haled up and down (2.5.64 s.d.), and threatened with a knife (2.5.73 s.d.). The luxuriant poetic tone of the passage has now issued into the physical violence of the stage action. This is all part of the style of Cleopatra's "infinite variety," which runs the gamut from "music, moody food" to "Rogue, thou hast liv'd too long" with the stage direction *"Draw a knife."*

In contrast to this scene we have the "infinite variety" of Cleopatra's suicide, which is not quite done in the "high Roman fashion" (4.15.87), but with a priestly deliberateness and an aesthetic enjoyment of robe and crown and the effect of the asp-bite. Shakespeare here takes advantage of all the richness of the Elizabethan staging to enforce the poetic splendor of Cleopatra's final scene. She is to be shown "like a queen" (5.2.227) in elaborate stage ritual and costume, and we know from Henslowe's account books and other sources how important gorgeous robes were to an Elizabethan production.

26

In her death Caesar affirms her magnificence:

> she looks like sleep,
> As she would catch another Antony
> In her strong toil of grace.   (5.2.349–51)

Part of the effectiveness of this passage rests in the manner of portrayal. Cleopatra must really look "like sleep," with an indefinable expression of grace — perhaps a smile. In Elizabethan English "grace" is a complex word whose meanings range from physical attraction and charm of personal manner to pre-eminence of nobility, moral rightness, and divine blessing. Cleopatra's "strong toil of grace" is a union of the queen who "beggar'd all description" (2.2.203) and the "serpent of old Nile" (1.5.25) — she could "catch another Antony" now as she caught the first one. We recall Cleopatra fishing in II,v; there the hooked fish was Antony, over whom she uttered the triumphant cry, " 'Ah, ha! y'are caught!' " (2.5.15). We should not overlook the violence in Cleopatra's "strong toil of grace" and its ability to "catch." The word "toil," for example, refers to a net or trap to snare game. Although Cleopatra is heightened by her death, her character and motives remain in a certain ambiguity even at the end. She is always both "queen" (female monarch) and "quean" (wench, whore), and in this covert pun [20] lies the secret of her attraction.

The rhapsodic and transcendental aspects of "infinite variety" are only too plain. Yet there is a strong sense in which the hyperboles of the play are constantly undercut. This is perhaps what Coleridge means when he says that Cleopatra's passion "springs out of the habitual craving of a licentious nature, and that it is supported and reinforced by voluntary stimulus and sought-for associations, instead of blossoming out of spontaneous emotion." [21] Such terms as "habitual," "voluntary," and "sought-for" convey a sense of the effort and ennui involved. But Coleridge safeguards the balance of his judgment by noting that "the sense of criminality in her passion is lessened by our insight into its depth and energy. . . ." [22] This is precisely the paradox of Cleopatra's "infinite variety," that it not only suggests an unlimited creative vitality, but also artifice and boredom. New pleasures are essential to a life of pleasure, as Antony says in the first scene of the play (where the whole Egypt-Rome conflict is stated in extreme form): "There's not a minute of our lives should stretch/ Without some pleasure now" (1.1.46–47). The concern for the new pleasure of every "minute" suggests Pater, who proposes in the Conclusion to *The Renaissance* "to give nothing but the highest quality to your moments as they pass, and simply for those moments' sake." Thus, behind the appearances of splendor and fulfillment in Egypt lies a burdensome compulsion: the life of the senses must have "infinite variety" or cease to exist.

Among Shakespeare's plays, *Antony and Cleopatra* is one of the richest in imagery and stylistic effects and *Julius Caesar* one of the most sparse. The two plays offer an illustrative contrast between a carefully limited and controlled "Roman" style and a hyperbolical and evocative "Egyptian" style. The imagery in *Antony and Cleopatra* tends to be implicit and its meanings suggested rather than stated. In this sense we may speak of its style as elliptical and complex, with an ability to suspend many ideas without seeking to resolve them into one. Its style demonstrates, to a remarkable degree, Shakespeare's "negative capability." This is not a quality that is much evident in *Julius Caesar*, yet the sharpness and clarity of detail in that play is a unique achievement. It proceeds deliberately rather than expansively, and it produces its effects, as in the appearance of Caesar's Ghost to Brutus, with an astonishing simplicity. There is a sense of distinct outline and completed form in this play that is absent from *Antony and Cleopatra*, but its perfection is attained at the expense of imaginative intensity and fullness of implication. The "Roman" style of *Julius Caesar* seems to involve Shakespeare in some basic contradictions, and he never again so consciously restricts his imaginative powers.

The style of *Coriolanus* stands in sharp contrast to both the other Roman plays, but perhaps most to *Antony and Cleopatra*, which was probably written only a year or so earlier.[23] We no longer find the richness and complexity of imagery of *Antony and Cleopatra*, but a curiously cold, aloof, and objective world. In this respect the sense of control in *Coriolanus* reminds us somewhat of *Julius Caesar*, although the two plays cannot be compared in the relative mastery of their dramatic verse.[24] Both plays also use a similar two-part form, but *Coriolanus* rises by a series of mounting climaxes to the high point of Coriolanus' yielding in V,iii, whereas *Julius Caesar* never builds to a second climax as strong as the murder of Caesar in the third act — this creates a certain imbalance in the development of the action. Despite the poetic and structural skill of *Coriolanus*, the play appears to be odd and anomalous and to point ahead to the last plays rather than back to the period of the great tragedies. It has not only not attracted critics, but it has seemed to represent an exhaustion of Shakespeare's powers. One way to answer these judgments is to examine the play in terms of its dramatic purposes; the strict application of expression to function makes its style quite different from that of *Julius Caesar* or *Antony and Cleopatra*.

As a basic premise we need to agree that the style of *Coriolanus* is closely linked to the character of the protagonist, about whom A. C. Bradley has said, "If Lear's thunderstorm had beat upon his head, he would merely have set his teeth." [25] Coriolanus is an unreflective man of action. His tragedy is massive and overwhelming, almost like fate, and it does not touch us very personally. We see him setting his teeth against the storm of Fortune when he appears in humble guise at the house of his former enemy, Aufidius. He expresses this great change from Rome's defender to Rome's chief enemy in terms of chance trivialities. Just as fast-sworn friends "on a dissension of a doit" (4.4.17) become enemies,

> So fellest foes,
> Whose passions and whose plots have broke their sleep
> To take the one the other, by some chance,
> Some trick not worth an egg, shall grow dear friends
> And interjoin their issues. So with me.
> My birthplace hate I, and my love's upon
> The enemy town. (4.4.18–24)

Enright finds this soliloquy strange because, "coming at the turn of the play, at the very hinge of the tragic action, it should refer us to 'some trick not worth an egg.' " [26] At a similar juncture Macbeth and Othello react entirely differently.

We have an even stronger example at the end of the play of the inadequacy of Coriolanus as a tragic protagonist. Although he yields to the family group, there is never any real recognition of the tragic folly of his betrayal; his climactic words are simply a realization of his own doom:

30

O my mother, mother! O!
You have won a happy victory to Rome;
But for your son — believe it, O believe it! —
Most dangerously you have with him prevail'd,
If not most mortal to him. But let it come. (5.3.185–89)

There is an awareness of the tragic consequences of mercy
here rather than any true self-awareness. The words have
none of the quality of Lear's emergence from madness:
"Pray, do not mock me./ I am a very foolish fond old
man . . ." (4.7.59–60). Although the character of Coriolanus is consistent throughout, his next appearance, proud
and choleric in Corioles (V,vi), comes as a surprise. Accustomed as we are to the effects of tragedy, we are not
ready to accept the fact that his yielding seems to have had
no influence on his moral being. But neither Coriolanus
nor any of the persons in this play is either inward or meditative or lyric, and there is not much self-awareness or tragic
recognition. Actually, only Menenius uses figurative language freely and naturally, as in the fable of belly and
members, but his role is limited to that of conciliator. In this
atmosphere a rich verbal imagery would defeat the dramatic purpose, whereas in such a play as *Richard II* it is just
this rich vein of poetic fancy that calls attention to the ineffectual and histrionic nature of the king.

When Coriolanus does use figures of speech, he inclines
to similes rather than metaphors, since they provide a
simpler and more explicit form of expression. Both the
vehicle and tenor of the image are very carefully balanced
and limited, usually by the connectives "like" or "as" (I
count ninety-three similes in the play, fifty-seven with "as"
and thirty-six with "like"). The similes do not suggest new
areas of meaning, but give points already stated an added

31

force and vividness. Their function is illustrative rather than expressive. In this respect *Coriolanus* seems to resemble *Julius Caesar* and Shakespeare's earlier plays, for the trend of Shakespeare's development is away from the simile form and toward a dramatically integrated type of metaphor.[27]

Volumnia makes good use of illustrative simile when she instructs her son in his role before the people: "Now humble as the ripest mulberry/ That will not hold the handling . . ." (3.2.79–80). Coriolanus must be "humble" before the people, and the simile emphasizes the exact sort of humility that is expected. Although the mulberry image makes a vivid and original illustration, it is an embellishment of the basic meaning and not at all indispensable. But the similes in *Antony and Cleopatra* — for example, Antony's "indistinct/ As water is in water" (4.14.10–11) — are themselves the meaning of the passages in which they occur and are not in any way dispensable. This sensitive image of the "ripest mulberry" has an important dramatic function. Its highly imaginative character suggests a false tone in what Volumnia is saying. In its context the image is overwrought, for Volumnia knows her son cannot feign any sort of humility, no less the supreme humility of the "ripest mulberry." It is too self-conscious and lush an image and hints that there is a servile, dishonorable aspect in what Volumnia is proposing. This type of figure raises interesting questions about the function of poetic language in the drama. If the mulberry image appeared isolated from its context in an anthology of lyric poetry, it would certainly seem striking and original, yet in the play its effect is insidious. The poetic quality of the image has been diverted to dramatic ends.

Another example of this principle is in Coriolanus' injunction against flattery in I,ix:

> When drums and trumpets shall
> I' th' field prove flatterers, let courts and cities be
> Made all of false-fac'd soothing! When steel grows
> Soft as the parasite's silk, let him be made
> An overture [28] for th' wars!   (1.9.42–46)

In the overturning of order that flattery brings, the steel of the soldier (probably his mail coat) will become as soft as the silk of the parasite. It is a vivid contrast of textures, but its imaginative tone is used to suggest the luxury of peace — as if one would expect the silk-clad parasite at court but not the steel-coated man of war to use similes. This pejorative connotation of silk is echoed in the final scene of the play when Coriolanus is accused of "Breaking his oath and resolution like/ A twist of rotten silk . . ." (5.6.94–95).

The images of peace and civil life put an unexpected music into Coriolanus' verse, although he uses them contemptuously. To prevent flattery, he terms his wounds "Scratches with briers,/ Scars to move laughter only" (3.3.51–52), which recalls his earlier speech in the Capitol as he escapes from Cominius' oration:

> I had rather have one scratch my head i' th' sun
> When the alarum were struck than idly sit
> To hear my nothings monster'd.   (2.2.79–81)

This passage is a graphic illustration of what it means to "voluptuously surfeit out of action" (1.3.28). War is "sprightly, waking, audible, and full of vent," while peace is "a very apoplexy, lethargy; mull'd, deaf, sleepy, insensible . . ." (4.5.237–39). In terms of these values (war is the positive force, peace the negative),[29] we find that the love imagery of the play is curiously transferred to military contexts. In I,vi Marcius greets Cominius in the language of the wedding-night:

3 3

O, let me clip ye
In arms as sound as when I woo'd, in heart
As merry as when our nuptial day was done
And tapers burn'd to bedward!   (1.6.29–32)

And in IV,v Aufidius welcomes his former enemy in these
same epithalamial terms:

But that I see thee here,
Thou noble thing, more dances my rapt heart
Than when I first my wedded mistress saw
Bestride my threshold.   (4.5.120–23)

But there is none of this sort of imagery between Coriolanus
and his wife Virgilia. In his first dialogue with her, for example, he addresses her as his "gracious silence" (2.1.192)
and asks somewhat bluntly: "Wouldst thou have laugh'd
had I come coffin'd home/ That weep'st to see me triumph?"
(2.1.193–94). The military context evokes a spontaneously
vivid imagery that ceases when we move "From th' casque
to th' cushion" (4.7.43).

Coriolanus' own attitude to words helps to shape the
character of the verbal imagery in the play. Suspecting he
will have the worst of it, he refuses to parry arguments with
the Tribune Brutus, for "oft,/ When blows have made me
stay, I fled from words" (2.2.75–76). Unlike Hamlet or
Richard II or even Othello, Coriolanus has a natural antipathy to eloquence that goes beyond the Elizabethan convention that a soldier should be a plain, if not rude,
speaker.[30] As Menenius tells the patricians, Coriolanus'
aversion to words is part of his hatred of flattery: "His
heart's his mouth;/ What his breast forges, that his tongue
must vent . . ." (3.1.257–58). He is "ill-school'd/ In bolted
language . . ." and "meal and bran together/ He throws
without distinction" (3.1.321–23). There is no subtlety in

this man, no use of language as an exploration of consciousness. He says what he thinks and feels and that is the end of it, for words are simply a means to express his bluff honesty. Remember Antony's ironic claim at the height of his oration: "I am no orator, as Brutus is . . ." (3.2.222). Coriolanus is emphatically "no orator," and in a play so thoroughly political as this, the inability to make speeches is a claim to integrity.

Coriolanus is also peculiarly oppressed by the reality of words, a weakness the fluent Tribunes and Aufidius know how to turn to their own ends. These antagonists of Coriolanus have, by the way, a striking similarity of function in the two parts of the play. Both display that extempore grasp of circumstance that is the mark of the Machiavel, and the "plebeian malignity and tribunitian insolence" [31] of Brutus and Sicinius are matched by Aufidius' guiding principle: "I'll potch at him some way./ Or wrath or craft may get him" (1.10.15–16). In III,i, for example, Sicinius baits Coriolanus in typical fashion:

> It is a mind
> That shall remain a poison where it is,
> Not poison any further.   (3.1.86–88)

Coriolanus seizes on this "shall" as if it were a menacing entity:

> Shall remain?
> Hear you this Triton of the minnows? Mark you
> His absolute 'shall'?
> Com.   'Twas from the canon.
> Cor.   'Shall'? (3.1.88–90)

And Coriolanus continues to rage against the "peremptory 'shall' " (3.1.94), the "popular 'shall,' " (3.1.106), which is

35

SHAKESPEARE'S ROMAN PLAYS

made to symbolize the whole patrician-plebeian conflict. In terms of the actual situation, Coriolanus' rage is excessive and strident; he is "fleeing from words" (2.2.76) rather than realities.

Aufidius uses the same trick as the Tribunes in V,vi, where he tempts Coriolanus to his doom with three contemptuous words: "traitor," "Marcius," and "boy." Coriolanus recoils from the verbal concussion and repeats the words unbelievingly as if they had power over him:

> Boy? False hound!
> If you have writ your annals true, 'tis there,
> That, like an eagle in a dovecote, I
> Flutter'd your Volscians in Corioles.
> Alone I did it. Boy? (5.6.112–16)

For the moment, the word and the thing are confounded, producing a crisis that can only be resolved by violence. The situation here is the reverse of that in *Antony and Cleopatra*, where Caesar mocks at Antony's insults: "He calls me boy, and chides as he had power/ To beat me out of Egypt" (4.1.1–2). The imperturbability of Caesar cannot be ruffled by mere words.

Coriolanus' normal speaking voice is often harsh and vituperative. In his tirades against the people he uses a few repeated image themes (especially food, disease, and animals), but our interest is not so much in the images themselves as in their expletive force. After the Romans are beaten to their trenches by the Volscians, for example, "Enter *Marcius*, cursing" (1.4.29 s.d.), and his volley of abuse begins:

> All the contagion of the South light on you,
> You shames of Rome! you herd of — Biles and plagues
> Plaster you o'er, that you may be abhorr'd

36

Farther than seen and one infect another
Against the wind a mile! You souls of geese
That bear the shapes of men, how have you run
From slaves that apes would beat! Pluto and hell!
(1.4.30–36)

What is important here is not the catalogue of disease and animal imagery, but the "thunder-like percussion" (1.4.59) of Marcius' wrath. The breaking off in "you herd of —" is not felt as a gap, but as part of a natural rhythm in which the histrionic stress is on sound rather than sense. These images are therefore "illustrative" because they are used as examples of Marcius' anger, and no single image nor the sequence of the group is absolutely necessary. We have the same sort of effect in Marcius' second speech in the play, an extended harangue to the plebeians:

He that trusts to you,
Where he should find you lions, finds you hares;
Where foxes, geese. You are no surer, no,
Than is the coal of fire upon the ice
Or hailstone in the sun. . . . (1.1.174–78)

These are metaphors but they could as easily have been similes, for the analogy that is drawn is very explicit and limited. The animals have traditional, proverbial associations that are fairly well fixed: the lion is valiant, the hare fearful, while the fox represents shrewdness and craft, and the goose foolish simplicity. We do not feel any breadth of meaning in these images. But we must remember that it is Marcius who is speaking, and he is neither a poet nor a politician, but only a straight-forward man of war. He tags plebeian faults with what is for him a suitable imagery, and if it seems familiar and trite, that in itself is a comment on his image-making powers.

It is significant, too, that the thirty-six lines of soliloquy in *Coriolanus* — the same number as in *As You Like It* — represent the minimal use of this device in Shakespeare. By itself, this proves nothing, but it keeps us aware of the lack of inwardness in the play and the fact that Coriolanus is the least articulate of Shakespeare's tragic heroes. At an opposite pole is the brooding, meditative Hamlet, who resorts to the soliloquy as a "natural" form of expression.[32] The few soliloquies in *Coriolanus* have a very particular dramatic effect. In a play so full of politics it is not often that we see a lone figure on stage speaking as if to himself. We have been accustomed to seeing troops moving about and crowds of plebeians and patricians wrangling with each other. In this context the soliloquy, the stage image of isolation, emphasizes Coriolanus' own inner state. The two soliloquies in IV,iv, for example, call attention to the spiritual alienation of Coriolanus as an exile and traitor in the country of the Volscians. In II,iii his proud soliloquy in the gown of humility sets him completely apart from his plebeian petitioners. He speaks to himself on stage not to unburden his conscience nor to express his inner purposes, but because he feels himself to be a lone and humiliated figure.

The style of *Coriolanus* is not so much "Roman," implying as this does a Stoic self-control, as objective and public. This is seen very vividly in the great amount of public ceremony in the play, with its accompanying music or noise. The ominous shouts of "mutinous *Citizens*" open the action, and these are reinforced by "*Shouts within*"(1.1.47 s.d.) from the mob on the other side of the city. We then have an elaborate range of sound directions for the battle scenes: "*They sound a parley*" (1.4.12 s.d.), "*Drum afar off*" (1.4.15

s.d.), *"Alarum far off"* (1.4.19 s.d.), *"Alarum, as in battle"* (1.8 s.d.), *"Flourish. Alarum. A retreat is sounded."* (1.9 s.d.), and *"A flourish. Cornets.* Enter *Tullus Aufidius* bloody, with two or three *Soldiers."* (1.10 s.d.). These directions graphically convey the changing fortunes of war. We also have a number of acclamations of Marcius' valor: *"They all shout and wave their swords, take him up in their arms and cast up their caps"* (1.6.75 s.d.) and *"A long flourish. They all cry,* 'Marcius! Marcius!' *cast up their caps and lances"* (1.9.40 s.d.). In Coriolanus' triumphal procession there is *"A shout and flourish"* (2.1.172 s.d.), *"A sennet. Trumpets sound."* (2.1.178 s.d.), and *"Flourish. Cornets. Exeunt in state, as before."* (2.1.220 s.d.). In the conflict between Coriolanus and the plebeians in Act III we have confused shouting as *"They all bustle about Coriolanus"* (3.1.185 s.d.), and when he is banished, *"They all shout and throw up their caps"* (3.3.135 s.d.). Coriolanus' decision to spare Rome is celebrated by musical jubilation: *"Trumpets, hautboys, drums beat, all together"* [33] (5.4.51 s.d.), *"Sound still with the shouts"* (5.4.60 s.d.), and *"A flourish with drums and trumpets"* (5.5.7 s.d.). The final scene of the play also puts strong insistence on public ceremony as *"Drums and trumpets sound, with great shouts of the people"* (5.6.48 s.d.), and Coriolanus enters "marching with *Drum* and *Colours* . . ." (5.6.69 s.d.). As in *Hamlet,* the play ends with solemn music: *"A dead march sounded"* (5.6.155 s.d.).

The public style of *Coriolanus,* so forcibly conveyed by the sound directions, is in some sense an expression of the imaginative limitations of the play; the characters use language and imagery that are natural and appropriate to them. Coriolanus himself renounces rhetoric and seems to equate a plain style with integrity, for the heroic virtues of war and the soldier do not demand an elaborate poetic imagery. Perhaps part of the difficulty in appreciating this play stems from an overemphasis on verbal imagery. If we consider the play from a dramatic point of view, it has surprising force and vitality, as the production directed by John Houseman at the Phoenix Theater in 1954 seemed to indicate. The poetic speech is remarkably tight and sinewy, from Volumnia's familiar "Pow, waw!" (2.1.157) to Marcius' formal renunciation of "acclamations hyperbolical" (1.9.50). There is also a brilliant use of short choric scenes which comment on the main action without making obtrusive analogies; for dramatic economy, I,iii and IV,iii are among the best scenes of this sort in all of Shakespeare. It is along these dramatic lines, I think, that we may understand the otherwise bewildering remark of Eliot that *Coriolanus* is, "with *Antony and Cleopatra*, Shakespeare's most assured artistic success." [34]

Chapter III

THE IMAGERY OF
Julius Caesar

I

THE position of *Julius Caesar* in Shakespeare's development raises interesting questions about its relation to the English history plays which it follows and the great tragedies which it precedes; it can be fairly certainly dated in 1599, probably just between *Henry V* and *Hamlet*.[1] In some sense its political issues resemble those of the English history plays, and it draws on a similar imagery of sickness and disorder in the body politic.[2] But it is a great oversimplification to call this play a "Morality of Respublica." [3] Such issues as Caesar's tyranny with its threatened destruction of republican liberties, the lawfulness of conspiracy, and the justification for political murder are hardly those of a morality play. In the Elizabethan period there was apparently no one traditional way of regarding either Caesar or Brutus. One may assemble a wealth of commentary on both sides of the question, although even if the texts were all pro-

Caesar and anti-Brutus, this would still not prove anything about Shakespeare's treatment of these historical figures.[4] Perhaps he was attracted to Caesar and Brutus and the events connected with them just because of their complexity; they offer a subject particularly suitable for handling in a tragedy. In this sense the "structure of sustained dramatic ambiguities"[5] of *Julius Caesar* and its "pervasive irony"[6] show its affinity with the great tragedies, especially with *Hamlet*. One obvious and often noticed similarity is that between Brutus and Hamlet, for both become tragically involved in a calculated and bloody murder which goes against the inclinations of their moral being. And the figure of Caesar, like the Ghost in *Hamlet*, always remains somewhat of an enigma. One may even go so far as to argue, as Schanzer does, that *Julius Caesar* is a "problem" play in the mood of *Measure for Measure*.[7] This judgment is at an opposite extreme from the simplified and one-sided views of earlier critics.

The chief image themes in *Julius Caesar* are the storm and its portents, blood, and fire. All of these have two opposed meanings, depending upon one's point of view. With reference to the conspirators, the storm and its portents indicate the evil of Caesar's tyranny in the body politic of Rome, while blood and fire are the means of purging and purifying this evil. But with reference to Caesar and his party, the storm and its portents indicate the evil of conspiracy that is shaking the body politic of Rome, while blood and fire are the signs of assassination and civil strife this evil brings in its wake. From either point of view, however, the action of the play moves from disorder (Caesar's tyranny or the conspiracy) to an uneasy restoration of order at the end (murder of Caesar or destruction of the conspiracy). These issues are never clearly resolved in the play. Although the defeat and death of the conspirators seem to be a comment on the futility of their enterprise, the rise of Antony and Octavius is by no means an affirmation of justice, truth, and human values.

The imagery of the storm and its portents allows Shakespeare to range freely among the correspondences of man, the state, and the cosmos. The tempest in nature reflects disturbances in man and the state, or, conversely, these disturbances are projected or externalized in the tempest. We need to revive some sense of the storm as it was presented in the Elizabethan theater. The storm poetry of *Julius Caesar* is not awesome and elemental as it is in *King Lear*, yet the storm in both plays was probably designed to create a similar theatrical effect. The stage directions of *Julius Caesar* indicate that the storm was represented chiefly by thunder and lightning. Act I, scene iii, opens with *"Thunder and lightning,"* and there is *"Thunder still"* at line 100. We have *"Thunder"* at the end of II,i, and the following scene begins with *"Thunder and lightning."* Although the stage directions may literally be reduced to four peals of thunder and two flashes of lightning, these effects seem to be much more prolonged — at 1.3.100 it thunders *"still."*

We are not certain how these storm effects were produced in the Elizabethan public theater, but the Prologue to Jonson's *Every Man in His Humour* gives us a clue when he tells us what his author will avoid:

> nor roul'd bullet heard
> To say, it thunders; nor tempestuous drumme
> Rumbles, to tell you when the storm is come.

We also learn from John Melton's *Astrologaster* (1620) that "Drummers make Thunder in the Tyring-house, and the twelve-penny Hirelings make artificiall lightning in their Heavens." [8] In both these examples thunder is a powerful noise made either with a rolled bullet or by drums, and lightning is a bright flash of fire. Lawrence thinks that "the approved method of making stage lightning" was to blow "rosin through a candle flame," [9] but it could have been done simply and effectively by fireworks. We ought to keep in mind, then, that the storm in *Julius Caesar* is not confined to words, and that the sights and sounds of the theater play an essential part in this imagery: it was possible to make a storm fairly impressive on the Elizabethan stage.

The final couplet of Cassius' soliloquy in I,ii serves as a prologue to the storm theme:

> And after this let Caesar seat him sure,
> For we will shake him, or worse days endure. (1.2.325–26)

The thunder and lightning of I,iii follow immediately as a comment of the heavens on Cassius' words; this is the beginning of "worse days" for Rome. After the thunder and lightning, Casca enters "breathless" and staring (1.3.2), with his sword drawn (1.3.19), and in great anxiety. This disordered entrance conveys an immediate visual impression of the storm's awesome power, for the present Casca is entirely different from the blunt and somewhat cynical figure of I,ii. He asks Cicero with obvious agitation: "Are not you mov'd when all the sway of earth/ Shakes like a thing unfirm?" (1.3.3–4). There has never been such a storm as this, so terrible and so full of unnatural prodigies, for

> never till to-night, never till now,
> Did I go through a tempest dropping fire.
> Either there is a civil strife in heaven,
> Or else the world, too saucy with the gods,
> Incenses them to send destruction. (1.3.9–13)

Casca seeks the meaning of the storm in the relations between the "gods" and the "world," and the "civil strife in heaven" will soon serve as a pattern for the conflict on earth.

Casca goes on to enumerate wonders — the slave with the burning hand, the lion near the Capitol, the men in fire seen by women, the screech-owl at noon in the market place — they are all impossible things that the gods have sent as signs and warnings to men:

> When these prodigies
> Do so conjointly meet, let not men say
> 'These are their reasons — they are natural,'
> For I believe they are portentous things
> Unto the climate that they point upon. (1.3.28–32)

These prodigies serve as a choric comment on the evil that is taking place (growing conspiracy) and on the evil that is about to occur (murder of Caesar and consequent civil war).

The entrance of Cassius marks a movement from description of the storm to an application of its meaning. Since it signifies so much, this is indeed "A very pleasing night" (1.3.43) to Cassius, who has walked about the streets

> And, thus unbraced, Casca, as you see,
> Have bar'd my bosom to the thunder-stone;
> And when the cross blue lightning seem'd to open
> The breast of heaven, I did present myself
> Even in the aim and very flash of it. (1.3.48–52)

Cassius does not remain in fear and trembling like Casca, because the "true cause" (1.3.62) of this "strange impatience of the heavens" (1.3.61) is at once apparent:

> Why all these fires, why all these gliding ghosts,
> Why birds and beasts, from quality and kind;
> Why old men, fools, and children calculate;[10]

45

Why all these things change from their ordinance,
Their natures, and preformed faculties,
To monstrous quality — why, you shall find
That heaven hath infus'd them with these spirits
To make them instruments of fear and warning
Unto some monstrous state.   (1.3.63–71)

This is a key passage for understanding the effect of the storm, and unnaturalness and disorder are emphasized in every line. These prodigies represent a twisting of things from their natural course ("ordinance") and essential being ("preformed faculties") into a "monstrous" sort. The word "monstrous" specifically links the condition of the state with what is occurring in external nature, and it is a strong indication of disorder. Remember that conspiracy wears a "monstrous visage" (2.1.81), and that the Ghost of Caesar is to Brutus a "monstrous apparition" (4.3.277). Cassius proceeds to identify the storm and its portents with Caesar, the ruler of the "monstrous state":

Now could I, Casca, name to thee a man
Most like this dreadful night
That thunders, lightens, opens graves, and roars
As doth the lion in the Capitol;
A man no mightier than thyself or me
In personal action, yet prodigious grown
And fearful, as these strange eruptions are.   (1.3.72–78)

The analogy is very close, and Cassius' identification is driven home by the naïve question of Casca: " 'Tis Caesar that you mean. Is it not, Cassius?" (1.3.79).

The sense of storm is maintained in II,i by several references, although it remains a minor motif. Brutus comments that "The exhalations, whizzing in the air,/ Give so much light that I may read by them" (2.1.44–45). Further, Cas-

46

sius wonders whether Caesar will stay away from the Capitol because of

> these apparent prodigies,
> The unaccustom'd terror of this night,
> And the persuasion of his augurers. . . . (2.1.198–200)

Cassius fears that Caesar may be interpreting the signs of the storm as he himself has done in I,iii. In the dialogue between Brutus and Portia atmospheric detail is added to our feeling of the storm by references to the "raw cold morning" (2.1.236), the "dank morning" (2.1.263), and the "rheumy and unpurged air" (2.1.266).

At the very end of the scene there is a stage direction, *"Thunder,"* and the next scene opens with *"Thunder and lightning."* Julius Caesar appears in his dressing gown ("nightgown") and comments on what is occurring:

> Nor heaven nor earth have been at peace to-night.
> Thrice hath Calphurnia in her sleep cried out
> 'Help, ho! They murther Caesar!' (2.2.1–3)

To Calphurnia the storm and its portents point to the murder of Caesar, and we should remember that this is the same storm in which Casca and Cassius have actually plotted his death, and in which Brutus has been won to the conspiracy. Calphurnia tries to dissuade Caesar from going forth by an account of unnatural prodigies: "O Caesar, these things are beyond all use,/ And I do fear them!" (2.2.25–26). "Use" is a word for what is to be expected, what is natural, the proper "ordinance" (1.3.66) of things. Calphurnia fears that the portents by their very magnitude cry out the death of Caesar; there is a proportion in these things, and portents are not the same for all men:

When beggars die there are no comets seen;
The heavens themselves blaze forth the death of princes.

(2.2.30–31)

Finally, we have Calphurnia's dream of Caesar's statue running pure blood, which she interprets as "warnings and portents/ And evils imminent" (2.2.80–81).

2

The central issue about the meaning of *Julius Caesar* is raised most forcefully and vividly by the imagery of blood.[11] If the murder of Caesar is indeed a "savage spectacle" (3.1.223), then the blood with which the conspirators are smeared "Up to the elbows" (3.1.107) is the sign of their guilt. But if the murder of Caesar is a ritual blood-letting of the body politic of Rome, then blood is the sign of purification and new life. The latter point of view marks the tragedy of Brutus, for he cannot foresee that his high-minded but specious motives will be drowned in the bloodiness of murder and civil strife. He is tragically unable to bridge the gap between reasons and acts.

The blood theme begins in II,i, where it becomes a powerful symbol for the conspiracy. The question of what to do with Antony after the murder of Caesar is a crucial one. The shrewd and practical Cassius wants to kill him, but Brutus objects and makes, according to Plutarch, the first great tactical error of his career.[12] This decision also indicates the rift between the other conspirators and Brutus, who argues his position from the analogy between the bodies human and politic:

Our course will seem too bloody, Caius Cassius,
To cut the head off and then hack the limbs,

48

Like wrath in death and envy afterwards;
For Antony is but a limb of Caesar.   (2.1.162–65)

He thinks of blood as the symbol of common murder, and he fears the stain of its guilt. The slaying of Caesar is a necessary and beneficial act, but Brutus wishes that there were no blood:

Let's [18] be sacrificers, but not butchers, Caius.
We all stand up against the spirit of Caesar,
And in the spirit of men there is no blood.
O that we then could come by Caesar's spirit
And not dismember Caesar! But, alas,
Caesar must bleed for it!   (2.1.166–71)

This is one of the most important passages in the play for showing the tragic wrongness of Brutus. The murder of Caesar proves to be not a loving sacrifice, but only a fruitless act of butchery, and its bloodiness is stressed as significantly as the murder of Duncan in *Macbeth*. When all is done, only the body of Caesar has been killed, not the spirit, which stays very much alive in Antony and Octavius and wins vengeance in civil strife. The meaning of the play can almost be formulated by taking the negative of all these statements of Brutus.

The tragedy of Brutus springs from his complete sincerity in preferring duty to Rome to his personal friendship with Caesar. In this sense his tragic course is ironic because his choice is essentially noble but misguided. It is an irony of his situation that things turn out quite differently from what he had anticipated. His inner conflicts are still strong in these early scenes, and it is from his paradoxically divided loyalties that he speaks of the murder of Caesar as a loving, sacrificial act:

49

And, gentle friends,
Let's kill him boldly, but not wrathfully;
Let's carve him as a dish fit for the gods,
Not hew him as a carcass fit for hounds.
And let our hearts, as subtle masters do,
Stir up their servants to an act of rage
And after seem to chide 'em. This shall make
Our purpose necessary, and not envious;
Which so appearing to the common eyes,
We shall be call'd purgers, not murderers.   (2.1.171–80)

Brutus persists in the analogy of the state as a body, which the conspirators by bleeding will restore to health. In this way the assassination of Caesar will be a purgation, a phlebotomy, and not a murder — it is a necessary though bloody act, and Brutus shrinks from the bloody stain of murder.

Among the portents in the next scene are two powerful signs of blood. Calphurnia warns Caesar of "Fierce fiery warriors" (2.2.19) who "drizzled blood upon the Capitol" (2.2.21). This blood prepares us for the actual murder of Caesar in the Capitol, and "Fierce fiery warriors" looks ahead to the antagonists in the civil strife. The concern with blood becomes more ominous in Calphurnia's dream, as Caesar relates it to Decius:

She dreamt to-night she saw my statuë,
Which, like a fountain with an hundred spouts,
Did run pure blood; and many lusty Romans
Came smiling and did bathe their hands in it.   (2.2.76–79)

This image, too, anticipates the later action in which the conspirators do actually bathe their hands in Caesar's blood after his murder. But Decius turns Calphurnia's dream to seemingly favorable omen:

Your statue spouting blood in many pipes,
In which so many smiling Romans bath'd,

Signifies that from you great Rome shall suck
Reviving blood, and that great men shall press
For tinctures, stains, relics, and cognizance. (2.2.85–89)

The image continues the analogy between Caesar's body and the body politic of Rome. There is a covert praise of Caesar's assassination here: the body politic of Rome will be revived by the murder of Caesar, although great men will press for memorials of him once he is dead. The last two lines are full of heraldic and religious imagery intended to flatter Caesar.

Blood imagery is of greatest importance in III,i, where it is not only a repeated verbal theme, but also enters into the stage action. Animal blood from concealed bladders or sponges was probably used to represent Caesar's murder on the Elizabethan stage, and, from all indications, there was a frank emphasis on the spectacular effects of murder scenes.[14] As Lisideius points out in Dryden's *Essay of Dramatic Poesy*, it is because the English audience enjoys these bloody scenes that it will not tolerate the French neo-classical practice of narrating deaths that occur off-stage.

A number of blood images in III,i show Caesar in the height of pride just before his fall. He thrusts aside Metellus Cimber, who "might fire the blood of ordinary men" (3.1.37), but not Caesar's. He does not bear "such rebel blood" (3.1.40) that can be melted by emotional persuasion, and the chief connotation of "blood" is the passion that Caesar forswears. The world is full of men who are "flesh and blood, and apprehensive" (3.1.67), but only Caesar remains in cold, unchanging constancy. Yet ten lines later he is stabbed to death as readily as any mortal, and the blood that would not be fired or thawed now flows freely from the dagger wounds of the conspirators.

From this point until the end of the play the fact of Caesar's assassination is kept constantly before the audience, and this is done to a large extent by blood imagery. Of course, Caesar's bloody and rent body is on stage through all of this scene, and at a number of important moments (3.1.148–50, 194–210, 254–75) Antony addresses it as if it were a living presence; Octavius' Servant does the same (3.1.281). In the next scene it is absent only for the short time of Brutus' oration. At line 44 Antony and others enter with the body, which remains on stage until removed by the plebeians for the funeral pyre (3.2.264 s.d.). Thus Caesar's body dominates the scene for almost 450 lines after his death. The body plays a conspicuous role during Antony's funeral oration, but throughout the time it is on stage it serves as a visible indictment of the conspirators. Its commanding presence on stage, possibly on the elevated platform or dais on which the "throne" usually stood,[15] keeps the audience aware of the crime of assassination.

Shortly after the murder, Brutus directs the conspirators in a fearful blood ritual:

> Stoop, Romans, stoop,
> And let us bathe our hands in Caesar's blood
> Up to the elbows and besmear our swords.
> Then walk we forth, even to the market place,
> And waving our red weapons o'er our heads,
> Let's all cry 'Peace, freedom, and liberty!' (3.1.105–10)

This action fulfills the prophecy of Calphurnia's dream (2.2.76–79), and we may assume that stage blood was liberally used for these effects, since the conspirators' hands and swords need to remain very vividly bloody for about 150 lines (until the exit at 3.1.253). The blood ritual that

Brutus began at 2.1.166 seems now a sacrilege rather than a consecration. It is continued as Cassius takes up Brutus' invocation:

> Stoop then and wash. How many ages hence
> Shall this our lofty scene be acted over
> In states unborn and accents yet unknown! [16] (3.1.111–13)

And Brutus answers antiphonally in the same spirit of uncontrolled exaltation:

> How many times shall Caesar bleed in sport,
> That now on Pompey's basis lies along
> No worthier than the dust! (3.1.114–16)

The eyes of the conspirators are on posterity, which they are sure will approve their present acts. These speeches represent the highest point in the development of the conspirators; with the entrance of Antony's Servant their downward course begins.

Antony's speeches in this scene reiterate "blood" both as the symbol of the murdered Caesar and as the sign of the conspirators' guilt. The double emphasis is made almost in his first words:

> I know not, gentlemen, what you intend,
> Who else must be let blood, who else is rank.
> If I myself, there is no hour so fit
> As Caesar's death's hour; nor no instrument
> Of half that worth as those your swords, made rich
> With the most noble blood of all this world.
> I do beseech ye, if you bear me hard,
> Now, whilst your purpled hands do reek and smoke,
> Fulfil your pleasure. (3.1.151–59)

Antony's thoughts run on blood as he boldly dares the conspirators to kill him, too. Their hands and swords have been

53

bathed in Caesar's blood, whose visual signs they now flaunt to all Rome as justification of their deed. Throughout this scene Antony provides a bitter, sarcastic commentary on these "purpled hands" and swords, for they bear the stain of guilt upon them just as surely as Macbeth's hands and dagger do.

Brutus' reply to Antony acknowledges the blood, but attempts to offer reasons:

> O Antony, beg not your death of us!
> Though now we must appear bloody and cruel,
> As by our hands and this our present act
> You see we do, yet see you but our hands
> And this the bleeding business they have done.
> Our hearts you see not. They are pitiful. . . . (3.1.164–69)

The separation of "hands" from "hearts" echoes Brutus' earlier distinction between the body and the spirit of Caesar (2.1.166ff). In his tragic blindness he cannot see that the one ("hands") is not simply an instrument for the other ("hearts"): in the act of murder the body and its blood are inseparable from the spirit.

But it is the bloody hands of the conspirators that Antony is insisting on as the outward badge of their guilt. In a supremely ironic ceremony Antony shakes each of their hands:

> Let each man render me his bloody hand.
> First, Marcus Brutus, will I shake with you;
> Next, Caius Cassius, do I take your hand;
> Now, Decius Brutus, yours; now yours, Metellus;
> Yours, Cinna; and, my valiant Casca, yours.
> Though last, not least in love, yours, good Trebonius.
> (3.1.184–89)

This ceremony parallels the one by which Brutus entered

the conspiracy: "Give me your hands all over, one by one" (2.1.112). We need to supply the all-important expression and attitude of Antony here, the mingling of intense loathing and feigned reconciliation. From this handshaking Antony acquires "bloody fingers" (3.1.198), *les mains sales,* and he speaks as if to undo the guilty ritual in which he has participated:

> Pardon me, Julius! Here wast thou bay'd, brave hart;
> Here didst thou fall; and here thy hunters stand,
> Sign'd in thy spoil, and crimson'd in thy lethe.
> O world, thou wast the forest to this hart;
> And this indeed, O world, the heart of thee!
> How like a deer, stroken by many princes,
> Dost thou here lie! (3.1.204–10)

He has almost gone too far, and Cassius says menacingly "Mark Antony —" (3.1.211), but Brutus, who himself loved Caesar, will now shield Antony. The hunting imagery of this speech stresses butchery rather than the sacrifice Brutus hoped for in 2.1.166ff. A grotesque pun demonstrates that the "heart" of the world can be killed bloodily like a "hart." Perhaps "lethe," too, is a part of this imagery and refers to the marking of hunters with the blood of a slain deer.[17] When Cassius asks Antony if he will be a friend, Antony answers ironically: "Therefore I took your hands. . ." (3.1.218). By sharing in Caesar's blood he has seemed to condone the murder, but behind this mask vengeance for Caesar is being prepared.

Brutus' unshaken sense of his own rightness allows him to commit his second great tactical error according to Plutarch:[18] he gives Antony permission to speak a funeral oration for Caesar in the market place. We need to understand the tragic character of Brutus here. He has absolute confidence in his own rational power, for the conflict in him does not go beyond the alignment of motives leading to the decision to murder Caesar:

> Between the acting of a dreadful thing
> And the first motion, all the interim is
> Like a phantasma or a hideous dream. (2.1.63–65)

After the "acting" of the "dreadful thing," however (equivalent to the decision to murder Caesar, rather than the murder itself), the "phantasma" and "hideous dream" become things external rather than aspects of Brutus' mind. But in the case of Macbeth or King Lear the "phantasma" and "hideous dream" become acute only after "the acting of a dreadful thing," or in the case of Hamlet and Othello it is the process of decision itself which persists as "phantasma" and "hideous dream" throughout the action. The scope of Brutus' tragedy is limited by his own sense of rightness, for his decision to take part in the conspiracy seems to end his process of self-questioning. He is "arm'd so strong in honesty" [19] (4.3.67) that he cannot feel the world aright or admit the possibility of error, although the quarrel scene perhaps contains a subdued sense of guilt and tragic disillusion.[20] He will either give reasons to Antony for Caesar's murder, "Or else were this a savage spectacle" (3.1.223). But Brutus seems too sure of his reasons to allow for alternatives to his own course of action, and this is one of the chief sources of his tragic blindness.

Antony's soliloquy after the conspirators leave says directly and forcefully what has already been said ironically. The stage situation for this soliloquy is particulary impressive. Beginning with the meeting of the Senate and continuing with the murder of Caesar and its aftermath, the stage has always been crowded, especially with conspirators. Antony's aloneness, then, comes as a sudden contrast. It is a moment of unexpected quiet which indicates that the counteraction is already underway. Antony apologizes to the dead Caesar for his conciliatory role with "these butchers" (3.1.255), and he prophesies the vengeance of blood for blood that must follow:

> Woe to the hand that shed this costly blood!
> Over thy wounds now do I prophesy
> (Which, like dumb mouths, do ope their ruby lips
> To beg the voice and utterance of my tongue),
> A curse shall light upon the limbs of men;
> Domestic fury and fierce civil strife
> Shall cumber all the parts of Italy;
> Blood and destruction shall be so in use
> And dreadful objects so familiar
> That mothers shall but smile when they behold
> Their infants quartered with the hands of war,
> All pity chok'd with custom of fell deeds. . . . (3.1.258–69)

Antony's vision of civil war is like the Bishop of Carlisle's in *Richard II* (4.1.136–49), and both serve as turning points in the action. The conspirators have shed Caesar's "costly" (precious) blood, which will indeed prove "costly" (dear, expensive) to them.

In III,i we learn that Antony will use his funeral oration to see "how the people take/ The cruel issue of these bloody men. . ." (3.1.293–94), and the oration never allows us to forget the blood of Caesar. If Antony read Caesar's will, the commons would "go and kiss dead Caesar's wounds/ And dip their napkins in his sacred blood. . ." (3.2.138–39). This blood has now become that of a martyr or a saint. Brutus' "most unkindest cut of all" (3.2.188) burst Caesar's heart, and

> Even at the base of Pompey's statuë
> (Which all the while ran blood) great Caesar fell.
>
> (3.2.193–94)

We recall Caesar's triumphing "over Pompey's blood" (1.1.56) at the beginning of the play; now Pompey triumphs over Caesar's blood. Antony very artfully disclaims any power as an orator "To stir men's blood" (3.2.228). The "most bloody sight" (3.2.207) of Caesar's body and "sweet Caesar's wounds, poor poor dumb mouths" (3.2.230) speak for themselves and act as a powerful persuasion to vengeance.

There is a general slackening of the blood imagery in Acts IV and V. After Brutus' "bloody spur" (4.2.25) image for the civil war, the next significant use of "blood" is in the quarrel scene. Brutus counters Cassius' waspish indignation with the fact of Caesar's murder:

> Remember March; the ides of March remember.
> Did not great Julius bleed for justice sake?
> What villain touch'd his body that did stab
> And not for justice? (4.3.18–21)

If the purpose of the assassination were not justice, then Caesar's blood is the mark of butchery and murder. By the time of this scene the first flush of idealism has gone out of the conspiracy. It is seen here on the defensive, and Cassius' venality is a sign of disillusion. Only Brutus persists in his original uprightness, which is repeatedly expressed with all the insolent frankness of the morally sure. There is also a suggestion here that Brutus is beginning to be aware of the tragic betrayal of the original ideals of the conspiracy. This awareness creates a sense of doom and fatality in the scene, which is climaxed by the appearance of Caesar's Ghost.

58

The blood imagery of V,i sets the tone for the battle of Philippi in V,ii. A Messenger reports the enemy's "bloody sign of battle" (5.1.14) to Antony and Octavius. Further on, Octavius cuts off the ingenious conceits of the battle parley with the words of a practical man:

> Come, come, the cause! If arguing make us sweat,
> The proof of it will turn to redder drops.
> Look,
> I draw a sword against conspirators.
> When think you that the sword goes up again?
> Never, till Caesar's three-and-thirty wounds
> Be well aveng'd, or till another Caesar
> Have added slaughter to the sword of traitors.   (5.1.48–55)

This is the case against Brutus, Cassius, and their party: they are "conspirators" and "traitors" who must answer for it in battle; the arbitration of the issue will be in blood, not words. The final blood image is used by Titinius for the dead Cassius:

> O setting sun,
> As in thy red rays thou dost sink to night,
> So in his red blood Cassius' day is set!
> The sun of Rome is set.   (5.3.60–63)

So Cassius ends in his own "red blood," slain by the same hand and with the same sword that stabbed Caesar. This is the reciprocity of blood for blood.

3

The fire imagery of *Julius Caesar* follows the basic conflicts in the play in a manner similar to the themes of storm and blood. Here, too, the interpretation of the images depends on our attitude toward Caesar and the conspirators.

Does fire refer to Caesar's tyranny or to the evils of conspiracy? It is the conspirators' tragic error to think of the destructive power of fire as also being purgative and purifying. Brutus, for example, justifies the murder by a proverb: "As fire drives out fire, so pity pity" (3.1.171) — the fire of conspiracy will destroy the fire of Caesar's tyranny. But the conspirators are themselves consumed in the fire of civil war that avenges Caesar. These comments may serve as a schematic and simplified pattern of the fire imagery, in which there are also two distinct lines of development. First, "fire" is used in the sense of passion, emotional power, the ability to inflame or enkindle, as Antony's oration inflames the mob. Second, "fire" is considered as a destructive and purifying force. This is the literal sense of fire, and it is carried into the stage action when the mob which Antony has inflamed lights firebrands to burn the conspirators' houses. In this scene the two meanings of fire merge.

The theme of fire as passion and its kindling power begins in the dialogue of Brutus and Cassius in I,ii. Brutus is aware of the fact that Cassius is "working" him to conspiracy (1.2.163), so that there is a certain sense of triumph in Cassius' remark:

> I am glad
> That my weak words have struck but thus much show
> Of fire from Brutus. (1.2.175-77)

Brutus is the flint that the passionate Cassius strikes against in his effort of persuasion. The flint image is used again more explicitly in the quarrel scene, where Brutus confesses his weakness:

> O Cassius, you are yoked with a lamb
> That carries anger as the flint bears fire;

> Who, much enforced, shows a hasty spark,
> And straight is cold again.   (4.3.110–13)

This imagery points the contrast between the hot Cassius and the cold Brutus (compare the hot-cold contrast between Cleopatra and Octavia in *Antony and Cleopatra*).

The fire of conspiracy that Cassius ignited in Brutus is thoroughly confirmed in the fire imagery of II,i. Brutus shrinks from a formal oath, since the motives for conspiracy themselves should

> bear fire enough
> To kindle cowards and to steel with valour
> The melting spirits of women. . . .   (2.1.120–22)

The noble Brutus thinks of himself as kindled to conspiracy by justice alone. "Enkindled" (2.1.249) is indeed the word which Portia uses for her husband later in the scene (it is significant how often Portia uses Brutus' words — it strengthens the bond between them and attests to Portia's dependence on her husband). At the end of the scene Brutus is able to persuade Caius Ligarius to abandon his sickness for an "exploit worthy the name of honour" (2.1.317). Caius needs only the example of Brutus,

> And with a heart new-fir'd I follow you,
> To do I know not what; but it sufficeth
> That Brutus leads me on.   (2.1.332–34)

Brutus, fired to conspiracy by Cassius, is now able to fire others, and Caius Ligarius is a good example of Brutus' power to win an unquestioning assent. This passage suggests one obvious reason why Cassius was so anxious to gain the support of Brutus.

These images of fire as passion and its kindling power

61

SHAKESPEARE'S ROMAN PLAYS

are strongly associated with the conspiracy. It is interesting
to note that shortly before his murder in III,i Caesar renounces this sense of fire by asserting his cold constancy.
Metellus Cimber's suit "Might fire the blood of ordinary
men. . ." (3.1.37), but not Caesar's. He is "constant as
the Northern Star" (3.1.60), and fire to him implies in-
constancy:

> The skies are painted with unnumb'red sparks,
> They are all fire, and every one doth shine;
> But there's but one in all doth hold his place.   (3.1.63–65)

Caesar's murder follows soon after these declarations of
starry stability.

The second sense of fire, as a destructive and purifying
force, is developed in the theme of the storm and its portents. Casca has never until this night been through "a
tempest dropping fire" (1.3.10), nor seen a sight like this:

> A common slave (you know him well by sight)
> Held up his left hand, which did flame and burn
> Like twenty torches join'd; and yet his hand,
> Not sensible of fire, remain'd unscorch'd.   (1.3.15–18)

Shakespeare dramatizes Plutarch here with a personal
touch: the anonymous "common slave" becomes a figure
whom Cicero knows "well by sight." Among the prodigies
are also the "Men, all in fire," who "walk up and down the
streets" (1.3.25). In II,ii Calphurnia warns Caesar that
"Fierce fiery warriors fight [21] upon the clouds. . ." (2.2.19),
and the fiery comet portent of this scene (2.2.30–31) is a
heavenly emblem of Caesar's murder. To Cassius fire is a
symbol of the base passivity of Rome, which lets itself be
used as kindling matter for Caesar's tyranny:

62

Those that with haste will make a mighty fire
Begin it with weak straws. What trash is Rome,
What rubbish and what offal, when it serves
For the base matter to illuminate
So vile a thing as Caesar! (1.3.107–11)

This "monstrous state" (1.3.71) of Rome can only be righted by deeds "Most bloody, fiery, and most terrible" (1.3.130).

Both senses of fire — as passion and its kindling power, and as a destructive and purifying force — are brought together in the scene of Antony's funeral oration. At the end of this scene the fire imagery emerges into the dramatic action, which marks the culmination of the theme in the play. Antony's oration, by its persuasive rhetoric, enkindles and inflames the mob. When he pauses for tears, the Second Plebeian remarks: "Poor soul! his eyes are red as fire with weeping" (3.2.121). Antony's success depends on his ability to communicate the "fire" of his own emotions, and he has soon gained such hypnotic power over the mob that he is able to control their reactions. At line 174, for example, he says: "If you have tears, prepare to shed them now"; this achieves its effect some twenty-five lines further: "O, now you weep, and I perceive you feel/ The dint of pity" (3.2.198–99).

It is just this technique of suggestion that Antony uses in connection with Caesar's will:

You are not wood, you are not stones, but men;
And being men, hearing the will of Caesar,
It will inflame you, it will make you mad. (3.2.148–50)

With masterful rhetoric Antony suggests the effect if only he provide the cause, and he seems to take pleasure in playing with effects. In this respect both he and Cassius (com-

63

pare his soliloquy at the end of I,ii) have qualities of the Machiavel. Antony is able to withhold the will for almost a hundred lines while he himself stirs up the mob to cry for vengeance: "Revenge! About! Seek! Burn! Fire! Kill! Slay!/ Let not a traitor live!" (3.2.209–10). Fire now becomes the instrument of destruction as Antony's own insinuation of mutiny is taken up by the plebeians:

> *1. Pleb.*   We'll burn the house of Brutus.
> *3. Pleb.* Away then! Come, seek the conspirators.   (3.2.236–37)

When Antony reads the will, the incensed mob seeks fire to wreak havoc on its enemies:

> *1. Pleb.*   Come, away, away!
> We'll burn his body in the holy place
> And with the brands fire the traitors' houses.
> Take up the body.
> *2. Pleb.* Go fetch fire!
> *3. Pleb.* Pluck down benches!
> *4. Pleb.* Pluck down forms, windows, anything!
>   (3.2.258–64)

We recall that this same violent, enthusiastic mob was the hostile group of citizens before whom Antony began his oration. Antony observes his effect with all the aloofness of the successful plotter: "Now let it work. Mischief, thou art afoot,/ Take thou what course thou wilt" (3.2.365–66). He has finished with his inflammatory rhetoric, and he now speaks in the cold, political tone of the proscription scene (IV,i) some fifty lines further.

After the concentrated verbal imagery of fire in Antony's oration, we have the image of actual fire as the mob goes to burn Caesar's body and the houses of the conspirators. This stage imagery of fire is the logical climax of the theme. The

Second Plebeian's cry, "Go fetch fire!" suggests that firebrands are brought in from off-stage, but the mob could also ignite the firebrands right there in front of the audience. Actual fire at this hectic moment is a powerful image of the citizens' passionate and destructive temper, and there is a sense of poetic justice in the use of brands from Caesar's funeral pyre to burn the conspirators' houses. It shows the double aspect of fire: consecration and destruction. In an over-all view, fire, which was first identified with the conspiracy as a symbol of destruction, has now, after the murder of Caesar, become an instrument of vengeance. It thus takes on a purgative, consecrating role.

Act III, scene iii, shows us the mob in all its undiscriminating anarchy. It is on its way to burn the conspirators' houses, and the innocent Cinna the Poet is caught up in its savage fury. The scene is full of a grotesque humor, as in the string of preliminary questions and the single answer (3.3.5–19), or in the repeated adverbial tyranny of the mob: "directly," "briefly," "wisely," and "truly" — there is a farcical lack of understanding between the mob and its prey. But it is a terrifying scene, too, because Cinna is torn to pieces for his name and bad verses alone, only words. Again, fire symbolizes the violent mood of the mob:

> 3. *Pleb.* Tear him, tear him! Come, brands, ho! firebrands! To Brutus', to Cassius'! Burn all! Some to Decius' house and some to Casca's; some to Ligarius'! Away, go! (3.3.40–43)

As at the end of III,ii, this seems to indicate that firebrands are either brought on stage or lit there, and they are menacingly brandished by the mob. Poets do not seem to fare very well in the Roman world of *Julius Caesar*, and the Poet (the cynic philosopher Phaonius in Plutarch) who rushes in upon the quarrel of Brutus and Cassius is similarly threatened and unceremoniously driven out. Brutus' comment is in the style of Coriolanus: "What should the wars do with these jigging fools?" (4.3.137).

There is not much further use of fire imagery in Acts IV and V. In IV,iii Brutus tells Cassius of Portia's death by swallowing fire (4.3.156); the political events in their personal turn have been too much for her. The only reference to fire in the battle of Philippi is made when Cassius asks Titinius: "Are those my tents where I perceive the fire?" (5.3.13). This is a further indication of the destruction of the conspirators by fire, a point emphasized in III,ii and III,iii. The final fire image provides a significant conclusion to the theme. Strato, who held the sword for Brutus, affirms the honor of his master:

> The conquerors can but make a fire of him;
> For Brutus only overcame himself,
> And no man else hath honour by his death.   (5.5.55–57)

The fire of conspiracy, having been turned as an instrument of vengeance against the conspirators, now ends with the dead body of Brutus ready for the pyre. This is the final requiting of Caesar.

4

In a very direct sense the "image" of a dramatic character is the actor performing the role in the theater. It is his task to embody in his person the imagery of the text and to present this realization to the audience. This is the mimetic, presentational core of the drama. In the role of Caesar, for example, the crucial contrast between the great public figure and the infirm private man — or what Knights calls "the person and the public persona, the face and the mask" [22] — is largely a matter of acting and stage presentation. The contrast is certainly developed verbally, but the most effective image of Caesar's double nature is the one we receive from the actor in the theater.

Critics of *Julius Caesar* have been inclined to make strong and final judgments of the character of Caesar. Brandes calls him "a miserable caricature" and thinks "It was because of Shakespeare's lack of historical and classical culture that the incomparable grandeur of the figure of Caesar left him unmoved." [23] Schücking, however, believes it "quite absurd to suppose that Shakespeare diminishes the importance of Caesar. Rather must we say that *the vastness of his figure is tacitly or openly presupposed in all the happenings of the play*." [24] The truth about the paradoxical figure of Caesar cannot be resolved at either extreme, and his real character and intentions were debatable even in antiquity. The official Caesar of Shakespeare's play is presented with all the pomp and ceremony of a great public person. Yet he is curiously undercut by our image of Caesar the private man, full of physical infirmities and an irritating insistence on his own dignity. Dowden puts the matter very well when he observes that Caesar has become

to himself legendary and mythical. The real man Caesar disappears for himself under the greatness of the Caesar myth. He forgets himself as he actually is, and knows only the vast legendary power named Caesar. He is a *numen* to himself, speaking of Caesar in the third person, as if of some power above and behind his consciousness.[25]

The people love the public spectacle of Caesar and their acclamations tend to deify him. In the first scene of the play they have come out to welcome him home after his victory over Pompey's sons in Spain, "and to rejoice in his triumph" (1.1.36). They look upon this ceremony as a public entertainment or play with Caesar as protagonist; for, as Casca tells us,

If the tag-rag people did not clap him and hiss him, according as he pleas'd and displeas'd them, as they use to do the players in the theatre, I am no true man. (1.2.260–63)

This ominous image of the people as audience, essentially fickle and easily moved as Antony's oration shows us so conclusively, also underlies the interview of Brutus and Cassius in I,ii. Although we do not actually see the mob, we are kept aware of its dealings with Caesar in the market place by off-stage sounds: "*Flourish and shout*" (1.2.78 s.d.) and "*Shout. Flourish*" (1.2.131 s.d.). Both of these occasions are marked by Brutus' apprehensive comments: "What means this shouting? I do fear the people/ Choose Caesar for their king" (1.2.79–80); and afterward:

Another general shout?
I do believe that these applauses are
For some new honours that are heap'd on Caesar.
(1.2.132–34)

These shouts and flourishes are a good example of presentational images that are not visual. We do not see the people, but the noise we hear presents an image of them — an ambiguous one, too, which increases the tension of Cassius' effort to persuade Brutus and serves as an ironic commentary on it. These sound-effects images are linked with the verbal imagery by Brutus' comments.

That the people want a Caesar is most graphically illustrated by their reaction to Brutus' funeral oration. "Let him be Caesar" (3.2.56), shouts the Third Plebeian, and the

Fourth continues in the same spirit: "Caesar's better parts/ Shall be crown'd in Brutus" (3.2.56–57). The mob needs a Caesar, and now that Julius is dead, his assassin can easily supply the office. And he will be given the full imperial ceremony of a "triumph home unto his house" (3.2.54) and "a statue with his ancestors" (3.2.55). The mob is not concerned with Caesar the man, but only with Caesar as a public image. These exclamations also at once deny the whole political issue of the conspiracy.

The strongest images of Caesar's imperial splendor occur when he first appears in I,ii. His impressiveness here is emphasized by the staging. He is carried in a litter above the heads of all present, clearly set apart from his followers and from the crowd that has come to see him — and the crowd needs to be large enough to serve as a tribute to Caesar's magnificence. At the outset we observe that his power to command is instantaneous. His "Calphurnia" brings Casca's immediate "Peace, ho! Caesar speaks" (1.2.1). The music ceases at once and there is a general hush which isolates Caesar's words and directs attention to them. This ceremony is repeated when the Soothsayer calls "Caesar!" (1.2.12) from the crowd:

> *Caes.* Ha! Who calls?
> *Casca.* Bid every noise be still. Peace yet again!   (1.2.13–14)

Again the music ceases and Caesar addresses the Soothsayer in the imperial third person: "Speak. Caesar is turn'd to hear" (1.2.17). He then dismisses the Soothsayer and departs with an impressive line of imperatives: "He is a dreamer. Let us leave him. Pass" (1.2.24). In these twenty-four lines of I,ii we have all the essential characteristics of the official Caesar. He is strongly distinguished from his

69

followers and from the Roman mob by his physical appearance, his style of speech, and the attitude of deference in those around him.

In this scene, too, we have the magical use of the name "Caesar" that becomes significant later on. Granville-Barker observes that "We hear the name sounded — sounded rather than spoken — seven times in twenty-four lines." [26] The use of the third person, "Caesar," rather than the first person pronoun tends to merge Caesar the man with Caesar the political figure. This identification is one of the sources of the pride that leads to Caesar's murder, for by mingling the personal with the public, Caesar claims for himself as a man the greatness and objective power of a political function. The constant repetition of the name "Caesar" keeps us aware of this pride. Occasionally, the name seems to function as a potent and independent reality, as when Caesar dismisses his fears of Cassius:

> Yet if my name were liable to fear,
> I do not know the man I should avoid
> So soon as that spare Cassius. (1.2.199–201)

The name is here the reality: a Caesar should not admit fear and therefore Caesar the man is unafraid. This idea is repeated at the end of the speech:

> I rather tell thee what is to be fear'd
> Than what I fear; for always I am Caesar. (1.2.211–12)

The name "Caesar" has become a kind of talisman to ward off fear. Earlier in the scene Cassius had tried to dispel for Brutus the magical power of "Caesar":

> 'Brutus,' and 'Caesar.' What should be in that 'Caesar?'
> Why should that name be sounded more than yours?

Write them together: yours is as fair a name.
Sound them: it doth become the mouth as well.
Weigh them: it is as heavy. Conjure with 'em:
'Brutus' will start a spirit as soon as 'Ceasar.'
Now in the names of all the gods at once,
Upon what meat doth this our Caesar feed
That he is grown so great? (1.2.142–50)

By all tests there are no magical properties in the name; yet
even after Julius Caesar's murder, the name continues in
Octavius as a symbol of power.

Caesar's triumphal entry in I,ii is almost immediately
contrasted with an account of his physical infirmities. Although these are presented chiefly by Cassius, who speaks
with obvious malicious intent, they nevertheless serve to
undercut our picture of Caesar. In this, of course, the actor
who plays Caesar would also contribute very significantly.
It is by no means an heroic and imperial role, but rather
one which emphasizes a certain weariness and consciousness
of pretense. We should note that the shortcomings of Caesar
are "wholly or mainly the fabrications of Shakespeare." [27]
Cassius is trying to undeify Caesar by anecdotes of his
frailty, which gives a certain pettiness and envy to what he
says, and he very characteristically mixes important and
trivial matters:

I had as lief not be as live to be
In awe of such a thing as I myself.
I was born free as Caesar; so were you.
We both have fed as well, and we can both
Endure the winter's cold as well as he. (1.2.95–99)

Cassius then proceeds to illustrate this point with the story
of his swimming match with Caesar in the Tiber. Caesar's
strength failed and he had to be rescued by Cassius:

I, as Aeneas, our great ancestor,
Did from the flames of Troy upon his shoulder
The old Anchises bear, so from the waves of Tiber
Did I the tired Caesar. And this man
Is now become a god, and Cassius is
A wretched creature and must bend his body
If Caesar carelessly but nod on him. (1.2.112–18)

There is a boyish boastfulness in Cassius, especially in his playing Aeneas to the "old" and "tired" Caesar: Caesar is a man, not a god, and a weak and unfit man at that. Cassius continues with an account of Caesar's fever in Spain, when the great Roman general cried, " 'Give me some drink, Titinius,'/ As a sick girl!" (1.2.127–28). The argument, however vivid, is almost completely specious. Why should Caesar be incapacitated for office by these examples of his frailty as a man? The office is a question of spirit rather than body, and in this Caesar is supreme. Yet the mention of these physical infirmities, though not strictly relevant, has a way of remaining in the mind.

We also need to remember a few other infirmities not mentioned by Cassius — Caesar's epileptic fit, for example, which comes just after the mob has forced his third refusal of the crown:

> Casca. He fell down in the market place and foam'd at mouth and was speechless.
> Bru. 'Tis very like he hath the falling sickness.[28]
> Cass. No, Caesar hath it not; but you, and I,
> And honest Casca, we have the falling sickness. (1.2.254–58)

There is a vivid shock effect in the image of Caesar foaming at the mouth in an epileptic fit in the market place, even though it may only be a pretense, and Cassius seizes the figurative suggestion in "falling sickness."

The most effective example of this ironic contrast between Caesar the man and Caesar the great public figure is probably in Caesar's last words in I,ii; he is speaking to Antony of Cassius:

> I rather tell thee what is to be fear'd
> Than what I fear; for always I am Caesar. (1.2.211–12)

After this resounding declaration, Caesar's next words strike us as a thunderbolt:

> Come on my right hand, for this ear is deaf,
> And tell me truly what thou think'st of him. (1.2.213–14)

This deafness in the left ear is a detail that Shakespeare did not find in Plutarch, and for which there is no ancient authority.[29] It is also given particular dramatic prominence by being the last line Caesar speaks before the sennet sounds and he leaves the stage. It is logically true that deafness in one ear does not disqualify a man from political power, but in context it offers an ironic comment on Caesar's omnipotent and superhuman claims. The whole of the assassination scene is shot through with this same irony. While Caesar is claiming the passionless infallibility of a god, we cannot help thinking of Caesar the man and asking ourselves: Is this a god indeed? or are these claims the pretensions of an ordinary and weak mortal? There cannot humanly be a greatness in the man Caesar equivalent to the greatness he imagines for himself, and in this disproportion lies his fall of pride, which is in the *De Casibus* tradition of medieval tragedy.[30]

There is an interesting series of changes in our attitude toward Caesar from the moment of his murder to the end of the play. In the first confusion after the assassination,

SHAKESPEARE'S ROMAN PLAYS

we are acutely conscious of the fall of great Caesar. A moment ago he had made his highest and most superhuman claims, and now his body lies at the pedestal of Pompey's statue "No worthier than the dust!" (3.1.116). Caesar the man has been humbled to this, as pride goeth before a fall — we almost feel the inevitability of such a movement, and it points up the vanity of earthly glory. This attitude is implied in Antony's first words to the dead Caesar:

> O mighty Caesar! dost thou lie so low?
> Are all thy conquests, glories, triumphs, spoils,
> Shrunk to this little measure? Fare thee well.   (3.1.148–50)

They are among the most moving words Antony speaks for Caesar, and they anticipate what Hamlet says in the gravediggers' scene. Here, too, the greatness of Caesar is separated from the perishable physical substance:

> Imperious Caesar, dead and turn'd to clay,
> Might stop a hole to keep the wind away.
> O, that that earth which kept the world in awe
> Should patch a wall t' expel the winter's flaw!
> (Hamlet 5.1.236–39)

Both Antony and Hamlet comment on the theme of vanity, but Hamlet's words reach beyond Antony's towards dissolution and physical decay. In Julius Caesar the dead body of Caesar struck down in the height of his godlike pride is soon transformed into a symbol of Caesarism, and we become aware of the tragic failure of the conspirators: they have killed Caesar's body, but his spirit is still alive to execute vengeance.

Antony, who was "but a limb of Caesar" (2.1.165), and who Brutus thought could "do no more than Caesar's arm/ When Caesar's head is off" (2.1.183–84), emerges as the

74

dominant figure after the assassination. It is he who takes over the role of Caesar at this point, which involves a radical change in his character. He is no longer the reveler of Acts I and II: the runner of the course (1.2. s.d.), "gamesome" (1.2.28) and of "quick spirit" (1.2.89), a lover of plays (1.2.203), devoted "To sports, to wildness and much company" (2.1.189), and one "that revels long a-nights" (2.2.116). There is a new seriousness and importance in Antony here.

Antony's assumption of Caesar's role is symbolized by a significant stage action — Brutus gives him Caesar's body: "Mark Antony, here, take you Caesar's body" (3.1.244). It is at this point that Antony literally assumes the role of Caesar. This meaning is emphasized in the staging as the conspirators depart, leaving Antony suddenly alone with the body. He immediately addresses a formal soliloquy to Caesar in which he promises the vengeance of blood for blood. At the end of the scene Antony and Octavius' Servant carry off the body, and Antony re-enters with it after Brutus' funeral oration in the next scene. Throughout Antony's oration he keeps the mob aware of this body for whose sake he is speaking, and Caesar is transformed from a symbol of fallen pride to a saintly, martyred corpse.[4]

An obvious dramatic conflict is generated in the latter part of the play by the fact that Octavius also assumes the role of Caesar. We hear of him first from his Servant, who tells Antony that Octavius is coming to Rome (3.1.279), and at the end of III,ii we learn that he "is already come to Rome" (3.2.267). Our first sight of him is as a fully functioning Triumvir in the proscription scene (IV,i). But the real strength of Octavius is not felt until the fifth act. Here we find him beginning to take the power of command from

75

Antony and to act indeed as Caesar's personal successor. This action clearly parallels Brutus' overbearing of Cassius; in both cases divided command, like divided rule, has evil consequences and cannot long endure. The prominent part given to Octavius at Philippi is a marked change from Plutarch.[31] Note the way he asserts his will against Antony:

> *Ant.* Octavius, lead your battle softly on
> Upon the left hand of the even field.
>   *Oct.* Upon the right hand I. Keep thou the left.
>   *Ant.* Why do you cross me in this exigent?
>   *Oct.* I do not cross you; but I will do so.[32]   (5.1.16–20)

This use of "will" seems to echo the emphatic tone of Julius Caesar, for example in his words to Decius: "The cause is in my will: I will not come" (2.2.71). Octavius' words in V,i also insist on the imperial style, and he uses the familiar, and perhaps contemptuous, "thou" form for Antony. It is in this scene, too, that Octavius is called "Caesar" by both Antony (5.1.24) and Brutus (5.1.56), and he also refers to himself as "another Caesar" (5.1.54). The repetition of the same name for both Julius and Octavius tends to establish a strong phonetic link between the two in the ears of the audience. Octavius' self-conscious pride in being Caesar resembles that of Julius Caesar, and the fact that he is Julius' nephew and adopted son gives his situation an hereditary cast.

All these details point to the fact that in the fifth act Octavius is taking over the role of Caesar from Antony. Although Antony speaks the eulogy for Brutus at the end of the play, that is all he does say there. It is Octavius who takes care of the final business and utters the two concluding couplets. He tells Brutus' party: "All that serv'd Brutus,

I will entertain them" (5.5.60). It may be significant that
he uses "I" rather than "we," as though he alone were in
charge without Antony. There is a convention in Elizabethan tragedy that the noblest present, he who will restore
and maintain order, should speak the last words of the play.
In *Julius Caesar* this person is Octavius rather than Antony.
The conflict for power between them looks ahead to *Antony and Cleopatra,* where the succession to Caesar is finally
arbitrated and Octavius emerges supreme.

The ironic interplay between the images of Caesar the
man and Caesar the political figure suggests an important
distinction between Brutus and Cassius. The shrewd Cassius sees the conspiracy in terms of individual men, whereas
Brutus sees it in terms of principles unfortunately embodied
in men. Brutus is not concerned with Caesar the man as
Cassius is, but only with "the spirit of Caesar" (2.1.167):
this is the public Caesar, Caesarism, the principles for
which Caesar stands and their potentiality for evil. Brutus
considered and rejected the personal argument three separate times in his "orchard" soliloquy (2.1.10–12, 19–21,
28–29). For Brutus the conspiracy will destroy in advance
the tyranny that Caesar may bring, with its probable sup-
pression of republican liberties. The murder of Caesar the
man, no matter what one's personal attachment, is a necessary means to this end. Cassius, on the other hand, emphasizes the infirmities and tyranny of Caesar the man as if all
that were needed to right matters in Rome were the death
of Caesar; Cassius does not really seem to be at all concerned
with the issue of Caesarism. But the course of the dramatic
action reverses Brutus' plan and shows its tragic wrongness,
for the conspirators are only able to kill the body of Caesar
not the spirit. As a final comment on this theme, Antony's

7 7

speech over the dead Brutus clearly sets him apart from the other conspirators:

> This was the noblest Roman of them all.
> All the conspirators save only he
> Did that they did in envy of great Caesar;
> He, only in a general honest thought
> And common good to all, made one of them.   (5.5.68–72)

This is the judgment of Brutus and the conspirators that Shakespeare leaves us with.

Chapter IV

THE IMAGERY OF
Antony and Cleopatra

I

THE "hyperbolical" style of *Antony and Cleopatra* is expressed in a repeated imagery of dimension and scope, which presents the hyperbole of the play in dramatic terms. There is the sort of fitness in this imagery that Cleopatra indicates to Proculeius:

> If your master
> Would have a queen his beggar, you must tell him
> That majesty, to keep decorum, must
> No less beg than a kingdom. (5.2.15–18)

This is the decorum of majesty, which must have a style and objects suitable to its nature; we recall that Iras in I,ii asked Isis to "keep decorum" (1.2.78) in parceling out fortunes. Cleopatra observes the same measure when, fearing mishap to Antony, she refuses all comfort:

> Our size of sorrow,
> Proportion'd to our cause, must be as great
> As that which makes it.   (4.15.4–6)

And the imagery in this and the following scenes is pro·
portioned to the "size of sorrow." There is a final example
of this type of hyperbole in Charmian's words to Cleopatra:
"The soul and body rive not more in parting/ Than greatness going off" (4.13.5–6). It is spoken as an argument to
Cleopatra to lock herself in her monument; the image of
"greatness going off" (Cleopatra's reported death) will still
Antony's rage — as it actually does. But in a general sense
"greatness going off" is the pageant of Antony and Cleopatra's fate. Death rives soul from body as it will rive
Antony and Cleopatra from the world, and there can be
no loss greater than the body's of soul or the world's of
Antony and Cleopatra. The image follows the "decorum"
of majesty.

We are never allowed to forget the magnitude of the
issues in the play, and this is achieved to some extent by
the use of words of cosmic reference ("earth," "heaven,"
"sun," "moon"), a large imperial vocabulary ("empire,"
"majesty," "king," "queen," "noble"), and frequent mythological allusions.[1] But the imagery of dimension and scope
is most powerfully expressed in the world theme, whose
cumulative force (forty-five examples) is especially significant in this play.[2] I shall be particularly concerned with the
structural use of the world theme, the way its meanings
follow the course of the dramatic action. There are at least
three distinct movements in this imagery. Before Actium
the world is the material domain of the Roman Empire, in
which Antony is a "triple pillar"; after his defeat there is
only the memory of the world lost; and his death marks

a devaluation of the world, as if his departure removed its source of value.

In theatrical terms the area of the stage represents the "world," whether it be the scene of the medieval pageant wagon (with heaven above and hell below) or the "doll's house" of the middle-class drawing room. The action on the Elizabethan stage was backed by the tiring-house façade, which presented an elaborate symbolism of order:

there before the eyes of the audience, as always implied in the imagery of the dialogue, stood the columns, castle gates, parapet-balcony, canopy-heavens that for centuries had symbolized the social and cosmic order — man and realm, earth and heaven. . . . [which] put behind Hamlet and Lear symbols of the order from which they were displaced.[3]

In *Antony and Cleopatra* we feel the theatrical presentation of the world most specifically in IV,iii, where a group of soldiers *"place themselves in every corner of the stage"* (4.3.7 s.d.). The dimensions of the Elizabethan stage are quite relevant here; we know from the contract for the Fortune, for example, that its main acting area measured forty-three by twenty-seven and one-half feet.[4] It had quite distinct corners (especially the two in front), which were widely separated from each other and could be made to represent the four corners of the earth. In any case, the immediate picture that this scene conveys is one of isolation over a large area, and the *"Music of the hautboys"* (4.3.11 s.d.) from the underworld beneath the stage creates a sense of cosmic portentousness. The Elizabethans did not, of course, have the advantage of such modern machines as the revolving stage, which Michael Benthall used in his production of *Antony and Cleopatra* in New York in 1951 to show, conveniently, the world moving on its axis be-

81

tween Rome and Egypt. But the Elizabethan playwright, with a long rectangular stage that extended into the middle of the yard or pit and was surrounded by the audience on three sides, could appeal much more directly to the symbolic imagination of that audience. As many modern producers are discovering, the Elizabethan "open stage"[5] allows for a much closer rapport between actors and audience than is possible in the proscenium arch theater, where the audience sits in darkness and looks into the lighted and framed box of the stage.

The world theme begins in the first speech of the play, which is of crucial importance as one statement of the tragic conflict. Philo shows Demetrius the group which has just entered — "*Antony*, *Cleopatra*, her *Ladies*, the *Train*, with *Eunuchs* fanning her" (1.1.10 s.d.) — and comments:

> Look where they come!
> Take but good note, and you shall see in him
> The triple pillar of the world transform'd
> Into a strumpet's fool. Behold and see. (1.1.10–13)

Antony is one of the three Triumvirs of the Roman Empire, which is here equivalent to the "world," and it is both the scene of the action and its stake. Philo, the Roman, grieves to see so great a man as Antony turned before our eyes into so grotesque and servile an object as "a strumpet's fool." It is one way, and a powerful one, of considering Antony, but not the only one. A few lines further Antony uses the world image in a sense just opposite to Philo's:

> The nobleness of life
> Is to do thus; when such a mutual pair
> And such a twain can do't, in which I bind,
> On pain of punishment, the world to weet
> We stand up peerless. (1.1.36–40)

82

This is the world of lovers which defies that other quantitative world of the Roman Empire. From his personal point of view Philo is right about Antony, but he has not reckoned with the world of love.

We find a much-changed Antony in the next scene. His concern for his imperial domain draws him back to Rome, for Sextus Pompeius threatens "The sides o' th' world" (1.2.199). Even in Egypt Antony has not forgotten his material world and the need to protect his share in it. But Cleopatra tries to detain him by arguing their love in splendid terms:

> Eternity was in our lips and eyes,
> Bliss in our brows' bent, none our parts so poor
> But was a race of heaven. They are so still,
> Or thou, the greatest soldier of the world,
> Art turn'd the greatest liar. (1.3.35–39)

The cosmic images here ("Eternity," "heaven") insist on the play's magnitude in a manner similar to "world." Note also the superlatives, "greatest soldier" and "greatest liar," which are part of the familiar discourse of the play. But "world" is chiefly the Roman Empire, the domain of military conquest, and it is just this concern of Antony that forces his return to Rome.

"World" has an important role in the conference between Antony and Octavius in Act II. The guardianship of the world is literally the issue between them as they play at politics on a grand scale. The three uses of "world" in II,ii enter casually in the course of conversation, and this is as it should be where the power is assumed. Caesar has strong cause to be offended with Antony "Chiefly i' th' world . . ." (2.2.33), but Antony fends him off with admirable diplomacy. Antony's political ability, so conspicuous in *Julius Caesar*, shows at its best in this conference. He makes sport of his dead wife Fulvia's wars against Caesar: "The third o' th' world" (2.2.63) is Caesar's, which he may "pace" as easily as a horse, "but not such a wife" (2.2.64). The crucial issues are kept hidden in this familiar, domestic tone. Caesar declares that he would gladly seek "from edge to edge/ O' th' world" (2.2.117–18) some "hoop" to bind himself to Antony.

Caesar's sister Octavia is the "hoop" that is proposed and accepted. In the short scene with her that follows, Antony uses "world" in a deliberate, official way: "The world and my great office will sometimes/ Divide me from your bosom" (2.3.1–2). The "world" *is* Antony's "great office" as Triumvir. It signifies care and responsibility and asserts the public man. Antony is very "Roman" here with Octavia, but in Egypt the sequence will be reversed, and Cleopatra will "Divide" him from the "world" and his "great office." In his next speech Antony asks Octavia to be gracious in her judgment of him: "Read not my blemishes in the world's report" (2.3.5). This is "world" in the Elizabethan sense of reputation or honor, what we would call public opinion. Antony knows the report of "the general tongue" (1.2.109) in Rome, but he will prove that it is wrong. "Read not my blemishes in the world's report" is one answer to Philo: there is an inner meaning in Antony's tragedy that is not simply the predestined fall of "a strumpet's fool."

The most important and direct use of world imagery is in II,vii, where Pompey is very literally offered the world by his captain Menas, but refuses it. The character of Pompey is sharply defined by this refusal of the world, which we are prepared for by the style in which he addresses the Triumvirs:

> To you all three,
> The senators alone of this great world,
> Chief factors for the gods. . . . (2.6.8–10)

As the compliments indicate, the ineffectual Pompey has too great an awe for these world-sharers, and he already shows that he is quite incapable of world rule. He petulantly whispers in Menas' ear, "Forbear me till anon" (2.7.44 and s.d.), but Menas will not be put off and stuns Pompey by asking bluntly: "Wilt thou be lord of all the world?" (2.7.67). Menas repeats: "Wilt thou be lord of the whole world? That's twice" (2.7.68), and for a third time he says: "I am the man/ Will give thee all the world" (2.7.70–71). Notice how deliberately Menas accents "world" at the end of his sentences; it is the magical word of the scene. But the tipsy Pompey can only ask: "Hast thou drunk well?" (2.7.71) as Menas repeats his offer for the last time:

> No, Pompey, I have kept me from the cup.
> Thou art, if thou dar'st be, the earthly Jove.
> Whate'er the ocean pales, or sky inclips,
> Is thine, if thou wilt ha't. (2.7.72–75)

"Whate'er the ocean pales, or sky inclips" is one of the most powerful definitions of "world" in the play. "Show me which way" (2.7.75), says Pompey with some interest now, and Menas reveals the frightening simplicity of his plot:

> These three world-sharers, these competitors
> Are in thy vessel. Let me cut the cable;
> And when we are put off, fall to their throats.
> All there is thine. (2.7.76–79)

Like Julius Caesar, "These three world-sharers" are only men, from whom the world may be taken by murder. Pompey's answer is a protestation of honor longing for a *fait*

accompli, and he ends with "Desist, and drink" (2.7.86).
Menas' defection at this point begins the series of desertions
in the play that continues with Canidius, Alexas, and
Enobarbus, and ends in Seleucus' betrayal of Cleopatra. As
an ironic comment on II,vii, we learn later that Pompey has
been ignominiously murdered by one of Antony's officers
(3.5.19–20).

Menas is much disillusioned with the world theme, and
when Enobarbus says that the Servant carrying the drunk
Lepidus "bears the third part of the world" (2.7.96) on
his back, Menas replies bitterly: "The third part, then, is
drunk. Would it were all,/ That it might go on wheels!"
(2.7.97–98). Enobarbus makes the obvious joking comparison between the man (Lepidus' limp form) and the office
("the third part of the world"). The fall of Lepidus is
clearly foreshadowed in this scene, for he is a man whom
"the least wind i' th' world" (2.7.3) can blow down.

There is a final emphasis on the world theme as the
"Music plays" and Enobarbus places Antony, Caesar, and
Pompey *"hand in hand"* (2.7.117 s.d.). A boy sings the song
of "Plumpy Bacchus" (2.7.119) while they dance in a circle
and bellow out the refrain as loud as their "strong sides
can volley" (2.7.117):

> Cup us till the world go round,
> Cup us till the world go round! (2.7.122–23)

The world is indeed "going round" in drunken revelry —
it is Menas' world going "on wheels." The word "world"
has a curiously ironic ring in this refrain, for Pompey has
already refused his chance for the world, and Lepidus will
soon be dispossessed (III,v). In the starkly sober scene that
follows immediately (III,i), Ventidius halts his world con-

quest for fear of seeming a rival to Antony. It is an ominous note, and made the more so because the blatant sounds of the "world" refrain in II,vii still echo in our ears.

By III,iv Antony is preparing for war with Caesar. Octavia, torn between the two sides, tries to act as mediator:

> Wars 'twixt you twain would be
> As if the world should cleave, and that slain men
> Should solder up the rift. (3.4.30-32)

It is a violent image, unexpected from the modest Octavia and therefore of added force. Compare the similarly violent image Enobarbus uses in the next scene after learning of Caesar's dismissal of Lepidus:

> Then, world,° thou hast a pair of chaps, no more;
> And throw between them all the food thou hast,
> They'll grind the one the other. (3.5.14-16)

Without Lepidus, Caesar and Antony are now a "pair of chaps," and they will devour the world between them.

A new movement in the theme occurs after the battle of Actium, where "world" for Antony and his followers becomes the world they have lost, the symbol of former glory and power. Scarus, who has just witnessed Antony's shameful flight, states the motif directly:

> The greater cantle of the world is lost
> With very ignorance. We have kiss'd away
> Kingdoms and provinces. (3.10.6-8)

Antony is now "so lated in the world that I/ Have lost my way for ever" (3.11.3-4). It is Antony's downward course, full of strange pathos and compassion, and he makes the obvious contrast between his present humility and his former glory,

who
With half the bulk o' th' world play'd as I pleas'd,
Making and marring fortunes. (3.11.63–65)

Enobarbus does not understand why Antony followed Cleopatra from battle, "When half to half the world oppos'd,
he being/ The meered question" (3.13.9–10). All Antony
can do now is to insist that "the world should note/ Something particular" (3.13.21–22) from Caesar, and, in a mood
of desperate honor, he challenges him to single combat. The
repeated world imagery after Actium insists on the scope of
the conflict between the two men and the greatness of
Antony's loss.

Antony's victory on the second day of battle brings with
it a temporary revival in the world imagery, as when he
greets Cleopatra: "O thou day o' th' world,/ Chain mine
arm'd neck!" (4.8.13–14). "Day o' th' world" is the sun,
used here to indicate renewed life. Antony has returned
from "The world's great snare uncaught" (4.8.18), and he
now has delusive prospects of recouping his fortunes.

But after Antony's final defeat, the world once more
becomes the memory of past glory. His fate appears in the
Vesper pageant of the clouds "that nod unto the world/
And mock our eyes with air" (4.14.6–7). It is a mocking
vision of the world lost, the material world of the Roman
Empire. While he prepares to join Cleopatra, he thinks
of his former greatness:

I, that with my sword
Quarter'd the world and o'er green Neptune's back
With ships made cities. . . . (4.14.57–59)

And as he is about to die he is still occupied with the time
"Wherein I liv'd the greatest prince o' th' world,/ The
noblest . . ." (4.15.54–55).

There is a definite heightening of Antony at his death, and the world theme plays its part in this movement. Eros, for example, sees his master's "noble countenance" (4.14.85) as the place "Wherein the worship of the whole world lies" (4.14.86). This is "world" in the sense of reputation and public opinion, and its serves to answer Antony's request to Octavia: "Read not my blemishes in the world's report" (2.3.5). The death of Enobarbus affirms Antony's magnanimity in much the same way. He prays Antony's forgiveness, although in the eyes of "the world" (4.9.21) he knows he will be judged for what he is, "A master-leaver and a fugitive!" (4.9.22). This is the same world of reputation in which Antony stands condemned, but Enobarbus is calling attention to the greatness of his master.

Caesar's reaction to the death of Antony is expressed in cosmic generalities:

> The breaking of so great a thing should make
> A greater crack. The round world
> Should have shook lions into civil streets
> And citizens to their dens. The death of Antony
> Is not a single doom; in the name lay
> A moiety of the world.   (5.1.14–19)

Antony's death should have disrupted the universal order (compare the lions in the street portent of *Julius Caesar* 1.3.20–22), for the scope of his name itself was "a moiety of the world." The conflict between Caesar and Antony was an inevitable struggle for lordship:

> I must perforce
> Have shown to thee such a declining day
> Or look on thine: we could not stall together
> In the whole world.   (5.1.37–40)

Despite the homely and striking expression, "stall together,"

89

we are never allowed to forget that the magnitude of the issue in *Antony and Cleopatra* was no less than "the whole world."

The world theme is particularly prominent in the last scene of the play. When Cleopatra is surprised in her monument, she tries to stab herself, but Proculeius restrains her with hints of Caesar's bounty:

> Let the world see
> His nobleness well acted, which your death
> Will never let come forth.   (5.2.44–46)

The "world" will be the stage on which Caesar's bounty will be acted before the "world" as audience. But we already know that Caesar wants to stage Cleopatra in his triumph. She addresses him as "sole sir o' th' world" (5.2.120), but he possesses that world by conquest and not by right. When Caesar says, "I'll take my leave" (5.2.133), Cleopatra answers with very deliberate and bitter irony:

> And may, through all the world! 'Tis yours, and we,
> Your scutcheons and your signs of conquest, shall
> Hang in what place you please.   (5.2.134–36)

She is confirmed in what she has known before: there is to be no dealing with Caesar.

In contrast to Antony's toppling domain, the world of Caesar is secure and firm-seated, and he looks forward to the *pax romana* of the Augustan Age:

> The time of universal peace is near.
> Prove this a prosp'rous day, the three-nook'd world
> Shall bear the olive freely.   (4.6.5–7)

Caesar's "universal peace" reminds us, in the words of Thidias,[7] that he is "The universal landlord" (3.13.72).

We tend today, being not quite free from the rationalistic tradition of character analysis, to be too harsh to Octavius. Stapfer's "mean shivering creature," [8] for example, is a caricature of the Octavius of Shakespeare's play. We should bear in mind that in Elizabethan histories and comparable works, the reputation of Octavius was very high; he was seen as the ideal Roman emperor, the restorer of peace, and the ruler of the fourth earthly monarchy.[9] It would be more correct to say with Harold S. Wilson that Octavius

remains an enigmatic figure, implacable, menacing, cold, as the historical Octavius doubtless was; but a power rather than a person, a function of the developing action, the nemesis of Antony and Cleopatra, the tragic measure of their human limitation.[10]

These qualities make him suited for world rule in just those particulars that Antony lacks. As in the case of Henry V, admirable sovereigns need not also be admirable and sympathetic persons.

The devaluation of the world marks a third and final movement in this theme. Before Actium images of the world stressed Antony's power as Roman Triumvir, while after Actium they recalled the magnitude of his loss. But now that Antony, the source of value, is gone, the world is a poor and base place indeed. When Cleopatra sees the Guard bearing the dying Antony, she exclaims:

> O sun,
> Burn the great sphere thou mov'st in! Darkling stand
> The varying shore o' th' world! (4.15.9–11)

The fate of Antony is a matter that concerns the cosmos, and there is a suggestion that the world will stand "darkling" in mourning. For Cleopatra his death leaves the world empty and rank, a place not fit to live in:

> Noblest of men, woo't die?
> Hast thou no care of me? Shall I abide
> In this dull world, which in thy absence is
> No better than a sty?   (4.15.59–62)

This feeling is intensified in her next speech:

> It were for me
> To throw my sceptre at the injurious gods,
> To tell them that this world did equal theirs
> Till they had stol'n our jewel.   (4.15.75–78)

Antony is the "jewel" of the world, and this taken away, the world is no longer a match for the gods'. There is an invidious comparison between the world and Antony, which is also a motif in Cleopatra's dream of her lover: "His legs bestrid the ocean: his rear'd arm/ Crested the world" (5.2.82–83). The images insist that Antony is a greater being than this mere physical universe: he "*bestrid* the ocean" and "*Crested* the world," as if he and the world could not be compared at all.

The final uses of "world" are of this same devaluing sort. Cleopatra's kiss, without further means, brings Iras her death, and this "tell'st the world/ It is not worth leave-taking" (5.2.300–01). The praise of death is a dispraise of life in this world. It is not worth all this ceremony at departure, and one should dispatch forthwith. Cleopatra dies delicately and characteristically in the middle of a sentence,[11] "What should I stay —" (5.2.316), which Charmian completes: "In this vile [12] world? So fare thee well" (5.2.317). "Vile world" climaxes the devaluation of the world theme which began at Antony's death. Death is now a lover, and after Antony and Cleopatra are gone, this "vile world" is "not worth leave-taking." Thus the world theme ends with the tragic protagonists greater than the world they lost.

2

The world theme in *Antony and Cleopatra* represents the most general pattern of imagery in the play. Within this theme a strong symbolic contrast is made between the worlds of Egypt and Rome.[13] It is "symbolic" in the sense that the two localities represent different moral qualities and values, and a different rhythm and style of life. We are always conscious that Antony, for example, is a Roman in Egypt, and the Roman thoughts that strike him there develop his stature as tragic protagonist. The play is built around the movements of Antony between Egypt and Rome. If these were simply geographical events without symbolic interest, there could be no tragedy — perhaps only a splendid travelogue. But Rome and Egypt represent crucial moral choices, and they function as symbolic locales in a manner not unlike Henry James's Europe and America.[14]

The symbolic contrast of Egypt and Rome ought to be interpreted in terms of Elizabethan stagecraft, which did not try to create a pictorial illusion of an actual place or scene — this is the heritage of the Italian perspective theater. A large symbolic opposition between Egypt and Rome could thus be developed in the Elizabethan public theater without constant scene changes. Although this theater could not present any splendid perspective pictures, it did offer great flexibility of movement between scenes imagined to be in different places. The nearest equivalent on our modern stage to the unlocated or placeless scene of the Elizabethans is the "unit set" or "multiple setting," often a collection of stylized geometric forms that are made to serve for an entire play. The concept of unity of place does not apply here and actually only makes sense in a staging that insists on presenting distinct and identifiable places.

It is particularly important to re-create the possible Elizabethan staging of *Antony and Cleopatra* because criticism has often been leveled at the multiplicity of scenes and quick changes of place in the play,[15] as if this offered an almost insuperable barrier to production. Although the First Folio (1623) has only one act-scene division — *"Actus Primus. Scaena Prima."* — most modern editors follow Rowe and the eighteenth-century practice of parceling the play out into forty-two scenes, each of which is then tagged with a specific locality that could be represented by a set of flats and a painted backdrop. In Kittredge's edition, for example, III,iv is said to take place in *"Athens. Antony's house.,"* and III,v in *"Athens. Another room in Antony's house.,"* despite the fact that there is not a word in either scene about Antony's house or Athens. These very specific indications of places would have had no meaning in the Elizabethan public theater for which the play was written. To all intents and purposes, these scenes would have been presented as continuous and unlocalized; they do not occur in any place more definite than the stage itself backed by the symbolic façade of the tiring-house.

A performance of *Antony and Cleopatra* should try to create a symbolic rather than a literal sense of place. In the 1951 production with Laurence Olivier and Vivien Leigh, the rhythm and pace of the Egyptian scenes were clearly distinguished from the scenes in Rome. Egypt was characterized by splendor and languor, with great variety in tempo and movement; Rome, the place of public affairs and business of state, was presented quickly and directly. Costume offers another effective means for defining symbolic place. It was one of the chief expenses of an Elizabethan play,[16] and when, for example, Cleopatra puts on her robe to appear "like a queen" (5.2.227), we can be sure that the most splendid costume in the wardrobe would be used here — the immediate standard of comparison would be to the sumptuous apparel of the great nobles and the court. We ought to keep in mind that costume in the Elizabethan period had a much more specific symbolic character than it has today. Different occupations and stations in life had their appropriate dress, and the robe of a queen, the highest being in the social order, had to have a suitable hierarchic magnificence. Costume offers one of the most direct means to express the substantial austerity of Rome and the aesthetic splendor of Egypt.

Although the play develops a symbolic conflict between Egypt and Rome, the imagery of Egypt is set forth in much greater detail than that of Rome; perhaps the qualities of Egypt lend themselves more readily to metaphorical expression. All of Acts I, IV, and V, with the exception of I,iv, take place in Egypt, whereas only Act II, with the exception of II,v, is located in Rome or Roman places. Act III is divided between Roman and Egyptian places with the latter more extensive; actually, many of the scenes in Act III are difficult to classify. Since the Egyptian action is almost twice as long as the Roman, I shall use it as the focus for the imagery of the play. The quality of Egypt is rendered in the themes of the Nile and its serpents, eating and drinking, hotness, and indolence. The quality of Rome is seen partly in terms of stated opposites of Egypt, as in the themes of temperance, coldness, and business, but the implied opposites, to which only passing reference is made, are perhaps even more important.

i

To Shakespeare's contemporaries Egypt was the symbol of oriental luxury, a place where one could fully enjoy a life of the senses. The splendors of Egypt were proverbial, and, as Cawley notes, "Egypt shared Asia's fame for luxurious living, rich cloths, fine carpets, silks, and spices, and 'wealthy' was as familiar an epithet as 'fertile.' " [17] Egypt was also thought of as a strange land of wonders, the home of soothsayers and the source of many magic charms and drugs. These conceptions were supported by the authority of the Old Testament and the reports of the voyagers.[18] In Elizabethan English "Egyptian" was used interchangeably with "gypsy," since it was believed that the gypsies originally came from Egypt. They migrated to England about the beginning of the sixteenth century and "quickly established a reputation for themselves as fortune-tellers and sorcerers; besides being shrewdly suspected of petty thefts." [19] "Gypsy" also meant a loose, cunning, fickle, or deceitful woman.

The Nile River is at the center of our conception of Egypt, just as the Tiber is of Rome. We are kept aware of the fact that the Nile's annual overflow brings great fertility; as Antony tells Caesar:

> Thus do they, sir: they take the flow o' th' Nile
> By certain scales i' th' pyramid. They know
> By th' height, the lowness, or the mean, if dearth
> Or foison follow. The higher Nilus swells,
> The more it promises. As it ebbs, the seedsman
> Upon the slime and ooze scatters his grain,
> And shortly comes to harvest.   (2.7.20–26)

The "foison," the promise, the "harvest" of the Nile mud
are all terms of fruitfulness, the lush and luxuriant growth
of a tropical country. There is an extended play on fruitfulness in the colloquial and bawdy scene of Cleopatra's
court in I,ii. As Charmian observes, Iras' palm as little
"presages chastity" (1.2.47) "as the o'erflowing Nilus pre-
sageth famine" (1.2.50). And she defends her ability to tell
fortunes in similar terms: "Nay, if an oily palm be not a
fruitful prognostication, I cannot scratch mine ear" (1.2.
52–53).

But there is also a baleful and death-dealing aspect of
the Nile's fruitfulness, for its mud yields not only rich
harvests, but a swarm of insects and serpents which are
bred in it by the spontaneous generation of the sun. We
recall that at his departure from Egypt, Antony swears his
devotion to Cleopatra "By the fire/ That quickens Nilus'
slime . . ." (1.3.68–69). To "quicken" is to fill with teem-
ing life. We have the same commonplace from Lepidus:
"Your serpent of Egypt is bred now of your mud by the
operation of your sun; so is your crocodile" (2.7.29–31),
and, as he tells us further on, " 'Tis a strange serpent"
(2.7.54) — this mouthful of sibilants is almost too much
for the tipsy Lepidus.[20] The fertile Nile mud also breeds
carrion-eating flies and gnats. Rather than be thought cold-
hearted to Antony, Cleopatra would prefer to have herself,
her children, and her "brave Egyptians all" (3.13.164) "Lie
graveless, till the flies and gnats of Nile/ Have buried them
for prey!" (3.13.166–67). This scene is echoed in V,ii when
Cleopatra proposes violent alternatives to Caesar's triumph:

> Rather on Nilus' mud
> Lay me stark-nak'd and let the waterflies
> Blow me into abhorring! (5.2.58–60)

The terrible image of Cleopatra "stark-nak'd" on the Nile mud being eaten by waterflies shows us the sinister aspect of the river. The fertility of Egypt is further undercut by the eunuchs in the play: Mardian, Alexas, Seleucus (5.2. 174), the Eunuchs fanning Cleopatra (1.1.10 s.d.), and Photinus (referred to in 3.7.15) — they are unfruitful in a direct sense.

The ominousness of the Nile is reflected in the serpent, a typical product of its mud. This theme is important in the play, and it enters into the dramatic action with the asp Cleopatra uses in her suicide. The first serpent image occurs in Antony's resolution to leave Egypt, for he fears the "serpent's poison" (1.2.201) that will develop if he remains. The association of serpent and poison occurs again in I,v, where Cleopatra's imagination plays on the absent Antony:

> He's speaking now,
> Or murmuring 'Where's my serpent of old Nile?'
> For so he calls me. Now I feed myself
> With most delicious poison. (1.5.24–27)

Cleopatra luxuriates in the "delicious poison" of her own imaginings. The "serpent of old Nile" has a poisonous sting in her fascination, an element of inscrutability which Antony can neither fully accept nor repulse. He speaks to Caesar of his time in Egypt "when poisoned hours had bound me up/ From mine own knowledge" (2.2.90–91) — Cleopatra is imagined here as a Circe or Acrasia who draws her victims away from self-knowledge.

Her dialogue with the Messenger from Antony in II,v is full of serpent imagery; she suspects some mischance to her lover:

> If not well,
> Thou shouldst come like a Fury crown'd with snakes,
> Not like a formal man. (2.5.39–41)

The snakes are a dire symbol of evil, which is repeated in Cleopatra's words of misgiving to the Messenger:

> Some innocents scape not the thunderbolt.
> Melt Egypt into Nile! and kindly creatures
> Turn all to serpents! (2.5.77–79)

By a nice turn she is able to imply that she and the Messenger are both "innocents" struck by the thunderbolt of Antony's marriage to Octavia, for the innocent Messenger has been beaten and haled only for reporting it. All order is now gone; Egypt may melt into Nile and its natural ("kindly") creatures turn into the monstrous serpents. When the Messenger returns, Cleopatra's mind is still harping on serpents. She wishes he were lying: "So half my Egypt were submerg'd and made/ A cistern for scal'd snakes!" (2.5.94–95). Cleopatra seems to be using serpents as a symbol for evil in the world, and she is still thinking of them at the end of the scene when she says of Antony: "Though he be painted one way like a Gorgon,/ The other way's a Mars" (2.5.116–17). In this multiple-perspective picture the Antony who married Octavia is the hissing, serpent-locked Gorgon.

Finally, the serpent theme "gains powerful dramatic relevance" [21] through Cleopatra's death by the asp. The sight of the dying Antony calls forth her first declaration of suicide: "If knife, drugs, serpents have/ Edge, sting, or operation, I am safe" (4.15.25–26). Note how the serpent's sting, which actually does the deed, is artfully put last. Right after the conference with Caesar, Cleopatra's resolution for suicide is fixed, and she sends Charmian to fetch the Clown with the asps (5.2.194–96). In the matter of time sequence it appears as if they were already provided for before Cleopatra spoke with Caesar. The entrance of

99

the Clown with the asps concealed in a basket of figs (5.2.241 s.d.) juxtaposes the fruitful and death-dealing powers of the Nile: the figs and the asps are both products of the same fertility, and figs have strong sexual connotations. We may recall what the Soothsayer told Charmian in I,ii: "You shall outlive the lady whom you serve" (1.2.31), and Charmian's answer: "O excellent! I love long life better than figs" (1.2.32). These figs prove to be sinisterly prophetic, since Charmian applies an asp they conceal and outlives her lady by fifteen lines. When the Clown enters, Cleopatra asks endearingly for the asp: "Hast thou the pretty worm of Nilus there/ That kills and pains not?" (5.2.243–44). Now that death has become a good, the serpent is no longer a symbol of evil in the world, but the loved means of deliverance. It is the "pretty worm of Nilus" now, not the unkindly creature spoken of before.

The sequence with the Clown, a vulgar, well-meaning country fellow, provides a fine bit of comic relief. He makes his report of the worm with garrulous professional ease, while Cleopatra is anxious to be rid of him. With the intuitive wisdom of fools, the Clown relates that the "worm's an odd worm" (5.2.259) who "will do his kind" (5.2.264). It "is not to be trusted but in the keeping of wise people; for indeed there is no goodness in the worm" (5.2.266–68). Besides, "it is not worth the feeding" (5.2 270–71). Before the Clown leaves, he twice wishes Cleopatra "all joy of the worm" (5.2.261, 281). His speech in this scene is full of overtones of Eve and the serpent, with comic asides on man's mortality, and it raises the serpent theme to an important symbolic level.

Cleopatra's "Immortal longings" (5.2.284) recall the Clown's caution that the biting of the asp is "immortal"

(5.2.247). When she kisses her maids farewell, Iras falls and dies, but it is a sign of blessing:

> Have I the aspic in my lips? Dost fall?
> If thou and nature can so gently part,
> The stroke of death is as a lover's pinch,
> Which hurts, and is desir'd. (5.2.296–99)

This passage shows Cleopatra as the "serpent of old Nile" again — "Have I the aspic in my lips?" — to whom it is very fitting that the asp be brought. But the serpent now symbolizes the love-making of death, which will be aggressively consummated "as a lover's pinch" (compare the earlier Cleopatra "with Phoebus' amorous pinches black" 1.5. 28). She does indeed take "all joy of the worm" (5.2.261) as she applies it to her breast and speaks to it in terms of endearment:

> Come, thou mortal wretch,
> With thy sharp teeth this knot intrinsicate
> Of life at once untie. Poor venomous fool,
> Be angry, and dispatch. (5.2.306–09)

Cleopatra bids Charmian still her grief, for it is out of keeping with the beatific tone of the scene:

> Peace, peace!
> Dost thou not see my baby at my breast,
> That sucks the nurse asleep? (5.2.311–13)

Death is a lover in a maternal [22] as well as a sexual sense, and this speech suggests a kind of life-in-death. The poisonous asp as the means of death becomes the baby nursing at the breast, a potent symbol of life. The serpent theme culminates in a brilliant union of the fruitful and the lethal powers of the Nile.

ii

The indulgence of the senses in Egypt is represented chiefly by images of eating and drinking. This appetitive imagery characterizes Egypt as a place of pleasure and gives particular point to Cleopatra's sensuality, for, by an extension of meaning, sex is presented in terms of appetite — love is lust, a hunger.[23] The imagery of eating and drinking enters significantly into our stage picture of Egypt and helps to create an important symbolic contrast with Rome. Rome is a place of conference tables, armor, political decisions, and hard material objects, while Egypt is represented by food and drink, by music and colorful dress, and by a general sense of luxury and splendor. This contrast is implied in the opening scene of the play, where Antony and the Egyptian court are clearly set apart from the Roman observers, Philo and Demetrius. Antony's first entrance is intended to strike a strong Egyptian attitude, and it would perhaps be effective to see him carousing on stage. In I,ii Enobarbus orders a "banquet" (1.2.11), or light repast, to be brought in, and we know that the scene aboard Pompey's galley is filled with feasting and drinking — it "ripens towards" an "alexandrian feast" (2.7.101–02). At the end of III,xi Antony orders "Some wine, within there, and our viands!" (3.11.73), and in III,xiii he will

> have one other gaudy night. Call to me
> All my sad captains; fill our bowls once more.
> Let's mock the midnight bell.   (3.13.183–85)

Act IV, scene ii, closes in the same spirit of desperate bravado: "Let's to supper, come,/ And drown consideration" (4.2.44–45). After the victory in IV,viii Antony wishes all his troops could "sup together/ And drink carouses to the next day's fate . . ." (4.8.33–34). Besides these specific indications, the stage business of eating and drinking could be used to good effect throughout the Egyptian scenes. These presented aspects of Rome and Egypt make at least as striking an impression on an audience as the words of the text.

The effect of this imagery is felt most strongly in Enobarbus, who is a good example of the Roman indulging himself in the pleasures of Egypt. He will be as active in revelry as the next man: his fortune, "and most of our fortunes, to-night, shall be — drunk to bed" (1.2.45–46). But, like Octavius Caesar (compare 1.4.25ff), he separates pleasure from duty, as when he says: "Under a compelling occasion let women die" (1.2.141). He is the Roman in Egypt, who tries to impress Agrippa and Maecenas: "we did sleep day out of countenance and made the night light with drinking" (2.2.181–82). Maecenas asks innocently: "Eight wild boars roasted whole at a breakfast, and but twelve persons there. Is this true?" (2.2.184–85). And Enobarbus replies with an hyperbole of feasting: "This was but as a fly by an eagle. We had much more monstrous matter of feast, which worthily deserved noting" (2.2.186–88) — Maecenas cannot conceive how good things were in Egypt. The description of Cleopatra on the Cydnus, the greatest hyperbole in the play, follows naturally after this extended food imagery. Enobarbus has used his throat well in Egypt (2.6.144), and he is filled with wonder at what he has seen.

Food imagery is used principally for the sensual aspect of Cleopatra's attraction. To Caesar she was "A morsel for a monarch" (1.5.31), and she is now Antony's "Egyptian dish" (2.6.133) to which he must return. When Antony upbraids her for favoring Thidias, he speaks in the contemptuous sexual terms of food:

> I found you as a morsel cold upon
> Dead Caesar's trencher. Nay, you were a fragment
> Of Gneius Pompey's, besides what hotter hours,
> Unregist'red in vulgar fame, you have
> Luxuriously pick'd out. . . . (3.13.116–20)

These associations of food ought to be remembered when Enobarbus refers to Cleopatra's "infinite variety":

> Other women cloy
> The appetites they feed, but she makes hungry
> Where most she satisfies. . . . (2.2.241–43)

This is a heightened use of food imagery, and it stresses the energy and plenitude of Cleopatra's attraction, but there is also an unmistakable sexual tone in "appetites," "hungry," and "satisfies."

Antony's lust is similarly presented in terms of food. Pompey imagines him in Egypt as he "sits at dinner" (2.1.12), and hopes that his indulgence of appetite will immobilize him:

> Tie up the libertine in a field of feasts,
> Keep his brain fuming. Epicurean cooks
> Sharpen with cloyless sauce his appetite,
> That sleep and feeding may prorogue his honour
> Even till a Lethe'd dulness! (2.1.23–27)

Antony's "appetite" is in conflict with his "honour," but only the latter can recall him to Rome and the affairs of the world. Epicurus was a prototype for the life of the senses in the Elizabethan period, and Jonson's arch sensualist is fitly called Sir Epicure Mammon. A few lines further Pompey calls Antony "This amorous surfeiter" (2.1.33), which gives the food imagery an explicit double reference to the indigestion and disgust that come from overindulgence. As Barroll points out, among the Seven Deadly Sins Gluttony and Lust are usually linked: one is an effect and an aspect of the other, and both are also closely connected with Sloth.[24] Pompey returns to his food imagery in II,vi, when he assures Antony that

> first or last, your fine Egyptian cookery
> Shall have the fame. I have heard that Julius Caesar
> Grew fat with feasting there.   (2.6.64–66)

Antony suspects an innuendo, since Julius Caesar was Cleopatra's lover, but Pompey protests his innocence. Again, "fat" suggests the indolence of a life of the senses.

Caesar remembers the Roman counterpart of the Egyptian Antony, for after his defeat at Modena Antony endured famine with remarkable fortitude:

> Thou didst drink
> The stale of horses and the gilded puddle
> Which beasts would cough at. Thy palate then did deign
> The roughest berry on the rudest hedge.
> Yea, like the stag when snow the pasture sheets,
> The barks of trees thou brows'd.[25] On the Alps
> It is reported thou didst eat strange flesh,
> Which some did die to look on.   (1.4.61–68)

This Antony is utterly different from the feaster and reveler in Egypt, and the Rome-Egypt contrast here extends deeply into character. The point of Caesar's speech is to warn Antony to "Leave thy lascivious wassails" (1.4.56): Rome is "queasy" (3.6.20) with his insolence. In the scene of revelry aboard Pompey's galley Caesar tries to follow the model of Antony's austerity, for he "had rather fast from all four days/ Than drink so much in one" (2.7.107–08). He plays a rational, grave Malvolio in this scene, although he has had something to drink and is rather affected by it (note 2.7.128–29: "mine own tongue/ Splits²⁶ what it speaks"). Similarly, when Caesar feasts his army in IV,i, he sees it as a necessary "waste" (4.1.16), but when Antony feasts his army in the next scene, it is a "bounteous" (4.2.10) meal and a sign of his warmth and liberality. All of these examples make a symbolic contrast between the self-control of Rome and the self-indulgence of Egypt.

In the last scene of the play there is a distinct change in the imagery of eating and drinking for Cleopatra. Proculeius counsels, "O, temperance, lady!" (5.2.48), but Cleopatra will practice more than "temperance":

> Sir, I will eat no meat; I'll not drink, sir;
> If idle talk will once be necessary,
> I'll not sleep neither. This mortal house I'll ruin,
> Do Caesar what he can. (5.2.49–52)

The sensual theme is reversed as Cleopatra prepares for death, and Caesar's "Feed and sleep" (5.2.187) becomes pointless advice. "Temperance" is a specifically Roman virtue that Antony had earlier denied to Cleopatra:

> I am sure,
> Though you can guess what temperance should be,
> You know not what it is. (3.13.120–22)

But Cleopatra is now moving after "the high Roman fashion" (4.15.87) of Antony's death. The asp will eat her, and, as the Clown adds paradoxically, "a woman is a dish for the gods, if the devil dress her not" (5.2.275–76). Cleopatra ends by forswearing the mortal longings of the senses and negating the quality of Egypt: "Now no more/ The juice of Egypt's grape shall moist this lip" (5.2.284–85). We may recall an earlier Cleopatra who, "Ere the ninth hour," drank Antony "to his bed . . ." (2.5.21). The final movement in the imagery of food and drink is toward a Roman temperance.

iii

The symbolic conflict in the play is also seen in an imagery of hotness for Egypt and coldness for Rome. The prevailing atmosphere of Egypt is a sultry one, and Cleopatra shares in this quality. We feel the strong sun of Egypt when Antony swears "By the fire/ That quickens Nilus' slime" (1.3.68–69), and when Cleopatra tells us that she is "with Phoebus' amorous pinches black" (1.5.28). The theme is announced in the first speech of the play, where Philo complains that his master "is become the bellows and the fan/ To cool a gypsy's lust" (1.1.9–10). To this firm Roman, Cleopatra's hotness is lust, which Antony debases himself by satisfying ("cooling"). When a great general becomes a mere "bellows" and "fan," he is certainly guilty of "dotage." Right after these words there is a flourish, and Antony, Cleopatra, her Ladies and Train enter, "with *Eunuchs* fanning her" (1.1.10 s.d.). Just what Philo has been speaking about is now presented directly in the stage action, and it is an image of oriental luxury which sets the tone for Cleopatra's role. Most significant here is a tacit identification between Antony and the Eunuchs, for they both "fan" Cleopatra, the one figuratively, the others literally.[27] The implication is plain: Antony's manly will has been effeminated in Egypt. We have a similar image when Cleopatra is fanned in her barge on the Cydnus:

107

On each side her
Stood pretty dimpled boys, like smiling Cupids,
With divers-colour'd fans, whose wind did seem
To glow the delicate cheeks which they did cool,
And what they undid did. (2.2.206–10)

The aesthetic tone is more elevated than in the preceding examples, but the hotness is still there, as it is in the "hotter hours" Cleopatra has "Luxuriously pick'd out" (3.13.118, 120).

If hotness is the sign of passion, coldness represents the opposite Roman quality of temperance. Its exemplar is Octavia, whose "holy, cold, and still conversation" (2.6.130) is in sharp contrast with Cleopatra and with Antony, too. "Cold" is always used pejoratively for Cleopatra since it is a word strongly associated with death. Antony found her "as a morsel cold upon/ Dead Caesar's trencher" (3.13.116–17), and she loved Caesar in her "salad days,/ When I was green in judgment, cold in blood . . ." (1.5.73–74). There is an interesting play on these qualities in III,xiii, where Antony suspects her of duplicity with Caesar's servant Thidias. Antony picks up her tentative half-lines and asks: "Cold-hearted toward me?" to which she replies in an extended conditional image:

Ah, dear, if I be so,
From my cold heart let heaven engender hail,
And poison it in the source, and the first stone
Drop in my neck; as it determines, so
Dissolve my life! (3.13.158–62)

The poisoned hailstone is an image of destruction for the hot Cleopatra, and "death" and "cold" are both antonyms of the qualities of Egypt.

iv

A final aspect of Egypt is its indolence, full of shifting moods and sudden violence, and always seeking variety to stave off boredom. Indolence is, in fact, the psychological state the moralists called Sloth, a sort of paralysis of the will produced by Lust and Gluttony. In this sense Cleopatra is an "enchanting queen" (1.2.132) who holds Antony's will in bondage to the "idleness" of Egypt. For Shakespeare "enchanting" was a much more forceful and specific word than it is for us, with a literal reference to witchcraft that could be prosecuted by law. Antony thinks of Cleopatra specifically in these terms after Actium, when he calls her "charm" (3.12.16, 25), "spell" (3.12.30), and "witch" (3.12.47).

The languorousness of Egypt finds its chief symbol in sleep. When Antony is gone, Cleopatra asks for mandragora, "That I might sleep out this great gap of time/ My Antony is away" (1.5.5–6). Like poppy, mandragora is one of "the drowsy syrups of the world" (*Othello* 3.3.331), and it offers a narcotic solace to Cleopatra. The image of sleep enters again on the morning of the second day's battle; Antony will be up and doing, but Cleopatra tries to restrain him:

> *Ant.* Eros! mine armour, Eros!
> *Cleo.* Sleep a little.
> *Ant.* No, my chuck. Eros! Come, mine armour, Eros!
>
> (4.4.1–2)

This passage suggests a symbolic contrast between the activity of Rome and the indolence of Egypt, where Enobarbus and his cohorts "did sleep day out of countenance" (2.2.181), and where Pompey hopes that "sleep and feeding" will "prorogue" Antony's "honour/ Even till a Lethe'd

109

dulness!" (2.1.26–27). When Antony comes to Rome, he answers Pompey in kind:

> The beds i' th' East are soft; and thanks to you,
> That call'd me timelier than my purpose hither;
> For I have gain'd by't. (2.6.51–53)

Business of state has called Antony to Rome, but the image of the "beds i' th' East" prepares us for his return. The Egypt-Rome opposition is stated again in III,vii, where Cleopatra compares Caesar's "celerity" (3.7.25) with Antony's negligence and "slackness" (3.7.28).

We note a new movement in the sleep imagery as Antony makes himself ready for death: "Unarm,[28] Eros. The long day's task is done,/ And we must sleep" (4.14.35–36). The sleep of sensuous pleasure is giving way to the sleep brought on by the noble act of suicide. The latter meaning is very clear in Cleopatra's speech at the beginning of V,ii:

> And it is great
> To do that thing that ends all other deeds,
> Which shackles accidents and bolts up change,
> Which sleeps, and never palates more the dung,
> The beggar's nurse and Caesar's. (5.2.4–8)

The creature of "infinite variety" now rejects the mutable world of "accidents" and "change" for the sure and honorable sleep of death.

The climax of this movement is in Cleopatra's death: "As sweet as balm, as soft as air, as gentle — " (5.2.314). The euphoria of her end reflects Plutarch's description of the effect of the asp (see Chapter II), and her death is a most sensuous and luxurious kind of falling asleep. We feel this in the full slow rhythms and word music of her final speeches. The asp is Cleopatra's baby at her breast

"That sucks the nurse asleep," and Charmian tries to continue the illusion of sleep as the Guard comes "rustling" noisily in (5.2.322 s.d.):

1. Guard. Where is the Queen?
Char.   Speak softly, wake her not.
                                                               (5.2.323)

The queen's death is represented as a beatific state, a mood confirmed by Caesar when he says:

> she looks like sleep,
> As she would catch another Antony
> In her strong toil of grace. (5.2.349–51)

This imagery plays a significant part in the development of Cleopatra. Her final sleep is a moral act and a mark of her greatness, but it is brought on with the full sensuous effect of the asp's bite, the splendid robe and crown, and poetic speeches. The moral import of her suicide is Roman, yet its elaborate ceremony recalls the earlier, Egyptian sense of "sleep" as a luxury and gratification of the senses. It is indolence of a magnificent sort, a paragon and apotheosis of indolence.

We may note in passing the suggestion of a "business" theme for Rome as opposed to the idleness of Egypt. This contrast is perhaps most effectively made in the staging of the play. As we have already observed, there is a different pace and tempo in the Roman scenes, whose quick and determined movement is set apart from the graceful movement of Egypt. It is interesting, nevertheless, to note that all of the nine occurrences of "business" are either directly or indirectly "Roman." Fulvia's wars are "The business" (1.2.178) that cannot endure Antony's absence from Rome. In I,iv we have Caesar's concern with the "business" (1.4.80) of preparing against Pompey. The conference between Antony and Caesar in II,ii is literally "business of state," and Antony answers Caesar's accusation with: "You do mistake your business" (2.2.45). Octavia's marriage to Antony is dispatched between Antony and Octavius as "The business we have talk'd of" (2.2.169). The most important statement of the theme occurs in the drinking scene aboard Pompey's galley, in which the austere, duty-bound Caesar protests against the merriment: "Our graver business/ Frowns at this levity" (2.7.125–26). In III,iii Cleopatra finds the Messenger from Rome "Most fit for business" (3.3.40), and a few scenes further, a Messenger's "business" (3.7.54) with Antony is to announce that Caesar has taken Toryne. Antony speaks of the soldier's profession in these same terms: "To business that we love we rise betime/ And go to't with delight" (4.4.20–21). Finally, Caesar says of an Egyptian messenger from Cleopatra: "The business of this man looks out of him . . ." (5.1.50). These uses of "business" are quite casual and undeveloped, but they do call attention to the opposition of Egyptian and Roman values.

3

The basic issues in *Antony and Cleopatra* revolve to a large extent around the role of Cleopatra and her effect on Antony. From Philo's point of view this effect can be explained quite simply: Antony is "The triple pillar of the world transform'd/ Into a strumpet's fool" (1.1.12–13). This attitude echoes the moral judgment with which Plutarch begins his discussion of Cleopatra:

Antonius being thus inclined, the last and extreamest mischiefe of all other (to wit, the loue of *Cleopatra*) lighted on him, who did waken and stirre vp many vices yet hidden in him, and were neuer seene to any: and if any sparke of goodnesse or hope of rising were left him, *Cleopatra* quenched it straight, and made it worse than before.[29]

But Plutarch's whole account is not so simple as this, for he seems to be fascinated and puzzled by Cleopatra.

We have recently had a revival of the moral attack on Cleopatra, especially in a study of Shakespeare's love tragedies by Franklin M. Dickey, who, on the basis of extensive research, concludes that

classical and medieval authorities, Elizabethan moral philosophers, and the Senecan playwrights show us a picture of extravagance, gluttony, and intemperance. Cleopatra appears again and again as a wanton and a sorceress, who employed all the conscious arts of love to keep Antony ensnared.[30]

The hypothetical Elizabethan reader would have seen Antony and Cleopatra as "patterns of lust, of cruelty, of prodigality, of drunkenness, of vanity, and, in the end, of despair." [31] All of this is no doubt true, yet there is much more in Shakespeare's play than Dickey sees. His demonstration seems to me to suffer from an important logical fallacy: the establishment of a tradition does not in itself prove that any particular work is an expression of that tradition; or, even if it were, one must still show in just what particular ways it uses the body of accepted ideas. The fact that our era is interested in Freud, for example, does not automatically mean that all our writers are influenced by Freud; or, even if they are, we must still determine for all cases the particular mode of influence. This is where Dickey attributes a simple-mindedness to Shakespeare that does not at all accord with what we are presented with in

the plays. Yet Dickey's work is valuable for its documenta-
tion and justification of the Roman point of view of Philo,
who most closely resembles Dickey's typical Elizabethan
reader. May not Shakespeare's play be, after all, intended
to persuade Philo to revise his accepted ideas?

At an opposite extreme are the many romantic, rhapsodic,
even mystical adorations of Cleopatra's "ewige Weiblichkeit."
G. Wilson Knight, for example, almost completely discards
the Roman and moral aspects of the play, which "We watch
as though from the turrets of infinity, whence the ethical
is found unreal and beauty alone survives." [32] Far from
the disquieting realities of Rome and of Egypt, we see the
Wagnerian spectacle of "Cleopatra and her girls at Alex-
andria . . . as the Eternal Femininity waiting for Man. A
certain eternity broods over this still, languorous Alexan-
dria. The wars of Caesar and Antony seem a little childish
by these deeps of love. . . ." [33] This interpretation seems
even farther from the truth of Shakespeare's play than the
moralistic views we have just considered.

It is necessary, I believe, to hold both the Egyptian and
Roman themes in the play together in the mind as a tragic
unity. Either without the other makes for distortion and
incompleteness. Taken alone, the Roman point of view
simplifies the tragedy into a morality play, and the Egyptian
one transforms the tragedy into a paean of transcendental
love. If the tragic choices in this play are between different
kinds of rightness, then we need both of these views to
understand the meaning of the action. We must therefore
reject the facile argument of Schücking, who accuses Shakespeare of inconsistency in his presentation of Cleopatra:
she is a whore in the first three acts and a royal queen in
the last two.[34] I should say rather that she is both queen

and quean throughout the play (see Chapter II, Note 20).

Dryden's *All for Love; or, The World Well Lost* should set an example for critics against simplifying Shakespeare's play. In the spirit of Philo, Dryden reduces the morality of the play to a symmetrical conflict of love and honor, thus taking the obvious course that Shakespeare avoided, for in *Antony and Cleopatra* the central issues remain in a fundamental ambivalence.[35] We may gauge the difference between the two plays by Dryden's comment that Shakespeare's "whole style is so pestered with figurative expressions, that it is as affected as it is obscure."[36] But these "figurative expressions" in Shakespeare are not simply tricks of style which can be "refined" for a later age; they are the essential part of his imagination. As Benjamin Spencer has pointed out, the paradoxical metaphor is not just a figure of speech in *Antony and Cleopatra*, but an expression of the deepest meanings of the play.[37] We must conclude, then, that there is a quality of somber "realism"[38] here that is neither moralistic nor rhapsodic, and the tragic conflict is not conceived as an alternation between love and honor. If we cannot in some way justify Antony's return to Egypt as well as condemn it, there can be no tragedy, for tragedy is based on significant choices in situations which have some elements of a moral dilemma. If Antony's return to Egypt is simply moral weakness and no more, then the play may just as well end at this point. But it represents a significant choice, and even though it brings on Antony's tragedy, it shows a certain kind of strength.

In some sense we may say that Cleopatra controls Antony's movements, and although she is not a tragic figure, she remains an enigmatic force throughout the play. Admittedly, as Caesar says, she is a "whore" (3.6.67) and a "trull"

(3.6.95), yet she is also deliberately "heightened" in the play. Dickey's explanation — "Were sin not alluring, who would sin?" [39] — seems to me to miss the point, for it is hampered by a specifically Christian interpretation of Cleopatra as a sort of Jezebel. The intensifications of Cleopatra's poetry at certain crucial points and the affirmative and ascending movement of the dramatic action from Antony's suicide to the end of the play cannot be considered as mere incitements to sin gloriously.

The key passage for the poetic heightening of Cleopatra is Enobarbus' description of her as she sits in her barge on the Cydnus. Dryden, significantly, gives this speech to Antony, which shows a characteristic difference between his Antony and Shakespeare's, for the rhapsodic mood of Shakespeare's hero is expressed only at the very beginning of the play and at his death. In I,ii, which is an important analogue and preparation for the Cydnus passage, it is Enobarbus, not Antony, who thinks of idealizing Cleopatra, though perhaps only ironically. "She is cunning past man's thought" (1.2.150), says Antony, but Enobarbus defends her: "Alack, sir, no! Her passions are made of nothing but the finest part of pure love" (1.2.151–52). All Antony acknowledges in his answer is her fatal and irresistible attraction: "Would I had never seen her!" (1.2.158) — this sentence provides for his return to Egypt before he has even left — and his awareness of Cleopatra's perils helps to develop his tragic stature in the play. But to Enobarbus this attitude is folly: "O, sir, you had then left unseen a wonderful piece of work, which not to have been blest withal would have discredited your travel" (1.2.159–61). This absolutely separates Antony's personal involvement with Cleopatra from Enobarbus' objective enthusiasm.

To Enobarbus she represents one of the wonders of the East in the double sense of something admired but only partly understood. He cannot fathom why Cleopatra should want to appear in the wars "for a man" (3.7.19). "But why, why, why?" (3.7.2) he asks, and can think only of the distraction that must occur when horses and mares serve together. His comment, "the mares would bear/ A soldier and his horse" (3.7.9–10), seems to be a direct answer to Cleopatra's exclamation: "O happy horse, to bear the weight of Antony!" (1.5.21). Enobarbus is always the Roman in Egypt, fascinated, awed, enjoying, but never drawn from his basically Roman morality. He is of course very vulnerable to Eastern luxury and beauty just because of his blunt insistence on reason and common sense, the qualities that also establish his role as choric commentator. He sees only too well the destructive force of passion and the tragic process by which Antony makes "his will/ Lord of his reason" (3.13.3–4). Perhaps Enobarbus values reason and good judgment so highly because he feels such strong promptings of his own will. His reason and good judgment prove inadequate to the force of Antony, and, ironically, his advice to Cleopatra after the first sea battle, "Think, and die" (3.13.1.), echoes in the "swift thought" (4.6.35) of his own death.

The prelude to the barge-on-Cydnus passage is the talk about Egyptian revelry. Enobarbus, the traveler, is trying to impress the eager Romans, Maecenas and Agrippa, and the description of Cleopatra on her barge is his master stroke; he is very consciously dominating the scene with his hyperbole. It is characteristic of Shakespeare's mature style to provide a dramatic context for his set speeches. We may compare the oration of Henry V before Harfleur ("Once

SHAKESPEARE'S ROMAN PLAYS

more unto the breach . . ." 3.1.1–34). It is a model of
vigorous exhortation to battle, yet it is almost completely
impersonal. Its high flights are appropriate only because of
the greatness of the occasion, whereas the highly figurative
style of Enobarbus' speech grows out of the intimate play
of character in the immediate situation.

In the description of Cleopatra on the Cydnus (2.2.195–
223) the appeal is to all the senses mingled together. The
imagery of sight stresses color: the barge "like a burnish'd
throne" made to burn on the water by the intense reflection
of the sun; the "beaten gold" poop; the "purple" sails; the
"silver" oars; the pavilion "cloth-of-gold of tissue"; "divers-
colour'd fans"; and Cleopatra's glowing "delicate cheeks."
The tactile imagery includes material things such as "beaten
gold" or "cloth-of-gold of tissue," but it is used specifically
for the waiting gentlewomen:

> The silken tackle
> Swell with the touches of those flower-soft hands
> That yarely frame the office.

For sound, we have the "tune of flutes" to which the silver
oars keep stroke, and we smell the barge's "perfumed"
sails. This "strange invisible perfume hits the sense/ Of the
adjacent wharfs" and permeates the scene. The sense of
stately and delicate movement is conveyed by the "winds"
in the purple sails; the silver oars beating the water to the
"tune of flutes"; the "pretty dimpled boys" stirring a "wind"
with their fans; the gentlewomen making "their bends
adornings"; and the "seeming mermaid" who "steers." It is
a gorgeous spectacle, an example of the rich and almost
unreal opulence of the East and the triumph of art over
nature.

118

Cleopatra is also presented in this passage in a context of cosmic imagery; nature is seen as waiting in adoration upon her in her barge. There is an obeisance and gentle yielding of things without any physical effort. The purple sails were "so perfumed that/ The winds were lovesick with them. . . ." The silver oars made "The water which they beat to follow faster,/ As amorous of their strokes." The absence of purposive action is seen particularly in a detail about the fans,

> whose wind did seem
> To glow the delicate cheeks which they did cool,
> And what they undid did.

This paradox is at an opposite pole from the practical and efficient world of Rome. But the highest adoration of Cleopatra is experienced at the end of the passage: the air in the market place, where Antony sits whistling to it, is personified and

> but for vacancy,
> Had gone to gaze on Cleopatra too,
> And made a gap in nature.

She must indeed be a "wonderful piece of work" (1.2.159) for her effect to be so powerful.

Nothing is said directly about the person of Cleopatra except that "It beggar'd all description." This appears to me quite worthy of note, since the passage gives the impression of saying a good deal about her. Shakespeare very skillfully uses the splendor of the barge as a mirror for the Egyptian queen, so that it almost seems to reflect an external aspect of her person. She is thus deified by the quality of the poetry and by the richness and scope of the poetic reference. Mythology, for example, serves to endow this scene with a perfection beyond that of mere mortals. We are told that Cleopatra lies in her pavilion "O'erpicturing that Venus where we see/ The fancy outwork nature." This image uses the familiar hyperbole of invidious comparison (*"O'er*picturing" — compare 5.2.82, 83) to indicate that Cleopatra is in a category of excellence above Venus; this is indeed "nature's piece 'gainst fancy" (5.2.99). On each side of the more-than-Venus Cleopatra "Stood pretty dimpled boys, like smiling Cupids" fanning her. Her other attendants are mythologized in like manner:

> Her gentlewomen, like the Nereides,
> So many mermaids, tended her i' th' eyes,
> And made their bends adornings. At the helm
> A seeming mermaid steers.

Mythology gives this scene a static pictorial perfection, which is later remembered as the subject of a tapestry in Imogen's bedchamber (*Cymbeline* 2.4.69–74).

The vision of Cleopatra on the Cydnus shows us how Antony first saw her, and it functions as the source and nucleus of her attraction. It is placed very artfully just after Antony's reconciliation with Caesar and his proposed marriage to Octavia. But we are not to be led astray by these events: the picture of Cleopatra on the Cydnus provides reasons for Antony's return to Egypt. When Maecenas says, "Now Antony must leave her utterly" (2.2.238), Enobarbus very bluntly contradicts him: "Never! He will not" (2.2.239). Enobarbus' description of Cleopatra thus not only prepares our minds for Antony's return to Egypt, but also ensures it.

All the force of Octavia's "beauty, wisdom, modesty" (2.2.246) and "holy, cold, and still conversation" (2.6.130) will not be able to keep Antony in Rome. Octavia is a high-minded feminine counterpart of her brother Octavius, and this is one way to interpret Antony's attitude to her. In contrast to Cleopatra she is spoken of as a "hoop" (2.2.117), an "unslipping knot" (2.2.129), a "blessed lottery" (2.2.248), a "statue" (3.3.24), a "castaway" (3.6.40), an "abstract" (3.6.61), and a "gem of women" (3.13.108). Antony and Caesar enter in II,iii with "*Octavia* between them," and she becomes a "piece of virtue" set between them "as the cement of our love/ To keep it builded . . ." (3.2.28–30), not "the ram to batter/ The fortress of it . . ." (3.2.30–31). This is a Roman imagery of cold and hard material objects, which, though substantial in themselves, cannot compete with the "most triumphant lady" (2.2.189) in Egypt.

Cleopatra's stature is not only developed by the poetic quality of her lines and of those describing her, but also by the general movement of the dramatic action from Antony's suicide to the end of the play. Her choice of the "high Roman fashion" (4.15.87) of suicide rather than the base life of Caesar's triumph ennobles her, for it is a resolution of moral courage, and it indicates a new and final movement in the dramatic action. When Antony hears the report of her death, there is a sudden transformation of tone. From a strident reviling, he now becomes still and resigned to his fate:

> *Ant.*   Dead, then?
> *Mar.*   Dead.
> *Ant.* Unarm, Eros. The long day's task is done,
> And we must sleep.   (4.14.34–36)

The simple, quiescent tone makes an absolute contrast with Antony's previous words.

The heightening of Cleopatra begins at this "turn" in

the action and continues until the end of the play. Her suicide is proof to Antony that she did not betray him to Caesar, and she sets an example of nobility for Antony to follow. But he can only inflict a mortal wound on himself, and, as he lies there, Diomedes enters and informs him of Cleopatra's ruse: she is alive and locked in her monument. It would have been possible for the action at this point to move in an entirely different direction from the one Shakespeare took. The discovery of Cleopatra's trickery could have been the crowning irony of her character: false at Actium, false at the final naval battle, and now false even in death — the "serpent of old Nile" at her most perfect. But instead, this important discovery is completely minimized. Antony shows the same resignation as at the "turn" in the action; there is not even an indication of surprise. He says only, "Too late, good Diomed. Call my guard, I prithee" (4.14.128). We should not overlook the interrelations of these final scenes. Cleopatra's feigned suicide provides a means for giving us Antony's reaction to her death, although he dies before her. This response, as well as Antony's actual death, echo in Cleopatra's suicide in V,ii with the effect of a theme and variations: we feel the force of Antony working in Cleopatra. Shakespeare is thus able to play the death scene over three times.

The repeated mention of the nobility of Cleopatra's suicide and the frequency with which she is addressed by her royal titles — "Royal Egypt!/ Empress!" (4.15.70–71), "Queen of Egypt" (5.2.9), "Most sovereign creature" (5.2.81) — are part of a larger emphasis on her majesty and queenliness in death. All this repetition of imperial imagery culminates in the stage action before her death, where we see her literally putting on royalty by its symbols of robe and crown. She sends Iras to fetch her regal attire:

> Show me, my women, like a queen. Go fetch
> My best attires. I am again for Cydnus,
> To meet Mark Antony. Sirrah Iras, go.
> Now, noble Charmian, we'll dispatch indeed;
> And when thou hast done this chare, I'll give thee leave
> To play till doomsday. — Bring our crown and all.
>
> (5.2.227–32)

At this point Iras leaves to fulfill her errand, and the noise of the Clown is heard within. Death is certain now, but it is not done in the abrupt Roman manner of sword or dagger. Cleopatra's suicide is a Roman act only in its moral implications, for it is staged with the full splendor and ceremony of Egypt. Her "I am again for Cydnus,/ To meet Mark Antony" should orient our aesthetic awareness. That event was only reported by Enobarbus, whereas Cleopatra will now be *shown* "like a queen." We may use this example to mark the difference between verbal and presentational imagery, although the symbolic languages of words and staging are used together for a unified effect.

When Iras brings the robe and crown "and all" (possibly jewels from the regalia),[40] Cleopatra makes herself ready for death:

> Give me my robe, put on my crown. I have
> Immortal longings in me. Now no more
> The juice of Egypt's grape shall moist this lip.
> Yare, yare, good Iras; quick. Methinks I hear
> Antony call. (5.2.283–87)

We need to supply the stage action for this passage: Iras is helping Cleopatra robe herself, and Cleopatra is impatient to be finished ("Yare, yare, good Iras; quick"). In her haste Iras appears to put the crown on awry (Charmian straight-

ens it at 5.2.321–22). The end of the dressing is marked
by Cleopatra's question: "So, have you done?" (5.2.293).
When Cleopatra kisses her, Iras suddenly falls dead at the
feet of her queen. The fact of Iras' death at this point should
give some indication of her manner while dressing Cleopatra; it is her final, hieratic service to her mistress.

After the death of Cleopatra, Charmian pays a final
tribute to her royalty:

> Now boast thee, death, in thy possession lies
> A lass unparallel'd. Downy windows, close;
> And golden Phoebus never be beheld
> Of eyes again so royal! Your crown's awry.
> I'll mend it, and then play —   (5.2.318–22)

She closes Cleopatra's "royal" eyes and straightens her
crown. The last bit of stage business is one of those marvelous details so frequent in Shakespeare and so characteristic of his dramatic art. By its psychological truth it calls
attention to the crown as symbol of the dead queen's royalty.
The First Guard's question, "Where's [41] the Queen?"
(5.2.323), also draws our attention to Cleopatra, who dominates the stage after her death until she is carried off at the
very end of the play — the staging here bears some re-
semblance to the use of Julius Caesar's body. We learn
later from this Guard just how Charmian is to act her
part: "Tremblingly she stood,/ And on the sudden dropp'd"
(5.2.346–47). The word "Tremblingly" — its only occurrence in Shakespeare — [42] indicates the ineffably devoted
manner of Charmian as she performs these last rites for her
mistress. When the Guard asks her if this is well done, she
once again affirms Cleopatra's noble act:

> It is well done, and fitting for a princess
> Descended of so many royal kings.
> Ah, soldier! (5.2.329–31)

Death is the final "decorum" for Cleopatra's majesty: the suicide is "fitting" and the triumph is avoided. The "Ah, soldier!" at the end indicates how little he can understand of these matters.

Caesar's reaction to Cleopatra's death is also a praise of her majesty:

> Bravest at the last!
> She levell'd at our purposes, and being royal,
> Took her own way. (5.2.338-40)

Caesar has played for her and lost, and there is no bitterness in his admission that her suicide was "royal" and the "Bravest" course. The word "Bravest" is a particularly good one for Cleopatra here, since in Elizabethan English it meant not only moral courage, but also splendor of personal appearance, especially the splendor of dress (the royal robe and crown would be "brave" apparel). These notions implied in the word include both the Roman and Egyptian aspects of her suicide: it is a noble and moral act achieved with magnificent ceremony. Each of these qualities serves to complete the meaning of the other.

Suicide is Cleopatra's tragic choice, and she is ennobled by it, although she does not become a full-scale tragic protagonist as Antony does. Her tragedy is very clearly focused on this choice, whereas Antony is made to bear the burden of choice, responsibility, and guilt throughout the play. We may say, then, that Cleopatra begins as a temptress or enchantress rather than a tragic figure, but she is drawn up into tragedy by Antony's death.

4

Shakespeare's Antony resembles Hamlet in at least this one respect: both have an acute awareness of their moral situation, but they are seemingly without the power to change it. Their tragedies do not come from a blindness or error of judgment, but from a deep-seated defect of will. Hamlet, however, is catapulted into a tragedy to which he remains alien and unreconciled, whereas Antony seems to choose his fate deliberately and knowingly. He goes through the motions of suicide, for example, only to learn that Cleopatra is "playing" dead in her monument. But this ruse seems to make no difference to him, and his dying wish to be carried to her is an acknowledgment and acceptance of his fate. In this way the death scene in IV,xv passes from tragedy to rhapsodic affirmation, and "the visions of comedy and tragedy merge." [43]

These movements in the fate of Antony grow out of the tragic conflict between the values of Egypt and Rome and may be illustrated in three image themes: sword and armor, vertical dimension, and dissolution. The sword and armor Antony wears are the visible signs of his soldiership and empire; but as the play progresses, the power of Antony's sword is undercut by his association with Cleopatra, and his unarming is a formal dumbshow for his renunciation of Rome. This pattern of Antony's tragedy is also reflected in images of lowness and height and in a very characteristic imagery of dissolution. Out of many possible themes, these three express the fate of Antony with most significance and originality.

Antony is visibly present in sword and armor for a good part of the play. This is a presentational image of his role as soldier and triumvir, his "royal occupation" (4.4.17), and the verbal imagery helps to support this impression. We see him in military dress throughout the scenes of war (from III,vii to IV,xiv,35, when he begins to disarm), and probably also in the conferences with Caesar (II,ii, III,ii) and with Pompey (II,vi, vii) — the formal dress of sword and armor would be in keeping with the gravity of public affairs in these scenes. As a matter of fact, Lepidus very specifically indicates "soldier's dress" (2.4.4) for the scene with Pompey. Antony is also probably in sword and armor when he first appears in the play. This would give Philo's allusions to "plated Mars" (1.1.4) and "The buckles on his breast" (1.1.8) an immediate reference to the Antony we see enter a few lines further. Philo wishes to indicate that the sword and armor are only a false appearance for Antony's present "dotage."

The basic application of sword and armor imagery is to the Roman concerns of war and soldiership. These are part of that public world of hard material objects and practical business that stands in sharp contrast to the luxuriousness and indolence of Egypt. Originally, it is the "civil swords" (1.3.45), or civil war, in Italy that calls Antony back to Rome. But after his shameful flight from battle at Actium, his sword becomes only an image of his former glory. He recollects that the now triumphant Octavius

> at Philippi kept
> His sword e'en like a dancer, while I struck
> The lean and wrinkled Cassius; and 'twas I
> That the mad Brutus ended. He alone
> Dealt on lieutenantry and no practise had
> In the brave squares of war. Yet now — No matter.
> (3.11.35–40)

Now Caesar, whose sword served no more function than a dancer's ornament, has defeated Antony, and the extent of Antony's present shame is indicated by the prolonged and

127

emphatic "now." Antony tries to restore the power of his sword by challenging Caesar to single combat:

> I dare him therefore
> To lay his gay comparisons apart
> And answer me declin'd, sword against sword,
> Ourselves alone.   (3.13.25–28)

It is an unreal, histrionic effort, for Caesar is not interested in this public display of bravery; he has, indeed, already refused Antony (3.1.31–35). The aside of Enobarbus serves as chorus here:

> Yes, like enough high-battled Caesar will
> Unstate his happiness and be stag'd to th' show
> Against a sworder!   (3.13.29–31)

"Sworder" is a contemptuous word, and it signifies that Antony now wears his sword "e'en like a dancer"; the power of war has gone out of it. Enobarbus, tragically divided between the qualities of Antony and Caesar, decides at this point to desert his master. His ominous and incisive comment closes the scene:

> When valour preys on reason,
> It eats the sword it fights with. I will seek
> Some way to leave him.   (3.13.199–201)

The Roman virtue of "reason" is valor's true sword, and Caesar's conquest of the "three nook'd world" (4.6.6) shows how well he has learned this lesson.

There is an ironic comment on the ineffectiveness of Antony's sword in his suicide scene. He entreats Eros to draw "thy honest sword" (4.14.79) and kill him, but Eros takes his own life instead. This gives Antony the courage to fall on his sword, but he is only able to inflict a mortal wound. He prays the Guard, then Diomedes, to make an end of his blundering work: "Draw thy sword and give me/ Sufficing strokes for death" (4.14.116–17). Antony's sword is powerless even for death — a graphic image of his tragedy. The inadequacy of his sword reflects the abandonment of his Roman role of soldier and world conqueror.

Our final image of Antony's sword balances the fall of Antony against the rise of Caesar. Once again the sword enters significantly into the stage action. As Antony lies dying, Decretas [44] steals his sword, which "but shown to Caesar, with this tidings,/ Shall enter me with him" (4.14.112–13). We see Decretas again at the beginning of Act V, where his portentous entrance with the bloody sword of Antony in his hand gives Caesar a sudden fright — it is a final reflection of the power of Antony. This sword, once the symbol of his Roman virtue and dominion, is handed over to Caesar, who is now indeed "Sole sir o' th' world" (5.2.120). Compare the symbolic stage business in *Julius Caesar*, where both Cassius (5.3.45–46) and presumably Brutus (5.5.50–51) stab themselves with the same swords they used to kill Caesar. This ironic reciprocity presents the poetic justice of the play in strong theatrical terms. In *Antony and Cleopatra* the presentation of Antony's sword to Octavius acts out the tragic transfer of power that is a central issue in the play, and the ritual stage business serves as a brusque investiture for Caesar.

In a sense "sword" has one set of connotations in Egypt and another in Rome. This difference reflects Antony's tragedy, for his sword in its Roman role is rendered powerless in Egypt, and his association with Cleopatra develops the sexual overtones of the image. Although the theme is directly stated only two or three times in the play, it underlies a good part of the action in Egypt. As Agrippa tells us, Cleopatra has the ability to charm swords to inaction: "She made great Caesar lay his sword to bed./ He plough'd her, and she cropp'd" (2.2.232–33). This utterly un-Shavian Julius Caesar is the model for Antony, and the strong connotations of "sword" here indicate its transformation from a military to a procreative term. The passage suggests Cleopatra's recollection of the time she drank Antony to his bed, "Then put my tires and mantles on him, whilst/ I wore his sword Philippan" (2.5.22–23). In both passages Cleopatra's dominance involves control of her lover's sword, the symbol of his manliness and soldiership. There is perhaps an allusion to Hercules' enslavement by Omphale here, for Omphale forced Hercules to wear her clothes, while she dressed in his lion-skin and carried his club.[45] The identification is very specifically indicated in the "Comparison" that follows the life of Antony in North's Plutarch:

we see in painted tables, where Omphale secretlie stealeth away Hercules clubbe, and tooke his Lyons skinne from him. Even so Cleopatra oftentimes unarmed Antonius, and intised him to her, making him lose matters of great importaunce, and verie needeful jorneys, to come and be dandled with her, about the rivers of Canobus, and Taphosiris.[46]

This is the sort of effemination that Cleopatra has inflicted on Antony, and it is no wonder that when Cleopatra enters in I,ii, Enobarbus says sardonically: "Hush! Here comes Antony" (1.2.83).[47]

The reversal of roles between Antony and Cleopatra is illustrated by the battle of Actium: it is to please her and against all reason that Antony accepts Caesar's dare to fight at sea. A Soldier warns him against it, but the Soldier's "sword" and "wounds" (3.7.64) cannot persuade Antony against the whims of Cleopatra, who insists on appearing at Actium "for a man" (3.7.19). Antony blames her for his defeat at the same time as he acknowledges his own "dotage" in Egypt:

> You did know
> How much you were my conqueror, and that
> My sword, made weak by my affection, would
> Obey it on all cause. (3.11.65–68)

"My sword made weak by my affection" is a key statement for the tragedy of Antony. His power to act, represented by the Roman sense of "sword," has been overwhelmed by his power to feel ("affection"). Enobarbus, too, blames "affection" for the defeat at Actium. When Antony followed Cleopatra from battle, "The itch of his affection should not then/ Have nick'd his captainship . . ." (3.13.7–8). The word "nick'd" implies that Antony's "captainship" is conceived as the blade of a sword, which Cleopatra has damaged and made useless. He is thus being made aware of the price of Egypt, and this gives a tragic dimension to what began as frivolity and indulgence of the senses.

There is a final reflection of the theme in the scene of Antony's suicide. The entrance of Cleopatra's Eunuch, Mardian, sends Antony into a rage: "O, thy vile lady!/ She has robb'd me of my sword" (4.14.22–23). This is another way of stating the tragedy of Antony. Cleopatra has deprived him of the power to act and conquer that made him "triple pillar of the world." "Sword" is being used in its obvious Roman sense, but there is also a play on the sexual connotations of the word. From a Roman point of view, Antony has become as impotent as the Eunuch Mardian: his sword is only an instrument of "affection," the symbol of his dominance by Cleopatra. But in the values of Egypt this is sufficient and in itself can offer a transcendence. When Antony learns that Cleopatra has not betrayed him to Caesar but has committed suicide in her monument, there is a marvelous change in his attitude. His sword is no longer his concern, nor is any temporal thing, as he prepares to follow his lady. It is a final, tragic acceptance of the values of Egypt, and it marks a strong poetic heightening for Antony.

The "turn" in the dramatic action begins with his request to Eros: "Unarm, Eros. The long day's task is done,/ And we must sleep" (4.14.35–36). Antony by disarming now visibly abandons his Roman role of soldier just as Cleopatra assumes the role of queen by putting on robe and crown; both are the final symbolic acts of the protagonists, and in both costume has strong thematic significance. Antony's arming on the morning of the second battle prepares us for the symbolic tone of the later passage. Cleopatra insists on helping in spite of his protest: "Ah, let be, let be! Thou art/ The armourer of my heart. False, false! This, this!" (4.4.6–7). Cleopatra, the "armourer" of Antony's "heart," is improperly assuming a Roman role in trying to arm his body, and the "False, false!" and "This, this!" refer to her ineptness at this sort of arming. It is another way of indicating that Antony's sword has been made weak by "affection," and the ill omen of "False, false!" echoes in his final defeat: "O this false soul of Egypt!" (4.12.25).

Antony's public position of Roman soldier and triumvir has been expressed by sword and armor throughout the play, so that his unarming in IV,xiv marks a new, and final, movement in the action. The bitterness and misgivings of tragic conflict are gone; there is only a desire for haste (compare Cleopatra and Iras 5.2.283ff):

1 3 2

Off, pluck off!
The sevenfold shield of Ajax cannot keep
The battery from my heart. O, cleave, my sides!
Heart, once be stronger than thy continent,
Crack thy frail case! Apace, Eros, apace. —
No more a soldier. Bruised pieces, go;
You have been nobly borne. (4.14.37–43)

"No more a soldier" indicates the end of the unarming, and Antony feels that he is now suddenly entering a new spiritual state. It is as if he had put off some external Roman self with this "sevenfold shield of Ajax" and these "Bruised pieces." His mortal body ("continent," with a play on the etymological and geographical senses) is now in itself too much armor to bear against death, and he prays that the "battery" from his "heart" be strong enough to "Crack" his "frail case" and "cleave" his "sides." And he eagerly anticipates the fate of his unarmed self, the lover of Cleopatra. Her death set him an example of nobility, which evokes memories of his former glory as he prepares to follow her:

I, that with my sword
Quarter'd the world and o'er green Neptune's back
With ships made cities. . . . (4.14.57–59)

But he is now "No more a soldier," and his world-quartering sword is only a recollection of the past.

The fall of Antony is also marked by a persistent imagery of vertical dimension, which is a simpler and more literal theme than sword and armor, but keeps us vividly aware of the movement of the action. The basic pattern here is the contrast in vertical dimension between high and low, up and down, in a manner quite similar to that used in *Richard II*.[48] This is best seen in two presentational images. Antony's

SHAKESPEARE'S ROMAN PLAYS

despair and remorse after Actium are summed up in a significant stage direction: *"Sits down"* (3.11.24). The action here is in absolute contrast to the movement of the battle scenes, and its tone suggests the homely opening of *Coriolanus* I,iii: "Enter *Volumnia* and *Virgilia*, mother and wife to *Marcius*. They set them down on two low stools and sew." It is not part of the "decorum" of majesty for Antony to be sitting down, and the action becomes a literal stage image for his lowness at this point: "He is unqualitied with very shame" (3.11.44). Similarly, one of the symbolic suggestions of Pompey's lowness in the political world is his reluctance to obey Menas' pregnant aside, "Rise from thy stool" (2.7.62). One may easily overlook these presentational images in reading the play, but in the theater they are an effective and eloquent expression, perhaps just because of their extreme simplicity. The image of Antony sitting down is supported by verbal references that do not allow us to forget his position. Cleopatra wishes to join him: "Let me sit down. O Juno!" (3.11.28), but Antony protests bitterly: "No, no, no, no, no!" (3.11.29) — the comment in its intensity recalls the "never's" of *King Lear* (5.3.308). And Antony is still seated at 3.11.46, when Eros says: "Most noble sir, arise. The Queen approaches." It is not presumably until a few lines further (3.11.50) that Eros, after four unsuccessful attempts (3.11.30, 34, 42, 46–48), is finally able to draw Antony's attention to Cleopatra and to compel him to stand. Antony deliberately turns his back to the queen (3.11.52), but the action of standing brings with it a recovery of equilibrium.

Antony reaches a different kind of height from Caesar's in IV,xv, when he is lifted, dying, to Cleopatra's monument. The action, *"They heave Antony aloft to Cleopatra"* (4.15.

134

37 s.d.), presents a literal image of height in the use of the upper stage. We see Antony being raised by his Guard, and they are assisted by Cleopatra and her girls from "aloft." The theater thus provides us with a metaphor of elevation for Antony's death, which is accompanied by a corresponding heightening of style. Cleopatra's speech is full of ironic puns about the stage business:

> Here's sport indeed! How heavy weighs my lord!
> Our strength is all gone into heaviness:
> That makes the weight. Had I great Juno's power,
> The strong-wing'd Mercury should fetch thee up
> And set thee by Jove's side.   (4.15.32–36)

Antony's heaviness as he is raised to the monument is made the symbol of heavy grief; we can see that Cleopatra very obviously does not have "great Juno's power." She uses "sport" ironically to fit in with the action, as if all the Egyptian pleasures should end in this final sport, the awkward manual labor of lifting a dying captain to his place of death. There are also obvious sexual overtones in "sport" and "heavy." But Antony's place is an elevated one (both literally and figuratively) and in its own way defies the temporal height of Caesar. The note of fulfillment and reconciliation in this image places the fate of Antony outside the toils of tragedy.

The language of this scene suggests that Antony was simply lifted "aloft" by his Guard, with some help from Cleopatra and her girls, but without the distracting use of a crane or pulley or hoist operated by stagehands from the "huts." The fact that North's Plutarch mentions "certaine chaines and ropes" [49] does not seem to me to have any bearing at all on the Elizabethan staging. It is possible to "heave Antony aloft" even if the upper stage were twelve

135

feet above the main stage, and it may well have been only eight or nine.[50] If, for example, Antony were carried in on a long shield mounted on four short poles, these could be lifted together by the bearers, who could easily reach the upper stage even at a height of twelve feet. Perhaps the most practicable plan for the staging of this scene is that of C. Walter Hodges, who suggests a property "monument" with two levels that would resemble the traditional strolling actors' booth. It would stand against the tiring-house wall throughout the play, and its lower level would also serve as a curtained inner stage. The upper level would be seven or eight feet from the stage and would have no balustrade in front. Antony could thus be raised without any difficulties and in full view of the audience.[51]

Antony's fallen state is represented most brilliantly by the imagery of dissolution. The pattern in the play is one of melting, fading, dissolving, discandying, disponging, dislimning, and losing of form that marks his downward course after Actium, "for indeed I have lost command" (3.11.23). As Antony says, "Authority melts from me" (3.13.90), and this is clearly acted out when he orders Caesar's servant, Thidias, to approach (I supply in brackets what the stage action appears to be):

> Approach there! — [*Thidias stands insolently still*] Ah, you
> kite! — [*Spoken to Cleopatra: you are responsible for this*]
> Now, gods and devils!
> Authority melts from me. Of late, when I cried 'Ho!'
> Like boys unto a muss, kings would start forth
> And cry 'Your will?' Have you no ears? [*Thidias is still insolently ignoring Antony*] I am
> Antony yet.   (3.13.89–93)

It was Antony who once declared with so much disregard:

136

"Let Rome in Tiber melt and the wide arch/ Of the rang'd empire fall!" (1.1.33–34). Now Antony's Rome has indeed melted and his own "rang'd empire" fallen, for his authority is gone. Thidias refuses ceremony to what is no longer a reality, so that the use of politeness or its denial becomes an important dramatic means for indicating an attitude. To the dismay of Enobarbus, Antony's power in this scene expresses itself only in the empty form of violence: "Take hence this Jack and whip him" (3.13.93). Incidentally, we are already prepared for Thidias' insolence by Cleopatra's comment just before his entrance:

> What, no more ceremony? See, my women!
> Against the blown rose may they stop their nose
> That kneel'd unto the buds. (3.13.38–40)

The declaration at the end of Antony's speech, "I am/ Antony yet," forces a contrast between the name and the reality. The real commanding presence of "Antony" — "That magical word of war" (3.1.31) as Ventidius called it — has melted away, has suffered dissolution, while the name itself remains as hollow reminder of the past. In the same mood Antony in his next speech questions the reality of "Cleopatra": "what's her name/ Since she was Cleopatra?" (3.13.98–99). The resolution of this play on names comes at the end of the scene in a reaffirmation of reality: "since my lord/ Is Antony again, I will be Cleopatra" (3.13.186–87).

The dissolution theme is acted out on a mythological plane in IV,iii, where the god Hercules, Antony's supposed ancestor and tutelary deity, abandons him. Shakespeare develops this scene from a marginal note in Plutarch: "*Strange noyses heard, and nothing seene.*" [52] One company

137

of soldiers is relieving another on the night before the second day of battle, and *"They place themselves in every corner of the stage"* (4.3.7 s.d.). The sense of isolation and dispersal over a large area would be intensified on the rectangular Elizabethan stage, which projected into the middle of the audience. Suddenly, after the Third Soldier has said, " 'Tis a brave army,/ And full of purpose" (4.3. 10–11), *"Music of the hautboys is under the stage"* (4.3.11 s.d.). This muffled, distant-sounding oboe music belies the false optimism of the soldiers.[53] It is a striking, portentous effect, and they listen with attentive fear:

2. *Sold.*		Peace! What noise?	
1. Sold.			List, list!
2. *Sold.*	Hark!		
1. Sold.		Music i' th' air.	
3. *Sold.*			Under the earth.
4. *Sold.*	It signs well, does it not?		
3. *Sold.*		No.	
1. Sold.			Peace, I say!

What should this mean?
2. *Sold.* 'Tis the god Hercules, whom Antony lov'd
Now leaves him.   (4.3.11–16)

This scene is in the symbolic tradition of the medieval pageant wagon, where the stage itself represented the world, with heaven above and hell below. As a matter of structure, the departure of Hercules occurs at almost the same time as the desertion of Enobarbus; in some sense Enobarbus has been Antony's Hercules, and IV,iii gives his desertion a mythological compulsion. By the strange voice of oboes from the underworld we are being prepared for Antony's defeat and tragic end. The image is harbinger of the "discandying" and "dislimning" that are to follow.

138

After his final defeat Antony speaks again in the imagery
of dissolution:

> All come to this? The hearts
> That spaniel'd me at heels, to whom I gave
> Their wishes, do discandy, melt their sweets
> On blossoming Caesar. . . . (4.12.20-23)

Antony's fawning and fickle allies now "discandy" and
"melt" and make Caesar flourish while Antony languishes.
Compare Cleopatra's melting imagery in III,xiii; if she be
cold-hearted to Antony,

> From my cold heart let heaven engender hail,
> And poison it in the source, and the first stone
> Drop in my neck; as it determines, so
> Dissolve my life! The next Caesarion smite!
> Till by degrees the memory of my womb,
> Together with my brave Egyptians all,
> By the discandying [54] of this pelleted storm,
> Lie graveless, till the flies and gnats of Nile
> Have buried them for prey! (3.13.159-67)

Cleopatra imagines death in Antony's terms as a dissolving
and a "discandying." The latter word is a vivid indication
that the sweetness and strength are going out of life. "Disponge" is used similarly for Enobarbus' death, when he
prays that

> The poisonous damp of night disponge upon me,
> That life, a very rebel to my will,
> May hang no longer on me! (4.9.13-15)

This is the earliest example of "disponge" (spelt "dispunge")
in the *Oxford English Dictionary*, and its status as an un-
familiar word strengthens its poetic effect; "discandy" also
appears to be a coinage of Shakespeare's.

The most extended imagery of dissolution is in the pageant of cloud shapes Antony sees in IV,xiv, which melt and dissolve into each other and cannot hold their form:

> That which is now a horse, even with a thought
> The rack dislimns, and makes it indistinct
> As water is in water. (4.14.9–11)

"Dislimns" is another of those arresting words of dissolution which give a characteristic quality to this play. Shakespeare seems to be creating his own vocabulary to establish the feeling of disintegration in the Roman world. The firm substance of life is being undone, things are losing their form, changing and fading with the indistinctness of water in water — this image is the essence of the dissolution theme. There is no bitterness here but only resignation and a certain aesthetic pleasure. The play of thought follows the same progress of forms, mingling as water in water. The complexity of the image lies in the fact that "water" and "water" are the same substance, yet in their being together, or in one's being in the other, subtle differences appear. Perhaps it is the idea of difference approaching similarity, as cloud shapes ("The rack") soon merge into simple clouds. The whole process of indiscernible change is expressed by "dislimning." Antony sees his own inner state reflected in this insubstantial show:

> My good knave Eros, now thy captain is
> Even such a body. Here I am Antony;
> Yet cannot hold this visible shape, my knave. (4.14.12–14)

It is ironic that the name remains — "Here I am Antony" — while the physical reality, "this visible shape," cannot be retained.

Finally, Cleopatra marks the moment of Antony's death with these words: "O, see, my women,/ The crown o' th' earth doth melt. My lord!" (4.15.62–63). Antony is not only her "lord" but the "crown o' th' earth"; the image attempts to objectify, to hyperbolize the personal dimension of the play. There is a peace and effortlessness in "melt," as if there were no barrier between life and death, and one could flow easily into the other. It is a fitting close for Antony. His end is not a "tragic" one as King Lear's is, or Othello's, or Macbeth's. Rather than being resolved, the conflict between Egypt and Rome ceases to exist, and the hard "visible shapes" of Rome are dissolved into an ecstatic, poetic reality. In this sense *Antony and Cleopatra* looks ahead to the mood of Shakespeare's last plays.

Chapter V

THE IMAGERY OF
Coriolanus

I

THE "unsavory figurative language" of *Coriolanus* and its "accumulation of derogatory comment" [1] prompted Oscar James Campbell to classify this play as a "tragical satire" rather than a tragedy. Although we may not accept this new category, nor Campbell's extreme judgments on the buffoonery of Menenius and the ridiculousness of Coriolanus, his account of the tone and mood of the play is quite convincing. He shows its affinity with such "disturbing" plays as *Timon of Athens, Troilus and Cressida, Hamlet,* and *Measure for Measure.* This affinity may also be demonstrated in their extensive imagery of food, disease, and animals. These image themes, which form the three dominant motifs in *Coriolanus*, help to establish the peculiarly satirical quality in all of these plays.

The imagery of *Coriolanus* is organized around the conflict between plebeians and patricians, which acts as a negative-positive force: the images that refer to the plebeians are generally pejorative, while those that refer to the patricians are favorable. But the play is by no means a defense of the old aristocracy. The prevailing tone is harsh and discordant, and the laudatory imagery is very sparse. It is clear that Shakespeare has no love for the plebeians, but it is equally clear that Coriolanus, the chief representative of the patricians, is not a sympathetic character. This makes for a balancing of forces in the play and gives it its tight and paradoxical character.[2]

The imagery of food and eating is perhaps the most extensive and important motif in the play. It calls attention to the appetitive nature of the plebeians, while the negative (images of temperance and austerity) represents an heroic aristocratic ideal. Another significant aspect of this imagery is the theme of war as a devourer; this develops the sense of "eat" as to devour, to destroy as prey. Shakespeare seems to be deliberately emphasizing this imagery to the exclusion of any talk about usury (there is one reference at 1.1.83–84), whereas in Plutarch usury and dearth of corn are linked as the two chief grievances of the citizens.[3] It has been suggested that Shakespeare's emphasis on food may be related to the enclosure riots in the Midlands in 1607.[4]

The most important and concentrated use of this imagery is in I,i. Like *Julius Caesar*, the play opens with a mob scene: "Enter a company of mutinous *Citizens* with staves, clubs, and other weapons." It is a violent beginning and a strong statement of the issues of the play, as can be seen in the First Citizen's question: "You are all resolv'd rather to die than to famish?" (1.1.4–5). This creates an immediate sense of urgency: it is a matter of life and death that is at stake. Caius Marcius is "chief enemy to the people" (1.1.8), whom the citizens resolve to kill in order to have "corn at our own price" (1.1.10–11). The propulsive force of the mutiny is checked for a moment by the First Citizen's statement of the case:

We are accounted poor citizens, the patricians good. What authority surfeits on would relieve us. If they would yield us but the superfluity while it were wholesome, we might guess they relieved us humanely; but they think we are too dear. The leanness that afflicts us, the object of our misery, is as an inventory to particularize their abundance; our sufferance is a gain to them. Let us revenge this with our pikes ere we become rakes; for the gods know I speak this in hunger for bread, not in thirst for revenge. (1.1.15–25)

In however low esteem Shakespeare's contemporaries regarded the people,[5] "I speak this in hunger for bread, not in thirst for revenge" elicits for the moment our sympathies. The patrician-plebeian class conflict is thus at the outset clearly expressed in terms of food, and the opening statements of the play point to an ominous disorder in the body politic of Rome.

When Menenius enters, he acknowledges the citizens' "wants" and "suffering in this dearth" (1.1.68–69), but insists that "The gods, not the patricians, make it" (1.1.75). This explanation does not satisfy the Second Citizen, who states the class conflict again in terms of food; the patricians

ne'er cared for us yet: suffer us to famish, and their storehouses cramm'd with grain; make edicts for usury, to support usurers; repeal daily any wholesome act established against the rich, and provide more piercing statutes daily to chain up and restrain the poor. If the wars eat us not up, they will; and there's all the love they bear us. (1.1.82–89)

In the last sentence "eat" is used in the negative sense of devour or destroy. This is an important aspect of the food and eating imagery, and it indicates that war and the patricians are both devourers. The image suggests the following sequence: we who have no food will be made to serve as food for war; we who have nothing to eat will be eaten by war, or if we stay at home the patricians will destroy us just as war does.

It is at this point that Menenius recites his "pretty tale" (1.1.93) of the belly and the members. Into the disorder of plebeian mutiny Menenius brings this fable of order, spoken in the prevailing food idiom. The citizens' grievances are seen within the larger framework of the idea of the state: it is a body in which each part must perform its particular and necessary function in order to maintain health. The immediate purpose of the tale is to still the plebeian mutiny, and it accomplishes this with great success. The fable begins with the accusation of the rebellious members against the belly:

> That only like a gulf it did remain
> I' th' midst o' th' body, idle and unactive,
> Still cupboarding the viand, never bearing
> Like labour with the rest. . . .   (1.1.101–04)

This complaint resembles that of the citizens, whose "leanness . . . is as an inventory to particularize" the "abundance" (1.1.20–22) of the patricians. The belly's answer, full of the commonplaces of Renaissance political theory,[6] is an epitome of the well-ordered state:

> 'True is it, my incorporate friends,' quoth he,
> 'That I receive the general food at first
> Which you do live upon; and fit it is,
> Because I am the storehouse and the shop

145

> Of the whole body. But, if you do remember,
> I send it through the rivers of your blood
> Even to the court, the heart, to th' seat o' th' brain,
> And, through the cranks and offices of man,
> The strongest nerves and small inferior veins
> From me receive that natural competency
> Whereby they live.' (1.1.134–44)

The belly then is not a tyrannical parasite on the body politic, but the necessary "storehouse and the shop" from which all "receive the flour . . ./ And leave me but the bran!" (1.1.149–50).

The fable is then applied point for point to the situation at hand:

> The senators of Rome are this good belly,
> And you the mutinous members. For, examine
> Their counsels and their cares, disgest things rightly
> Touching the weal o' th' common, you shall find
> No public benefit which you receive
> But it proceeds or comes from them to you,
> And no way from yourselves. (1.1.152–58)

By means of the imagery of body and food — the image literally is of digestion — Menenius states the proper function of patrician and plebeian in the state. The plebeians ("members"), in return for their services to the state, are beneficially ruled by the patricians ("belly"), whose natural function it is to rule. This innocent tale, placed in a commanding position in the first scene, provides a fable of order for the entire play. It is a point of reference for all the later disorder and distemper in the state.

Menenius shows no particular affection for the mob, yet he has earned the reputation of "one that hath always lov'd the people" (1.1.52–53). He is a thoroughly politic figure, shrewd and temperate in his dealings with the plebeians, and

146

acknowledging their vital function in the state. Throughout his speech the "humorous patrician" (2.1.51) shows all the skill of an Antony in dealing with the mob. Menenius is always conscious of his audience, whom he is able to manipulate with great skill. Notice how, as spokesman for the belly, he directs the tale to his listeners: "Your most grave belly was deliberate,/ Not rash like his accusers . . ." (1.1.132–33). And when he has made sure of his public at the end of his speech, he thoroughly insults the leader, or "great toe" (1.1.159), of the mob as "one o' th' lowest, basest, poorest/ Of this most wise rebellion . . ." (1.1.161– 62). Although some of Menenius' words for the people are almost the same as Coriolanus', the humorous, self-conscious tone in which they are spoken is quite different; he is con- ciliatory where Marcius is contemptuous.

Compare the opening speeches of the two men. When Menenius enters, the citizens are brandishing "staves, clubs, and other weapons" (1.1 s.d.) and preparing to mutiny; he asks:

> What work's, my countrymen, in hand? Where go you
> With bats and clubs? The matter? Speak, I pray you.
>
> (1.1.56–57)

Very cleverly, he does not ask them to cease, nor threaten them with destruction, but proposes to talk the matter over. Marcius, however, enters when the people are already pacified and stirs them up again with angry taunts:

> What's the matter, you dissentious rogues
> That, rubbing the poor itch of your opinion,
> Make yourselves scabs? (1.1.168–70)

These words are perhaps a more honest expression of per- sonal belief than Menenius', but they are absolutely wrong at this crisis; the state cannot subsist on the honesty or dishonesty of one's personal feelings. It is precisely the tragic dilemma of Marcius: his hatred of the people springs from a deep conviction of aristocratic worth. He cannot be politic and conciliatory like Menenius without being dishonest to himself, although this brings about his exile from Rome and the demonic revenge that follows.

Marcius' scorn of the people finds expression chiefly in the imagery of food and eating. The plebeians do not act from motives of honor as the patricians do, but merely from promptings of greed and hunger; their

> affections are
> A sick man's appetite, who desires most that
> Which would increase his evil. (1.1.181–83)

It is an image of the changeable and perverse will ruled by a destructive "appetite." Marcius asks the mob contemptuously why

> You cry against the noble Senate, who
> (Under the gods) keep you in awe, which else
> Would feed on one another? (1.1.190–92)

This view of the people is like that of Hobbes (although the *Leviathan* did not appear until the middle of the century): the people would "feed on one another" if not prevented by the Senate's overawing authority, and the patricians are therefore justified in exercising absolute control over their appetitive animal nature.[7] Food and eating imagery is taking on a violent tone — "feed" here is equivalent to "devour as prey."

Menenius, not tempted to Marcius' choleric vein, says simply that the people's seeking is "For corn at their own rates, whereof they say/ The city is well stor'd" (1.1.193–

148

94). But Marcius scorns their demands, as if it were presumption in them to make demands at all:

> They say there's grain enough?
> Would the nobility lay aside their ruth
> And let me use my sword, I'd make a quarry
> With thousands of these quarter'd slaves as high
> As I could pick my lance.   (1.1.200–04)

This directly negates Menenius' fable, and Marcius' report on the troop of people from whom he has just come is another caustic commentary on hunger as the plebeian motive for mutiny:

> They said they were anhungry; sigh'd forth proverbs —
> That hunger broke stone walls, that dogs must eat,
> That meat was made for mouths, that the gods sent not
> Corn for the rich men only. With these shreds
> They vented their complainings. . . .   (1.1.209–13)

As we have seen, the people's hunger is a real grievance, and to scorn it away is an act of human and political folly. Marcius' exaggerated and malicious contempt for the plebeians leaves him here at one of the lowest points in our sympathy; contrary to most of Shakespeare's other tragic protagonists, he alienates the audience on his first appearance in the play. And as a Messenger enters to announce that the Volsces are in arms, Marcius adds a final insult: "Go get you home, you fragments!" (1.1.226) — the last word means the worthless leftovers after a meal.

From this point through the battle scenes the themes of the people as food and of war as devourer are especially important. Marcius welcomes the news of war as a "means to vent/ Our musty superfluity" (1.1.229–30). The whole food issue is resolved by war, for the Volscians will either destroy the moldy excess of Rome or provide spoils to satisfy the base plebeian appetite. Marcius calls on the mutinous citizens with utter scorn:

> Nay, let them follow.
> The Volsces have much corn. Take these rats thither
> To gnaw their garners. Worshipful mutiners,
> Your valour puts well forth. Pray follow. (1.1.252–55)

The stage direction right after reads: *"Citizens steal away"* — a strong contrast to their bold entrance at the opening of the scene. This resembles *Julius Caesar*, where the hostile mob who began the action finally "vanish tongue-tied in their guiltiness" (1.1.67). In both plays the seeming docility of the mob has undercurrents of restive sullenness, already intimated at the end of the first scene of *Coriolanus* in the Tribune Brutus' reversal of the war-as-devourer theme: "The present wars devour him! He is grown/ Too proud to be so valiant" (1.1.262–63). It is Marcius, rather than the "musty superfluity" of Rome, who ought to be "vented" (1.1.229–30) in war.

I shall deal more briefly with the food and eating imagery that follows the opening scene. In I,iii Volumnia says that if she had a dozen sons, she would rather have "eleven die nobly for their country than one voluptuously surfeit out of action" (1.3.27–28). "Surfeit" means intemperate indulgence in food and drink with accompanying ill effects, and this is Volumnia's image for the life of peace, which is represented very unattractively throughout the play. Food and eating have unpleasant connotations because of their connection with the people, whose indulgence of appetite is the opposite of the aristocratic ideal of honor. The "surfeit" image is used in an opposite sense in IV,i, when

Cominius says that he is "too full/ Of the war's surfeits" (4.1.45–46) to accompany Coriolanus in exile. The image recalls the lines in I,ix where Cominius contrasts the passivity of the "fusty" (1.9.7) plebeians with Marcius' deeds for war the devourer: "Yet cam'st thou to a morsel of this feast,/ Having fully din'd before" (1.9.10–11). This "feast" (the praise of Marcius' deeds against the Volscians) is merely a "morsel" compared to his former deeds of valor ("fully din'd before"). The destructive sense of food and eating is being used here to indicate the aristocratic virtue of the warrior. Further on in the scene Marcius forswears flattery in the contemptuous imagery of food: "As if I lov'd my little should be dieted/ In praises sauc'd with lies" (1.9.51–52).

There are a few interesting food images in Menenius' conversation with the Tribunes at the beginning of Act II. He returns a figure in kind when he says that the wolf loves the lamb "to devour him, as the hungry plebeians would the noble Marcius" (2.1.10–11), and he observes satirically that the Tribunes' justice goes awry "if you chance to be pinch'd with the cholic" (2.1.82–83) — we are kept unpleasantly aware of the digestive functions of the plebeians. But the Tribunes have a remarkable insight into Marcius by which they can work his ruin; they know he considers the people no better than

> camels in the war, who have their provand
> Only for bearing burthens, and sore blows
> For sinking under them. (2.1.267–69)

It is a paraphrase of Marcius' own words at 1.1.253–54: the people are not concerned with honor in battle but only with "provand," a base image of the animal appetite. The contrast is clearly drawn in II,iii, where the First Citizen

151

dwells on corn (2.3.16–18), while Coriolanus in the gown of humility asserts his honor:

> Better it is to die, better to starve,
> Than crave the hire which first we do deserve.   (2.3.120–21)

A noble starvation is infinitely preferable to the feigned humility of soliciting the plebeians to be consul.

Food imagery becomes fairly important again in III,i, and the corn issue, which was the original cause of the plebeian mutiny, is remembered throughout this scene. Brutus, for example, accuses Coriolanus of opposing the free gift of corn to the people (3.1.43), which touches off Coriolanus' wrath: "Tell me of corn!" (3.1.61). There should be an explosive emphasis on the final word as if to make an absolute contrast in value between "corn" and "me." Coriolanus agrees that he opposed the free gift of corn, but he clearly states the reason:

> They know the corn
> Was not our recompense, resting well assur'd
> They ne'er did service for't. Being press'd to th' war
> Even when the navel of the state was touch'd,
> They would not thread the gates. This kind of service
> Did not deserve corn gratis.   (3.1.120–25)

The "navel of the state" reminds us once more of the physical reality of the body politic, in which to Coriolanus the formula for distribution can only be: "to each according to his merits."

Besides "corn" there are a number of other food and eating images in III,i. Coriolanus warns the patricians against "mingling" (3.1.72) their authority with the plebeians: "When, both your voices blended, the great'st taste/ Most palates theirs" (3.1.103–04). There is a natural antipathy between plebeian and patrician in Coriolanus' aristocratic order. Notice how all words connected with food and eating have taken on negative connotations. The original distribution of corn "nourish'd disobedience, fed/ The ruin of the state" (3.1.117–18). The decree of the Senate was thus an act of self-destruction. It was also a debasing act, which the people will interpret as a sign of weakness:

> How shall this bosom-multiplied [8] digest
> The Senate's courtesy? Let deeds express
> What's like to be their words: 'We did request it;
> We are the greater poll, and in true fear
> They gave us our demands.' (3.1.131–35)

"Bosome-multiplied" is the Folio reading for line 131, and in this context "digest" not only means "interpret," but also literally refers to the digestion of food, a repeated theme for the people. They are imagined collectively as a great digestive mechanism, a "bosom-multiplied," that suggests an aspect of the Hydra monster.

These tirades arouse the immediate demand for Coriolanus' death. Menenius tries to pacify the people lest Rome, "like an unnatural dam/ Should now eat up her own!" (3.1.293–94). "Eat" means "destroy" here, with Senecan overtones — the "hungry plebeians" (2.1.10–11) of Rome are threatening to devour their chief defender. Finally in this scene, Menenius uses food imagery to apologize for Coriolanus' rash words; he is a soldier

> ill-school'd
> In bolted language; meal and bran together
> He throws without distinction. (3.1.321–23)

The pejorative food images are meant to define Coriolanus' aristocratic virtue; he is not at all to be associated with such base plebeian matters. There is another example of this in his defiance of the people at the end of III,iii. He would not "buy/ Their mercy" (3.3.90–91) with flattery even if he were "pent to linger/ But with a grain a day . . ." (3.3.89–90). The "grain a day" is the ascetic strain in the aristocratic ideal of honor.

The depreciative and violent tone of the food imagery grows more pronounced with Coriolanus' exile. Volumnia will not dine with Menenius because "Anger's my meat. I sup upon myself,/ And so shall starve with feeding" (4.2. 50–51). Her anger at her son's banishment is self-consuming. Food is also one of the images of worthlessness in Coriolanus' soliloquy at Antium: "Fellest foes" (4.4.18) grow dear friends by "Some trick not worth an egg . . ." (4.4.21). At the very beginning of this scene a strong contrast is made between Coriolanus "in mean apparel, disguis'd and muffled" and the sound and bustle of the feast going on offstage in the house of Aufidius. Coriolanus addresses the plebeian servants in contemptuous food imagery: "Follow your function, go and batten on cold bits" (4.5.35–36). As he tells Aufidius, only his name "Coriolanus" remains, for the "hungry plebeians" (2.1.10–11) of Rome "hath devour'd the rest" (4.5.81). The last food images here are those the servants use to indicate Coriolanus' superiority to Aufidius:

   1. Serv. Before Corioles he scotch'd him and notch'd him like a carbonado.
   2. Serv. An he had been cannibally given, he might have boil'd ° and eaten him too. (4.5.197–200)

A "carbonado" was a piece of meat scored by the cook for roasting on the coals, and both images develop the violence of the war-as-devourer theme.

The news of Coriolanus' approach to Rome with a Volscian army pricks the bubble of optimism blown up at the beginning of IV,vi. The Tribunes' petty empire of "Our tradesmen singing in their shops and going/ About their functions friendly" (4.6.8–9) crumbles before an overwhelming force. It was "The breath of garlic-eaters" (4.6. 98) that banished Coriolanus, and retribution is now coming for it as Menenius forebodes in his repeated refrain, "You have made good work" (4.6.95, 100, 117, 118, 146–47, and 5.1.15).

Aufidius' own revenge on his rival is being prepared in the next scene, where a Lieutenant tells him what he himself knows only too well about Coriolanus:

> Your soldiers use him as the grace fore meat,
> Their talk at table, and their thanks at end;
> And you are dark'ned in this action, sir,
> Even by your own.   (4.7.3–6)

The association of Coriolanus and eating is curiously positive here, something we have not noticed before. It is perhaps part of the twisted values in these scenes of revenge.

The food imagery of V,i echoes the corn issue at the beginning of the play. Cominius' mission to Coriolanus has been a failure, and he reports his unsuccess to Menenius and the Tribunes:

> I offered to awaken his regard
> For's private friends. His answer to me was,
> He could not stay to pick them in a pile
> Of noisome musty chaff. He said 'twas folly,
> For one poor grain or two, to leave unburnt
> And still to nose th' offence.   (5.1.23–28)

Coriolanus now sees all Rome in the food imagery of the

plebeians — not even food, but "a pile/ Of noisome musty chaff." The "poor grain or two" is absolutely lost in this evil-smelling heap and must burn with it. Menenius cannot believe this inhumanity:

> For one poor grain or two?
> I am one of those! his mother, wife, his child,
> And this brave fellow too — we are the grains. . . .
>
> (5.1.28–30)

And he accuses the Tribunes of being responsible for the present catastrophe:

> You are the musty chaff, and you are smelt
> Above the moon. We must be burnt for you! (5.1.31–32)

As we soon see, these poor grains become the test of Coriolanus' mercy, for he has already condemned the chaff of the plebeians out of hand.

Menenius uses a curious, extended food image as he prepares to visit Coriolanus; he attributes Cominius' failure to trivial matters:

> He was not taken well; he had not din'd.
> The veins unfill'd, our blood is cold, and then
> We pout upon the morning, are unapt
> To give or to forgive; but when we have stuff'd
> These pipes and these conveyances of our blood
> With wine and feeding, we have suppler souls
> Than in our priest-like fasts. Therefore I'll watch him
> Till he be dieted to my request,
> And then I'll set upon him. (5.1.50–58)

The hypothetic image of Coriolanus "stuff'd . . . With wine and feeding" is almost impossible to conceive — "priest-like fasts" would be more typical of him. This is one of the few places in the play where Coriolanus is favorably associated with eating (see also 4.7.3–6). I suspect a note of strong irony in Menenius' tone here. It is a desperate attempt to explain away Cominius' refusal by irrelevant reasons, a way of trying to avert the impending disaster and make ready for his own possible rejection. He continues in this vein in V,ii when he asks the First Watchman: "Has he din'd, canst thou tell? For I would not speak with him till after dinner" (5.2.36–37). This represents a fussy uncertainty, which is exacerbated by the guards' humiliation of Menenius; his appeal to them is only "the palsied intercession" of "a decay'd dotant" (5.2.46–47).

These are the last significant food images in the play, and it is perhaps a comment on the character of this imagery that it is excluded from the climax in V,iii. There are actually only two places in the play (I,i and III,i) where it is used with much sense of a deliberate effect, yet in both these places it is of crucial importance. Elsewhere, the repeated images of food and eating serve as a commentary on the plebeian-patrician conflict and on the function of war as a devourer. Although any particular example of this imagery may seem trivial in itself, the cumulative effect of all the examples, taken together with the imagery of disease and animals, is very strong. These image themes make only a few points about the tragedy of *Coriolanus*, but they make them so often that they cannot possibly be overlooked, and they do much to create the harsh and satirical mood of the play.

2

In *A Comparative Discourse of the Bodies Natural and Politique* (1606), Edward Forset develops an elaborate and exact parallel between the maladies of these bodies. Beginning with Menenius' fable of the belly and the members, he shows how desperate diseases of the state require desperate remedies.[10] Forset's analogy is a traditional one, which Shakespeare employs very frequently to express political and moral disorder. Perhaps *Hamlet* and *Troilus and Cressida* use disease imagery more significantly than *Coriolanus*,[11] but in all three plays it helps to impart a strident tone. In *Coriolanus* these images are an important part of the vocabulary of vileness and worthlessness Marcius uses for the people, although they are occasionally turned against him. Behind this imagery lies Menenius' fable, which serves as a reference point for the healthy functioning of the body politic.

The theme begins with the entrance of Marcius, who reviles the mutinous plebeians:

> What's the matter, you dissentious rogues
> That, rubbing the poor itch of your opinion,
> Make yourselves scabs? (1.1.168–70)

"Scabs" means both "sores" and "worthless fellows": the vileness of the plebeians makes disease imagery appropriate for them. Their "affections" are no more dependable than "A sick man's appetite . . ." (1.1.182). Toward the end of the scene Titus Lartius, like Caius Ligarius in *Julius Caesar* (2.1.310ff), will throw off his sickness at Marcius' behest:

> *Mar.* What, art thou stiff? Stand'st out?
> *Tit.*   No, Caius Marcius.
> I'll lean upon one crutch and fight with t'other
> Ere stay behind this business. (1.1.245–47)

The wars have become a sudden healer here, for they are

the positive force opposed against the negative power of illness. Similarly, in II,i Marcius' letter gives Menenius "an estate of seven years' health . . ." (2.1.125–26). There is a clear division of the imagery of the play into disease for the plebeians and health for the patricians.

One side of this division is forcefully illustrated in I,iv when Marcius enters "cursing" (1.4.29 s.d.) his retreating soldiers:

> All the contagion of the South light on you,
> You shames of Rome! you herd of — Biles and plagues
> Plaster you o'er, that you may be abhorr'd
> Farther than seen and one infect another
> Against the wind a mile! (1.4.30–34)

It is a violent catalogue, overfull and excessive, but typical of Marcius, and the "agued fear" (1.4.38) of the soldiers' flight expresses their diseased sense of honor. This retreat is meant to be contrasted with Cominius' in I,vi, which is presented in an entirely different tone; Cominius says:

> Breathe you, my friends. Well fought! We are come off
> Like Romans, neither foolish in our stands
> Nor cowardly in retire. (1.6.1–3)

It would be inconceivable for Marcius to utter such a rational and temperate judgment, but we must remember that it is he who is the hero of the battle, however harsh, inhuman, and foolhardy his attitude may be. The excess in Marcius that makes him different from Cominius' mean is the source at once of virtues and defects. In I,iv the virtues are most evident, for Marcius as a warrior has the power to make his "enemies shake, as if the world/ Were feverous and did tremble" (1.4.60–61). But he is so little willing to hear his virtues commended that his hatred of flattery verges on ingratitude. When he tells Cominius that his wounds "smart/ To hear themselves rememb'red" (1.9.28–29), Cominius comments:

> Should they not,
> Well might they fester 'gainst ingratitude
> And tent themselves with death. (1.9.29–31)

The suggestion here is an insidious one: Marcius' attitude is a diseased condition that threatens to "fester." His hatred of flattery, which should be a virtue, becomes through excess something harsh and egotistical, "a way of holding people at a distance, of refusing to admit relationship." [12] The most important and concentrated use of disease imagery is in III,i. Coriolanus will not restrain his wrath against the people, and his "lungs" will continue to

> Coin words till their decay against those measles
> Which we disdain should tetter us, yet sought
> The very way to catch them. (3.1.78–80)

"Measles" has a double reference similar to "scabs," for it means both "skin disease" and "foul wretches," with the literal disease word serving as a metaphor for vileness. The people are an infection that endangers the body politic, but Coriolanus' remedy here, as in I,i, is to deny the plebeians any part in this body. He advises the Senate

> To jump a body with a dangerous physic
> That's sure of death without it — at once pluck out
> The multitudinous tongue; let them not lick
> The sweet which is their poison. (3.1.154–57)

The word "poison" in the last line may be interpreted either actively or passively: the "sweet" of the people's new authority gives them a venomous power (the "poison" they can inflict), although it will eventually be their undoing (a "poison" to them).

The political power of the people is vested in the Tribunes, the "multitudinous tongue" Coriolanus wants to "pluck out." It is a declaration of open conflict between himself and them, and when they try to apprehend him, he resists Sicinius with contempt: "Hence, rotten thing! or I shall shake thy bones/ Out of thy garments" (3.1.179–80). "Rotten" was a stronger word than it is today, especially in its suggestion of disease. We may recall the "rotten dews" (2.3.35) of the South and the "reek o' th' rotten fens" (3.3.121). Menenius, truly concerned for the state, stands in the center and insists on a moderation that Brutus objects to:

> Sir, those cold ways
> That seem like prudent helps are very poisonous
> Where the disease is violent. (3.1.220–22)

The Tribunes' violence is like Coriolanus', except that it springs from self-defensive "policy" while his is deeply honest.

The patricians, wishing to "cure" (3.1.235) the body politic rather than destroy it, persuade Coriolanus to leave; for, as Menenius says, " 'tis a sore upon us/ You cannot tent yourself" (3.1.235–36). In the debate between Menenius and the Tribunes that follows, disease imagery is used very deliberately to describe the disordered state. Menenius defends Coriolanus against the penalty of death:

> Sic. He's a disease that must be cut away.
> Men. O, he's a limb that has but a disease:
> Mortal, to cut it off; to cure it, easy. (3.1.295–97)

161

The course of events is to prove Menenius correct, for the cutting-off of Coriolanus almost proves "mortal" to Rome. Some lines further Menenius asks ironically:

> The service of the foot,
> Being once gangren'd, is not then respected
> For what before it was. (3.1.306–08)

Brutus picks up Menenius' acknowledgment of disease and calls for immediate action against Coriolanus, "Lest his infection, being of catching nature,/ Spread further" (3.1.310–11). Coriolanus' own disease imagery for the people is now being turned against him. By a reversal of roles he, and not the plebeians, is now the "infection," and the Tribunes have become physicians to the body politic. Brutus will "pluck" (3.1.309) Coriolanus from his house with the same violence Coriolanus himself invoked to "pluck out/ The multitudinous tongue" (3.1.155–56). Sicinius knows that Coriolanus has always sought means "To pluck away" (3.3.96) the power of the people, and the spy Nicanor in IV,iii reports that the nobles are "in a ripe aptness to take all power from the people and to pluck from them their tribunes for ever" (4.3.23–25). The blatant word "pluck" seems to be very closely associated with the Tribunes in these scenes.

Act III, scene ii, marks a pause between two violent appearances of the mob; it is the schooling of Coriolanus in the ways of restraint. There is no other "remedy" (3.2.26), as one Senator says; for the fate of the city depends upon Coriolanus' ability to pacify the people. This is the "cure" Menenius spoke of previously, for "The violent fit o' th' time craves it as physic/ For the whole state . . ." (3.2.33–34). He advises Coriolanus to

> Speak fair. You may salve so,
> Not what is dangerous present, but the loss
> Of what is past.   (3.2.70-72)

"Salve" is the medication that Coriolanus has not humility enough to apply, and his failure here brings on his banishment.

The Tribunes have gained their victory only at the price of violence to the organism of the state. It is therefore an illusory triumph, which is undercut in Coriolanus' banishment speech by powerful suggestions of disease:

> You common cry of curs, whose breath I hate
> As reek o' th' rotten fens, whose loves I prize
> As the dead carcasses of unburied men
> That do corrupt my air, I banish you!   (3.3.120-23)

Rome has now become the place of disease, but there is an ominous note here that is fulfilled when Coriolanus returns to destroy his "cank'red country" (4.5.96). The remaining images of disease in the play are fairly incidental and will not be discussed. Although this imagery is of least importance in the fourth and fifth acts, its reiteration helps to keep us aware of the ubiquitous analogy between the human body and the state which was so powerfully presented in Menenius' fable. Disease signifies disorder in both of these bodies, and it is also, in some sense, an archetypal image for tragedy. In terms of his dramatic character Coriolanus' rejection of all "remedies" and "cure" is inevitable, but it also entails tragic consequences.

3

The main function of the animal imagery [13] in *Coriolanus* is to express the base nature of the plebeians, and this gives

163

it a strongly negative tone. A large group of worthless animals is used for the people, while a few noble animals are associated with the patricians. At a number of points a contrast is made between plebeian and patrician by means of a pair of animals, one noble and the other ignoble. There is also an animal imagery of violence which represents Coriolanus' valor and wrath. Since this theme overlaps the two themes already discussed, I shall deal only with examples of some special significance.

The classical image of the people as a Hydra, the nine-headed serpent slain by Hercules, lies behind the animal imagery of the play, especially in III,i, where Hydra and the body politic of Rome are seen in conflict. This image first appears in the Citizens' conversation at the beginning of II,iii. The Third Citizen insists they must deal justly with Coriolanus because

Ingratitude is monstrous; and for the multitude to be ingrateful were to make a monster of the multitude, of the which we being members, should bring ourselves to be monstrous members.

(2.3.10–14)

Menenius' fable comes to mind here: the Third Citizen will not have the people be "monstrous members" of a Hydra. "Monstrous" implies the unnatural and grotesque, something to be exhibited as a curiosity. But the First Citizen cannot abide this deference to Coriolanus, who "himself stuck not to call us the many-headed multitude" (2.3.17–18).

The image of the people as a Hydra is nowhere more insistently implied than in III,i, and it is represented there as an organism threatening the existence of Rome. Coriolanus calls the Tribunes "The tongues o' th' common mouth"

(3.1.22), and he is particularly concerned with tongues and mouths and voices in this scene.[14] We may recall the earlier comment of the Third Citizen, the most strikingly vulgar image in the play: "for if he show us his wounds and tell us his deeds, we are to put our tongues into those wounds and speak for them" (2.3.6–8). When the tongues and voices forswear themselves in III,i, Coriolanus knows it is the work of the Tribunes, whom he asks bitterly:

> Are these your herd?
> Must these have voices, that can yield them now
> And straight disclaim their tongues? What are your offices?
> You being their mouths, why rule you not their teeth?
> Have you not set them on? (3.1.33–37)

As if to confirm this accusation, the First Citizen says that Coriolanus shall be made to know that "The noble Tribunes are the people's mouths,/And we their hands" (3.1.271–72). This is an image of multitudinousness in the state rather than unity, with the Tribunes as "mouths" and the people as "hands" and "teeth" — the last image suggests a biting viciousness.

Hydra is mentioned directly only once, when Coriolanus warns the Senate of the dangerous plebeian power:

> Why,
> You grave but reckless senators, have you thus
> Given Hydra here to choose an officer
> That with his peremptory 'shall,' being but
> The horn and noise o' th' monster's, wants not spirit
> To say he'll turn your current in a ditch
> And make your channel his? (3.1.91–97)

The Hydra monster threatens the state, and Coriolanus is preparing for the open conflict that will soon follow. The resolution of these fears comes in his exile: "The beast/

With many heads butts me away" (4.1.1–2). The multitudinousness of the people is also suggested in images of the herd (1.4.31, 2.1.105, 3.1.33, 3.2.32) and of generation. Coriolanus cannot flatter the "multiplying spawn" (2.2.82) "That's thousand to one good one" (2.2.83), or their Tribune Sicinius, "this Triton of the minnows" (3.1.89).

The most frequent animal insults for the people are dogs, hounds, and curs. In I,i Marcius calls the mob "curs,/ That like nor peace nor war" (1.1.172–73). He contemptuously reports one of their proverbs as: "that dogs must eat . . ." (1.1.210). In his exile speech he rejects the people as "You common cry of curs . . ." (3.3.120), and his cutting scorn is emphasized by the alliteration. The last scene of the play shows us the same Coriolanus again, full of derogatory and violent animal imagery. He answers Aufidius' accusation with blunt rage, calling him "cur" (5.6.106) and "False hound" (5.6.112). He will not let the Volscians forget that it was he who conquered their city and held it "Even like a fawning greyhound in the leash,/ To let him slip at will" (1.6.38–39). Coriolanus' point of view is Hobbesian in its assumption of servility in the plebeians. The Tribune Brutus clearly understands this when he warns the people that they

> have chose a consul that will from them take
> Their liberties; make them of no more voice
> Than dogs, that are as often beat for barking
> As therefore kept to do so. (2.3.22–25)

Coriolanus' dog image for the people is being turned to his own undoing here: the animal imagery has become inflammatory political propaganda. He is indeed "a very dog to the commonalty" (1.1.28–29); on the other hand, to

defeat him, predicts Sicinius, will be "as easy/ As to set
dogs on sheep . . ." (2.1.272–73).
The pairing of noble and ignoble animals to show the
contrast between patrician and plebeian may be seen in
Coriolanus' speech to the Senate. He fears that the rabble

> will in time break ope
> The locks o' th' Senate and bring in the crows
> To peck the eagles.   (3.1.137–39)

The worthless and gross "crows" have an entirely different
value from the kingly "eagles." The eagle image occurs
again in a contrast Coriolanus makes between himself and
the Volscians:

> If you have writ your annals true, 'tis there,
> That, like an eagle in a dovecote, I
> Flutter'd your Volscians in Corioles.
> Alone I did it.   (5.6.113–16)

The noble eagle fought the Volscians as if they were so
many doves. We recall the image of Virgilia's "dove's eyes"
(5.3.27) and the absolute peace-war antithesis it makes
with this passage, for to be a dove in battle is cowardly and
contemptible.

The animal imagery used for Coriolanus is full of violent
action and intense movement. This is seen most characteristically in the figure of the butterfly; three of the six references in Shakespeare are in this play. In the first Valeria
gives us a vivid prose account of how she saw young
Marcius, the son of Coriolanus,

> run after a gilded butterfly; and when he caught it, he let it go
> again, and after it again, and over and over he comes, and up again;
> catch'd it again; or whether his fall enrag'd him or how 'twas, he
> did so set his teeth and tear it! O, I warrant, how he mammock'd it!
> (1.3.66–71)

167

"One on's father's moods" (1.3.72), says Volumnia, a point abundantly confirmed by the battle scenes that follow immediately. In IV,vi the full terror of the rumors about a new war is confirmed by Cominius; Coriolanus leads the Volscians

> Against us brats with no less confidence
> Than boys pursuing summer butterflies
> Or butchers killing flies. (4.6.93–95)

The Romans are the prey that Coriolanus and his Volscians will now unnaturally tear and mammock. The father is taking up the sport of butterfly hunting on a larger scale, and both passages have a common violence. They also echo Gloucester's despairing comment in *King Lear*: "As flies to wanton boys are we to th' gods./ They kill us for their sport" (4.1.36–37).

Finally, the powerful images of Coriolanus' pride in V,iv provide an ironic commentary on the mercy already shown in V,iii. Menenius speaks of the change in Marcius:

There is a differency between a grub and a butterfly; yet your butterfly was a grub. This Marcius is grown from man to dragon. He has wings; he's more than a creeping thing. (5.4.11–14)

Coriolanus' pride has gone through a cycle of development that is now at its height as "butterfly" and "dragon." It is a curious sort of imagery, particularly because so frail and delicate a thing as a butterfly is made to represent the height of violence; perhaps the butterfly is apt just because it is so vulnerable. The association of butterfly and dragon recalls the dire image of Coriolanus' exile, to which he prefers to

> go alone,
> Like to a lonely dragon, that his fen
> Makes fear'd and talk'd of more than seen. . . . (4.1.29–31)

1 6 8

The foreboding here is fulfilled in Coriolanus' return to Rome, when he "is grown from man to dragon" (5.4.13) and "fights dragon-like" (4.7.23) for the Volscians.

The animal imagery of *Coriolanus* is used more consistently and for more specific purposes than the imagery of food or disease, and it is more evenly distributed over the course of the play. Animal images refer chiefly to the plebeians, who are dogs, hounds, curs, rats, rascals (lean deer not fit to be hunted), hares, geese, asses, mules, camels, wolves, crows, goats, foxes, cats, kites, minnows, a multiplying spawn, and a beastly herd. The patricians, however, as represented by Coriolanus, have only a few noble and violent animals to indicate their power — lion, bear, eagle, dragon, osprey, tiger — but this power is also the implied opposite of the plebeian images. Most of these animals, including the osprey, represent traditional primacies.[15] There is also a good deal of interplay in the animal imagery, especially when the Tribunes turn Coriolanus' base images for the people against him.

4

The themes of food, disease, and animals relate Coriolanus to the basic conflicts of the play. We may approach his dramatic character more directly, however, in the extensive imagery of acting and of isolation. Both themes rely much more significantly on presentational images than the ones already discussed. Too few critics have recognized that the art of acting is one of the most important subject matters of Shakespeare's imagery. To act in a play is to seem something other than what one is; it is deliberately to play a role, to feign, to counterfeit, to dissemble. Cleopatra, for

SHAKESPEARE'S ROMAN PLAYS

example, baits Antony with his coldness toward Fulvia's
death in terms drawn from the playhouse:

> I prithee turn aside and weep for her;
> Then bid adieu to me, and say the tears
> Belong to Egypt. Good now, play one scene
> Of excellent dissembling, and let it look
> Like perfect honour. (1.3.76–80)

Even if Antony wept for Fulvia it would only be "excellent
dissembling," not true feeling. In this sense Shakespeare's
most accomplished actor is Iago.[16] One of his early statements in *Othello* keynotes his dedication to illusion: "I am
not what I am" (1.1.65); he is one person to Othello, another to Cassio and Roderigo, and yet another to his wife
Emilia. He has been schooled in the tradition of the Shakespearean villain, whose histrionic abilities are exemplified
by Buckingham, the agent of Richard III:

> Tut, I can counterfeit the deep tragedian,
> Speak and look back, and pry on every side,
> Tremble and start at wagging of a straw,
> Intending deep suspicion. Ghastly looks
> Are at my service, like enforced smiles;
> And both are ready in their offices,
> At any time to grace my stratagems. (*Richard III* 3.5.5–11)

The ability to act or to dissemble is one of the chief resources of the Machiavel, and his language is often specifically that of the theater. In this respect Shakespeare
follows the traditional identification of acting with hypocrisy
and moral disguise, as in the description of the Player in
Micrologia: "He is a notable hypocrite, seeming what he is
not, and is indeed what he seems not." [17]

For Coriolanus images of acting and the theater are
used negatively to stress his honesty: he cannot betray the

170

truth of his own nature at any price, and he would rather suffer banishment from Rome than flatter the people. His hatred of the mob may arise from a narrowly aristocratic ideal, yet his devotion to it makes the moral issue of the play a complex one, for it is an uncompromising devotion which excludes easy alternatives.

The acting imagery begins when Cominius reviews Marcius' career in a formal speech to the Roman Senators. As a youth against Tarquin,

> When he might act the woman in the scene,
> He prov'd best man i' th' field and for his meed
> Was brow-bound with the oak.   (2.2.100–02)

At sixteen Marcius scorned to play a woman's role (as boy actors did in the Elizabethan theater) on the "scene" of battle, although he might have done so without dishonor. Now, in peace, he cannot act the part of flatterer to the people. He gives an unwilling consent to wear the gown of humility and beg the plebeians' voices:

> It is a part
> That I shall blush in acting, and might well
> Be taken from the people.   (2.2.148–50)

The "blush" is for shame at the dissembling involved. And throughout the gown of humility scene, he is conscious of acting "most counterfeitly" (2.3.107).

These same issues arise in III,ii, except that here Coriolanus' life is at stake. The Tribunes have already condemned him to death, but they will allow him to appear before the people to defend himself; III,ii is the preparation for this appearance. At the very beginning of the scene we notice a conflict developing between Coriolanus and his mother, which is sharpened by the fact that they resemble each

171

other so closely. His first words to her are a strong declaration of belief:

> I talk of you.
> Why did you wish me milder? Would you have me
> False to my nature? Rather say, I play
> The man I am. (3.2.13–16)

He will not play penitent to the people no matter what fate they have in store for him, for to be "false" to his "nature" is of greater weight than any punishment. The moderation Volumnia and Menenius advise does not make sense to Coriolanus, a creature of extremes without that neutral middle state between honesty and dishonesty. His simple working principle — "I play/The man I am" — is at an opposite pole from Iago's "I am not what I am." It is also at once a source of weakness and strength, for it ensures his integrity but leaves him vulnerable to attack.

The counsel Volumnia offers of "Honour and policy" (3.2.42) seems particularly specious and dishonorable. It insists that her son suspend his honesty to meet the crisis, then return to it later. She will teach him the role he has to play:

> Because that now it lies you on to speak
> To th' people, not by your own instruction,
> Nor by th' matter which your heart prompts you,
> But with such words that are but roted in
> Your tongue, though but bastards and syllables
> Of no allowance to your bosom's truth. (3.2.52–57)

This is the prepared part that Coriolanus must be taught in order to pacify the people, but it is at the price of what his "heart prompts" and his "bosom's truth." The issue is very clearly drawn, for good acting here is "policy": "to

seem/ The same you are not . . ." (3.2.46–47). Volumnia
very specifically rehearses the gesture and diction of the
humble role:

> I prithee now, my son,
> Go to them, with this bonnet in thy hand;
> And thus far having stretch'd it (here be with them),
> Thy knee bussing the stones (for in such business
> Action is eloquence, and the eyes of th' ignorant
> More learned than the ears), waving thy head,
> Which often, thus, correcting thy stout heart,
> Now humble as the ripest mulberry
> That will not hold the handling — or [18] say to them
> Thou art their soldier. . . .   (3.2.72–81)

In this context, as much as in Antony's funeral oration or
in Menenius' fable, "Action is eloquence" and the stage
business is intended to produce calculated emotional effects.
Coriolanus is to hold his hat in his hand and then stretch
his hand out to the people; he is to kneel on the stone platform where he speaks; he is to wave (or shake) his head to
indicate humility — he is instructed in his part as if
he were an absolute novice in acting. And Cominius assures him that if he forgets what to do or say, "we'll prompt
you" (3.2.106). This passage, along with Hamlet's advice
to the players, is one of Shakespeare's few commentaries on
the art of acting, and it plainly emphasizes visual, nonverbal persuasion, for the "eyes of th' ignorant" are "More
learned than the ears. . . ."

The arguments of his mother, Menenius, and Cominius
force a strained and rebellious consent from Coriolanus:

> Must I go show them my unbarb'd sconce? Must I
> With my base tongue give to my noble heart
> A lie that it must bear? Well, I will do't.

Yet, were there but this single plot to lose,
This mould of Marcius, they to dust should grind it
And throw't against the wind. To th' market place!
You have put me to such a part which never
I shall discharge to th' life. (3.2.99–106)

The "policy" of this humble role is a "base" thing, a "lie,"
which Coriolanus doubts his ability to perform effectively
or naturally ("to th' life"). But his mother offers powerful
emotional persuasion: "To have my praise for this, perform
a part/ Thou hast not done before" (3.2.109–10).

Against this he can offer no arguments, although his sense
of shame and baseness persists to the end of the scene. He
answers his mother's image of "Thy knee bussing the
stones" (3.2.75) with strong exclamations of distaste:

A beggar's tongue
Make motion through my lips, and my arm'd knees,
Who bow'd but in my stirrup, bend like his
That hath receiv'd an alms! (3.2.117–20)

We have already seen with what contempt Coriolanus
played beggar in the gown of humility (2.3.75–87). The
servile imagery works here as a counter-persuasion, and he
is led to revoke his consent:

I will not do't.
Lest I surcease to honour mine own truth
And by my body's action teach my mind
A most inherent baseness. (3.2.120–23)

This is, in its way, a noble and sympathetic speech — something not too common for Coriolanus. He fears that the
part will become merged with the reality, but he is once
again driven by his mother to agree in a manner that anticipates V,iii:

> Pray be content.
> Mother, I am going to the market place.
> Chide me no more. I'll mountebank their loves,
> Cog their hearts from them, and come home belov'd
> Of all the trades in Rome. (3.2.130–34)

Although he consents to go, "mountebank" suggests that he thinks of himself in terms of the trickery and deceit of the market-place performer.

The next scene shows us what we have been led to expect: Coriolanus is unable to play the role he has been instructed in. His first exchange with Menenius echoes the scornful tone of the preceding scene:

> *Men.* Calmly, I do beseech you.
> *Cor.* Ay, as an hostler, that for th' poorest piece
> Will bear the knave by th' volume. (3.3.31–33)

Coriolanus is still preoccupied with the venality of what he is doing — the "hostler" working for his tip is a kind of beggar — and "Calmly" here recalls "mildly" of 3.2.139, 142, 144, 145; both suggest the same base hypocrisy of acting. Coriolanus is able to begin his encounter calmly enough, but the charge of "traitor" (3.3.66) dissolves his pose of mildness into a torrent of abuse, and he is soon banished.

Unlike Coriolanus, the crafty Tribunes can easily dissemble to gain their ends. They can "make faces like mummers" (2.1.82), and after Coriolanus is banished they can change their role:

> Now we have shown our power,
> Let us seem humbler after it is done
> Than when it was a-doing. (4.2.3–5)

The Tribunes can "seem humbler" at will, following the politic way that Coriolanus has so violently forsworn.

175

There is a final echo of acting imagery in V,iii. Here the parts are reversed from III,ii, and Coriolanus cannot play the role of revenger on his native city. He confesses his weakness to Virgilia:

> Like a dull actor now,
> I have forgot my part and I am out,
> Even to a full disgrace. (5.3.40–42)

As in III,ii, Coriolanus cannot maintain the pretense of acting, although mercy will mean his own destruction. He cannot feign a "part" so discordant with nature, and his yielding to his family is again a sign of inherent honesty. This is one way of regarding his mercy speech:

> Behold, the heavens do ope,
> The gods look down, and this unnatural scene
> They laugh at. (5.3.183–85)

If "unnatural scene" is a theatrical metaphor, it indicates the role Coriolanus has just rejected: it was "unnatural" for the defender of Rome to be acting as the destroyer of his native city. There is also a suggestion that "unnatural scene" may refer to Coriolanus' present role of mercy: it is "unnatural" for the proud and godlike Coriolanus to be playing this "scene" of humble yielding. The latter sense looks ahead to quite a different figure in V,vi, one who seems to have recovered very quickly from his experience of mercy.

5

As Harry Levin has noted, "alone" is repeated more often in *Coriolanus* than in any other play of Shakespeare, and the protagonist seems to suffer from Captain Ahab's "desolation of solitude." [19] This comment shares Plutarch's concern with the uncivil aspects of his hero:

wilfulnesse is the thing of the world, which a gouernour of a commonwealth for pleasing should shun, being that which *Plato* called solitarinesse. As in the end, all men that are wilfully giuen to a selfe opinion and obstinate minde, and who will neuer yeeld to others reason, but to their owne; remaine without companie, and forsaken of all men.[20]

Coriolanus' "solitarinesse" or isolation offers one way of understanding his pride, but his aloneness is the source of his excelling strength as well as the cause of his tragic ruin.

I shall deal with the isolation theme in terms of a number of presentational images, for which the Elizabethan stage was an especially suitable medium. The use of an "open stage" that projected far into the audience would allow for effective contrasts between the single figure Coriolanus and the antagonistic groups he is set against. If, for example, he took a position far downstage, he would be standing quite close to the spectators and could address them directly.[21] Or if the mob were downstage and Coriolanus diagonally opposite upstage, a feeling of conflict could be created in which the mob on stage would seem to be continuous with the crowd standing in the "pit." The close contact with the audience possible in an Elizabethan public playhouse gives the isolation theme special significance: this sort of theatrical situation intensifies the illusion of actuality and presses the audience to identify with the characters and issues of the play.

i

Our first example of Marcius' isolating pride occurs in the battle scene of I,iv. When the Volscians retreat, Marcius follows them through their gates and is shut in, and, as the First Soldier reports, he "is himself alone,/ [22] To answer all the city" (1.4.51–52). The action here was probably indicated by an exit through one of the stage doors, which in the Swan drawing seem solid and massive enough to represent city gates. Another way of staging this scene would be to use removable property gates especially set up for the occasion.[23] There may also have been off-stage noises for the battle within the gates, although none are mentioned in our printed text. The important point for the isolation theme is that Marcius fights alone against the whole city of Corioles. He is an isolated figure here, just as he is against the Roman plebeians and in his exile. But "alone" in this context means "not needing the help of others," and it emphasizes Marcius' valor as contrasted with the cowardly soldiers who remain behind: "Foolhardiness! Not I." (1.4. 46) says the First Soldier. But after Titus Lartius has already spoken a formal eulogy for him, Marcius suddenly reappears, "bleeding, assaulted by the *Enemy*" (1.4.61 s.d.). This is the first sight we have had of him fighting single-handedly against the Volscians, and it is a powerful heroic image.

The feat in I,iv is remembered throughout the play as the chief example of Marcius' valor, and "alone" is stressed in each instance. In his encounter with Aufidius, Marcius taunts him with this deed:

> Within these three hours, Tullus,
> Alone I fought in your Corioles walls
> And made what work I pleas'd. 'Tis not my blood [24]
> Wherein thou seest me mask'd. (1.8.7–10)

And the fact that "all alone Marcius did fight/ Within Corioles gates . . ." (2.1.179–80) is announced by a Herald

178

in the triumphal procession. In Cominius' formal and detailed report to the Senators "alone" is again emphasized:

> Alone he ent'red
> The mortal gate of th' city, which he painted
> With shunless destiny; aidless came off,
> And with a sudden reinforcement struck
> Corioles like a planet. (2.2.114–18)

Coriolanus' valor is being put in violent terms ("shunless destiny," "planet"), and "aidless" serves to define "Alone" as the mark of military worth. He has become at this point a sort of "human war-machine," a "mechanical warrior, a man turned into an instrument of war. . . ." [25]

But the most important reference to the fight within Corioles' gates is at the end of the play, where Coriolanus tells Aufidius how he "Flutter'd your Volscians in Corioles./ Alone I did it" (5.6.115–16). Coriolanus' isolation in this scene is that of a traitor; he is an alien from Rome and an alien in Corioles.[26] His proud remembrance of his victory in I,iv only points up the desperation of his present plight. Once more "He is himself alone,/ To answer all the city," but he is defenseless against the Volscians he himself has provoked. Within a few lines the conspirators have killed him, and the stage direction reads: "*Aufidius stands on him*" (5.6.131). This is the triumph Aufidius prepared for in IV,vii, and the image of his victory and Coriolanus' defeat gains in strength from being presented as a simple, barbarous tableau. Its powerful symbolism of dishonor is emphasized by the Volscian lord who calls Aufidius to reason: "Tread not upon him" (5.6.134). The stage action here is an ironic reversal of Volumnia's heroic vision of her son: "He'll beat Aufidius' head below his knee/ And tread upon his neck" (1.3.49–50).

ii

The theme of isolation is developed in another variation in II,iii, where Coriolanus stands in the gown of humility to beg the voices of the people. In this scene costume is used significantly to express the dramatic meaning. Although we have lost some of the explicitness of the Elizabethan symbolism of dress, I think we are still sensitive enough to its connotations to receive something of a shock when Coriolanus appears in the gown of humility. This effect is apparent as soon as the actor walks on stage, for his costume is a violation of social decorum. Coriolanus must go through the ceremony in order to be consul, but he does it unwillingly and with heavy mockery. There is a real discordance between his inner hatred of the people and the outward signs of his humility, and costume is used ironically to show that he is not the man he seems. The physical uncomfortableness of the gown expresses a moral state, which it is up to the actor to convey by the proper gesture and stage business.

The pattern of action in II,iii is already carefully laid before the scene begins. Brutus knows that Coriolanus is too proud to wear "The napless vesture of humility . . ." (2.1.250), and Coriolanus himself insists that he "cannot/ Put on the gown, stand naked, and entreat" (2.2.140–41) the people. On the one side, the people will not "bate/ One jot of ceremony" (2.2.144–45), and on the other, Coriolanus cannot follow the advice of Menenius to mingle his "honour with the form" (2.2.148).

Although Coriolanus enters in the gown of humility, his mood is one of blank and intransigent defiance. The tone of all three of his encounters with the citizens is much the same: mocking insults mingled with veiled threats. The antagonism between him and the plebeians completely isolates him on stage. His pose of beggar has only the external sign of the gown to represent it, while the words he speaks are a sarcastic parody of humility — "There's in all two worthy voices begg'd. I have your alms. Adieu" (2.3.86–87). As Coriolanus scornfully tells the second group of citizens: "Pray you now, if it may stand with the tune of your voices that I may be consul, I have here the customary gown" (2.3.91–93). But the "customary gown" is indeed only a "form," and he manages never publicly to show his wounds, which, as he hints to the First Citizen, "shall be yours in private" (2.3.83).

The heart of the matter is that Coriolanus should not have to beg for a reward that is rightly his. Either he deserves to be consul or he does not, but this is not a question to be decided by the base plebeians. As he says in his soliloquy in II,iii,

> Better it is to die, better to starve,
> Than crave the hire which first we do deserve.
> Why in this wolvish toge [27] should I stand here
> To beg of Hob and Dick that do appear
> Their needless vouches? (2.3.120–24)

He cannot understand why he should have to flatter the people for an approval which is "needless" in the sense that it has nothing to do with his true merit. Like the Prince of Arragon in *The Merchant of Venice*, who rejects the gold casket because he fears it is connected with the multitude, Coriolanus also "assumes desert"; neither has any doubts about his own intrinsic worth. The image of the "wolvish toge" implies the hypocrisy of the wolf in sheep's clothing, for Coriolanus is using the humble gown as a disguise in

1 8 1

which to stalk his prey. But it also suggests that the people are trying to make Coriolanus seem to be a wolf by clothing him in sheep's wool; in this sense they are forcing him to be their prey. There is a large body of Elizabethan proverbs based on the relations of wolf and sheep which imply not only hypocrisy, but also rapaciousness and guile.[28] Incidentally, the Folio spelling, "Wooluish," would suggest to a reader the base woollen material of the gown — we recall that "woollen vassals" (3.2.9) is one of the scornful expressions for the people Coriolanus has inherited from his mother.

After the third group of citizens leaves, Coriolanus' chief anxiety is to be rid of the gown. "Is this done?" (2.3.149) is his first question, and a few lines further he asks Sicinius: "May I change these garments?" (2.3.154). It is something he will "straight do and, knowing myself again,/ Repair to th' Senate House" (2.3.155–56). These lines are a significant comment on the whole scene, for Coriolanus cannot recover his sincerity and honesty until the gown of humility is removed. Brutus' observation is therefore completely just: "With a proud heart he wore/ His humble weeds" (2.3.160–61). The Tribunes see in this attitude a way to provoke Coriolanus' banishment, for his failure in a humble role in this scene anticipates his failure in III,iii.

As a visual image of related interest, we may note that Coriolanus' hat (as well as his gown) enters into the action in II,iii. To remove one's hat, or to "uncover," was a sign of respect in the Elizabethan period as it is today. Thus *"Cominius and Lartius stand bare"* (1.9.40 s.d.) before Marcius after his refusal of "A bribe to pay my sword" (1.9.38), and in IV,v a servant reports that the Volscian senators "stand bald" (4.5.205) before Coriolanus. In II,iii

182

he tells the second group of citizens that he will flatter them if they wish:

since the wisdom of their choice is rather to have my hat than my heart, I will practise the insinuating nod and be off to them most counterfeitly: that is, sir, I will counterfeit the bewitchment of some popular man and give it bountiful to the desirers. Therefore, beseech you I may be consul.   (2.3.104–10)

We think of Bolingbroke's "courtship" of the commoners: "Off goes his bonnet to an oyster-wench . . ." (*Richard II* 1.4.31). There is a dishonest flattery in this seemingly democratic ceremony, for it is the sign of counterfeit humility, trying to appear something one is not. Coriolanus has won his honor by deeds, not by such politic flattery as taking his hat off to the people, as the Second Officer laying cushions in the Capitol says in his favor:

his ascent is not by such easy degrees as those who, having been supple and courteous to the people, bonneted, without any further deed to have them at all into their estimation and report. . . .
(2.2.28–32)

That is why Coriolanus cannot play the humble role artfully devised by his mother: to show the mob his "unbarb'd sconce" (3.2.99) and to go to them "with this bonnet in thy hand;/ And thus far having stretch'd it . . ." (3.2.73–74). Although occurring later, this passage provides a clue to the acting of the "wolvish toge" scene. The Third Citizen tells the Tribunes what he has actually witnessed there: "with his hat, thus waving it in scorn,/ 'I would be consul,' says he" (2.3.175–76). The hat imagery of III,ii explains the stage business of II,iii, and it works together with the image of the gown of humility to emphasize Coriolanus' inability to play a humble role.

iii

Coriolanus' banishment, which comes as the climax of his conflict with the plebeians, provides a third example of his isolation. His strong aloneness here is particularly emphasized by his readiness to fight the whole people of Rome; he will deal with them as he has dealt with the enemy within Corioles' gates. Thus, in III,i, when Brutus orders him to be seized and taken to the Tarpeian Rock, "*Coriolanus draws his sword*" (3.1.223 s.d.). This violent image represents an extremity of alienation and pride. Perhaps this is what Volumnia means when she tells her son: "You are too absolute . . ." (3.2.39), although being "absolute" is in itself an aristocratic virtue. In stage terms Coriolanus' isolation is seen in the contrast between the single figure and the hostile group; in such open conflict no one can be neutral.

These images of isolation culminate in the exile of Coriolanus at the end of III,iii, and his speech there is a denunciation of his fellow Romans:

> You common cry of curs, whose breath I hate
> As reek o' th' rotten fens, whose loves I prize
> As the dead carcasses of unburied men
> That do corrupt my air, I banish you! (3.3.120–23)

It is a strange denial of civil society, for the single man, the "enemy to the people" (3.3.118), is assuming a power above and beyond that of society. "I banish you!" is the height of Coriolanus' isolating pride. It is also a proof of his "solitarinesse," and it reverses the idea of a body politic in Menenius' fable. The nucleus of Coriolanus' revenge is already present in the curses he cries down on Rome (3.3. 124–33). They provide an outline of the action from IV,vi,

184

where we see "feeble rumour" shaking the hearts of the Tribunes, to V,iii (and part of V,iv), where Rome in "uncertainty" and "despair" threatens to be delivered "without blows" to her former defender. Coriolanus ends his speech with another kind of defiance:

> Despising
> For you the city, thus I turn my back.
> There is a world elsewhere. (3.3.133–35)

But it is a desolate defiance, for the "world elsewhere" is "vast," and the exile in it is a "single man" (4.1.42), alien and unaccommodated.

The spiritual isolation of Coriolanus' exile is expressed in visual terms when he appears at the house of Aufidius. The opening stage direction of IV,iv sets the tone: "Enter *Coriolanus* in mean apparel, disguis'd and muffled." We have not seen him since his departure from Rome in IV,i, and he now appears entirely changed from the heroic figure of the first part of the play. His stature is deliberately undercut by his fears "Lest that thy wives with spits and boys with stones/ In puny battle slay me" (4.4.5–6). Thus Shakespeare is able to jump boldly and without transition from Coriolanus in Rome to Coriolanus in Antium,[29] with only the intermediate scene of Adrian and Nicanor to suggest the momentous changes that have taken place. While the wolvish gown of II,iii expressed a false humility put on unwillingly, this "mean apparel" represents a true humbling of circumstance — it marks the low point to which Coriolanus has fallen. In both scenes the costume is inappropriate for the true character of the hero, and the constraint and uncomfortableness of it must be conveyed in the acting. "Muffled," for example, is not merely a descriptive term,

185

but has distinct connotations for the acting of the part. Compare Antony's oration in *Julius Caesar*, where Antony tells us how Caesar died "muffling up his face" (3.2.192) with his mantle.

In these scenes in Act IV the feast of Aufidius off-stage also isolates the ill-clad, somber Coriolanus: he is out of place in such surroundings. We never actually see the banqueting, but are kept aware of it by the bustle of servants carrying food and drink and by the sounds of music and revelry coming from within. It is undoubtedly good dramatic economy to keep this feast off-stage, since it only serves as a background for the appearance of Coriolanus. Similarly, the off-stage "noise of a sea-fight" in *Antony and Cleopatra* (3.10 s.d. and 4.12.9 s.d.) — represented by boisterous cannonading from the guns just outside the theater — [30] and the shoutings of the mob in *Julius Caesar* (1.2.78 s.d., 131 s.d.) also indicate Shakespeare's capacity to use sound effects as a setting for the main action. This imagery of sound is often more suggestive than a comparable visual imagery, and it reaches a kind of perfection in the "Music of the hautboys . . . under the stage" in *Antony and Cleopatra* (4.3.11 s.d.) and in the "noises" of *The Tempest*, but it is unfortunately most elusive for a reader of these plays.

Coriolanus enters into this festive atmosphere as a figure who is out of place, and his first words mark his alienation: "A goodly house. The feast smells well, but I/ Appear not like a guest" (4.5.5–6). These words gain added force from being spoken as a soliloquy, a rather uncommon form of utterance for Coriolanus. Further on, the servants' attempt to humiliate him is met with a patrician scorn that reminds us of the scenes in Rome. But his cryptic tone and the stale bawdy joke he makes (4.5.52–53) are unlike anything that has gone before, except perhaps his encounters with the citizens in the gown of humility. At the moment of discovery Aufidius draws an ironic contrast between the man and his costume:

> Thou hast a grim appearance, and thy face
> Bears a command in't. Though thy tackle's torn,
> Thou show'st a noble vessel. (4.5.65–67)

This innate nobility is confirmed by the Second Servant: "By my hand, I had thought to have stroken him with a cudgel — and yet my mind gave me his clothes made a false report of him" (4.5.155–57). It is interesting to note how Coriolanus gradually recovers his stature from the low point at the beginning of IV,iv. His clothes no longer express the humiliation of exile — they made a "false report of him" — and the inner man is not in any way mean.

iv

Our final example of Coriolanus' isolation shows him in his splendid godlike pride in V,iii. This pride in deifying itself rejects the ordinary limitations of man and thereby leaves itself open to a tragic fall, which is the breaking of insolence (or "hubris"). We are made to feel that there is no more terrible isolation than that of a god, so that the rejection of this unnatural role is also a reassertion of common humanity. The dictum from Aristotle's *Politics* should serve as a touchstone for the god theme: "He that is incapable of living in a society is a god or a beast. . . ."[31] Coriolanus' "solitarinesse," then, his inability to live in a civil society, becomes the motivating force for his imitation of "the graces of the gods" (5.3.150).

SHAKESPEARE'S ROMAN PLAYS

A brief review of the god imagery should help us understand its high point in V,iii. The first statement of the
theme is in Brutus' comment at the end of I,i: "Being mov'd,
he will not spare to gird the gods" (1.1.260). This implies
that Coriolanus, like Tamburlaine, has become a proud and
defiant rival of the gods. Brutus speaks in the same terms of
Coriolanus' entry into Rome:

> Such a poother
> As if that whatsoever god who leads him
> Were slily crept into his human powers
> And gave him graceful posture. (2.1.234–37)

Coriolanus for a moment has the attractiveness as well as
the power of a god, but there is an ominous note here, which
is taken up in III,i. Brutus answers Coriolanus' abuse of the
plebeians with a personal argument:

> You speak o' th' people
> As if you were a god to punish, not
> A man of their infirmity. (3.1.80–82)

This insight points to the source of Coriolanus' tragedy. In
their perspicacity and shrewdness the Tribunes resemble
Aufidius, whom they also follow in being able to turn their
insight to practical effect.

From the low point at Antium after his exile (IV,iv)
Coriolanus is raised to a height of pride unparalleled in the
first part of the play. But it is the pernicious and inexorable
pride of revenge, as of some baleful deity. The motif begins
when Aufidius chooses to welcome his old rival rather
than cut his throat; he recognizes in Marcius' voice an
authority no less than "Jupiter's" (4.5.108) and addresses
him as "thou Mars" (4.5.123). Toward the end of the scene
the Third Servant reports a deference shown to Marcius

188

as to a god, who "is so made on here within as if he were son and heir to Mars . . ." (4.5.202–03). Mars is in fact identified as Coriolanus' god throughout the play, which gives a special sting to Aufidius' final taunt: "Name not the god, thou boy of tears!" (5.6.100). Coriolanus has the immediate appeal of a god in IV,vii, as Aufidius' Lieutenant indicates:

> I do not know what witchcraft's in him, but
> Your soldiers use him as the grace fore meat,
> Their talk at table, and their thanks at end;
> And you are dark'ned in this action, sir,
> Even by your own. (4.7.2–6)

But this witchcraft is setting in motion a means to destroy itself. In IV,vi the discovery of Coriolanus' intention to burn Rome is marked by Cominius' positive statement in an atmosphere of rumor:

> He is their god. He leads them like a thing
> Made by some other deity than Nature,
> That shapes men better. . . . (4.6.90–92)

The nature and god themes are beginning to cross here, for Coriolanus is an unnatural and infernal deity, shaped better than by Nature, and in whom the "confidence" of destruction is assured. His perversely isolating pride is also developed by his rejection of Cominius and Menenius in Act V. We are ready for the family group of mother, wife, and son (and Valeria), which is the ultimate appeal to nature.

Act V, scene iii, shows us Coriolanus imitating "the graces of the gods" (5.3.150) and represents the climax of the god theme. His unexpected mercy comes then as a momentous act, a sudden return to things human and a recognition of his limitations. This is the general movement,

189

although the recognition itself is extremely limited. He begins the scene with a certain remorse for his treatment of Menenius, who "godded me indeed" (5.3.11); Menenius is the father figure [32] of this primarily maternal [33] scene. But the god Coriolanus has stooped a little to offer him the first conditions. It is through these little cracks in the mask that we see the human figure within. Coriolanus' reaction as he watches the family group approach shows a conflict of tenderness and deliberate resolution:

> But out, affection!
> All bond and privilege of nature, break!
> Let it be virtuous to be obstinate.
> What is that curtsy worth? or those dove's eyes,
> Which can make gods forsworn? I melt and am not
> Of stronger earth than others.   (5.3.24–29)

The two parts of the speech are in an entirely different tone. Virgilia's weakness has a power to "melt," and in this melting, this recognition of his human nature — he is "not/ Of stronger earth than others" — lies a true humbling of Coriolanus. We are being moved toward the final yielding at line 182.

The part played by Coriolanus' son in this movement is of strong dramatic interest. Although he speaks only two lines in the entire play (5.3.127–28), his presence in V,iii offers a powerful argument for "instinct," or Nature, as when Coriolanus first sees him:

> my young boy
> Hath an aspect of intercession which
> Great Nature cries 'Deny not.' — Let the Volsces
> Plough Rome and harrow Italy! I'll never
> Be such a gosling to obey instinct, but stand
> As if a man were author of himself
> And knew no other kin.   (5.3.31–37)

Coriolanus must now raise himself to the very height of pride in order to oppose the promptings to mercy in his own nature. The last sentence represents man in the absolute isolation of a god: "author of himself," without "kin," and an alien in human society. It is all he can oppose to the appeal of "Great Nature," but it is an impossible demand for a human being to make even on himself. Later in the scene the child kneels to his father (5.3.75) and Volumnia asks him to speak, for "Perhaps thy childishness will move him more/ Than can our reasons" (5.3.157–58). The essence of the child's part is in his presence on stage, which is a wordless affirmation of "kin." He thus serves as Volumnia's final argument before she makes ready to depart:

> This boy, that cannot tell what he would have
> But kneels and holds up hands for fellowship,
> Does reason our petition with more strength
> Than thou hast to deny't. Come, let us go. (5.3.174–77)

Volumnia clearly describes the stage action of young Marcius here, which makes a powerful dumbshow image of the appeal for mercy.

Act V, scene iii, is one of the few places in the play where the style is consciously "written up" to achieve a dramatic effect. Only here, for example, does Coriolanus use a highly imaginative simile without unfavorable overtones; his greeting to Valeria is formal and ornately eloquent:

> The noble sister of Publicola,
> The moon of Rome, chaste as the icicle
> That's curded by the frost from purest snow
> And hangs on Dian's temple! Dear Valeria! (5.3.64–67)

Considering how minor a role Valeria plays, this greeting may seem too elaborate, but Shakespeare is beginning to show us the breaking of Coriolanus' pride, and the use of a minor character keeps the movement from becoming intrusive. We need this marked change in rhetoric and rhythm to indicate the possibility of tenderness and humanity in Coriolanus. In his couplet aside a few lines further rhyme is used to make a similar effect:

> Not of a woman's tenderness to be
> Requires nor child nor woman's face to see.   (5.3.129–30)

This couplet represents a sudden change in tone from what has preceded, and the poetic form itself indicates the "woman's tenderness" that is growing in him. If he did indeed want "nothing of a god but eternity and a heaven to throne in" (5.4.25–26), he could not speak in this way. Tenderness is not the attribute of the warrior, and the infrequency of this tone underlines its dramatic significance: the pardon for Rome is being made inevitable in the texture of the verse itself.

Throughout V,iii there must be an acute awareness in Coriolanus of the price of yielding. This is particularly apparent in the theme of silence, which develops the dramatic tension in the scene from his inflexible resolution to the breaking of his pride. Consider the stage situation. Coriolanus is silent from his two lines at line 92 to the couplet and half-line at line 129, and from this point until his mercy speech more than fifty lines further (131–182). He speaks, in fact, only four and a half of these ninety crucial lines. His mother calls attention to this silence as an image of alienation: "Speak to me, son" (148), "Why dost not speak?" (153). The family's plea tries to penetrate this barrier: "Daughter, speak you./ He cares not for your weeping. Speak thou, boy" (155–56). There is obviously a pause after "Daughter, speak you," but Virgilia can only weep and Coriolanus remains inflexibly quiet. He leaves his mother to "prate" in vain "Like one i' th' stocks" (159–60). Coriolanus' silence is an image of the isolation that is about to be destroyed from within and is thus perhaps more difficult to act than any of his speaking part. The actor must not only present the tense inner conflict, but also register the effect of the family appeal. He may use any number of histrionic means, such as an expressionless impassivity in which the slightest gesture is a sign of emotion, or an abortive moving toward the family group then away as if to exit (but they hedge him in and prevent this).

The stage situation of V,iii also includes the insidious presence of Aufidius and his lieutenants as a sort of chorus or audience on stage to whom Coriolanus plays his role of unyielding revenger. He is very conscious of them throughout the action. When Volumnia asks to be heard, for example, he immediately turns to them and comments: "Aufidius, and you Volsces, mark; for we'll/ Hear naught from Rome in private" (5.3.92–93). Compare the earlier scene with Menenius, the rejection of whom Coriolanus boasts of as an act of integrity: "This man, Aufidius,/ Was my belov'd in Rome; yet thou behold'st" (5.2.98–99). The presence of Aufidius and his lieutenants deepens the conflict and sense of isolation in Coriolanus, for it forces him to stand alone against two hostile groups whose interests and appeals are entirely irreconcilable.

The final acting out of the imagery of silence comes at the climax of the play. Volumnia has been speaking compulsively as if to fill the void of her son's silence, but finally she, too, has no more to say and makes ready to leave: "I am hush'd until our city be afire./ And then I'll speak a little" (5.3.181–82). At this point occurs one of those marvelous bits of staging by which Shakespeare could express a moment of great intensity in the action: *"Holds her by the hand, silent"* [34] (5.3.182 s.d.). The language of dumb-show or pantomime presents the yielding of Coriolanus in strongly symbolic terms. The silence continues, but it is now the sign of mercy rather than of inscrutable hardness. All of Shakespeare's other tragic heroes are endowed with a special eloquence at the climax of the tragic action, but Coriolanus expresses himself best in an eloquence of action, and the words that follow only record his own wonder at what has happened:

> O mother, mother!
> What have you done? Behold, the heavens do ope,
> The gods look down, and this unnatural scene
> They laugh at.   (5.3.182–85)

The scene ends with the drinking of wine (5.3.203) to celebrate Coriolanus' newly recovered humanity, although the tone is hardly one of jubilation.

The actual yielding of Coriolanus is marked by the stage action: *"Holds her by the hand. . . ."* His fearful isolation has been broken, and the lone antagonistic figure who seemed by his silence to reject the family's appeal, now holds his mother's hand. Except for the kiss to Virgilia earlier in the scene (5.3.44–48), this gesture marks one of the rare physical contacts between Coriolanus and another human being in the play; [35] he is tragically reunited with the forces of "Great Nature" (5.3.33). Compare the reunion of King Lear with Cordelia: he kneels to her and fumblingly touches her cheeks. "Be your tears wet? Yes, faith. I pray weep not" (4.7.71). Since boy actors played the women's roles on the

Elizabethan stage, the playwrights tended to avoid these physical contacts. The sparing use of this type of stage action thus gives it a special significance.

The scene that follows V,iii offers a final comment on the god theme. Dramatic irony is used to good effect here, for neither Menenius nor Sicinius knows of Coriolanus' mercy, and Menenius speaks of his godlike pride as if it were something inviolable:

When he walks, he moves like an engine, and the ground shrinks before his treading. He is able to pierce a corslet with his eye, talks like a knell, and his hum is a battery. He sits in his state, as a thing made for Alexander. What he bids be done is finish'd with his bidding. He wants nothing of a god but eternity and a heaven to throne in.   (5.4.19–26)

The breaking of the time sequence in V,iv conveys a sense of simultaneity and a working-over of the climax, for Menenius speaks of Coriolanus' pride before his yielding, while we have already seen him humbled. This scene has perhaps the most imperious imagery in the play for Coriolanus as a god, but it serves structurally to emphasize his mercy. Further on Sicinius prays that "The gods be good unto us!" (5.4.33), but Menenius denies the possibility now that Coriolanus has become the gods' scourge:

No, in such a case the gods will not be good unto us. When we banish'd him we respected not them; and, he returning to break our necks, they respect not us.   (5.4.34–37)

Into this desperation the news of Coriolanus' mercy comes with a sudden joyous impact announced by music: "*Trumpets, hautboys, drums beat, all together*" (5.4.51 s.d.).

The upshot of the isolation theme is that Coriolanus is neither a god nor a beast, but a man like other men, and the assertion of common humanity marks a familiar tragic pattern. It is especially important in this play because the hero's "solitarinesse" lies at the heart of his tragedy. His harsh, aristocratic pride and uncompromising wrath separate him from the company of his fellow men, yet from this alienation spring his heroism in battle and his iron-bound integrity. These are harsh, inflexible virtues, yet virtues nevertheless, and we are left with a deeply paradoxical impression of him.

Chapter VI

CONCLUDING REMARKS

THE justification for a study of Shakespeare's imagery must ultimately be sought in the image-consciousness of the Elizabethans, their spontaneous use of analogy as a habit of mind. On these grounds one may make an historical argument for the symbolic interpretation of Shakespeare. The figurative view of reality assumed order and symmetry in the universe, which, in a schematic and simplified form, had fixed and proper places on the chain of being for man, the state or human society, and the cosmos.[1] Each of these planes of being was thought to be not only in flexible correspondence with the others, but also implicit in them, on the principle that all illustrate the copious workings of natural law and the inherent order of things. The natural analogy between the three planes of being is at the basis of the idea of the microcosm and the macrocosm: the great can be seen in the little and the small part represent the whole. There has been much recent debate whether Shakespeare's beliefs can indeed be reduced to the simplified scheme of an ordered universe or to any specific system at all. We do not need, however, to insist on personal belief to see that the traditional idea of analogous planes is pregnant with imaginative possibilities. The similitudes and correspondences in this world-picture reflect the same Elizabethan delight in the discovery of relations that is seen in an elaborate rhetoric of poetic figures and very unclassical intricacies of dramatic structure.

The Elizabethans were much more given to symbolism than we are, not only in literature, but also in their daily life. Clothes, for example, indicated a man's occupation and social position in a very specific, traditional way. We should also consider the emblematic nature of such daily items as colors, jewels, embroidery, heraldic badges and mottoes, and the posies of rings. The popularity of allegory and personification in this period is indicative of a certain way of thinking that is abundantly illustrated by masques, pageants, shows, emblem books, and by such huge poems as *The Faerie Queene* and *Poly-Olbion*. Analogy was also at work in the interpretation of history, with the past supplying important examples for the present. The currency of the history play as a form bears witness to this, and, more specifically, we know that the Essex conspirators had *Richard II* played on the day before their rising, since there was "an analogy present to the Elizabethan political imagination between the reign of Richard II and that of Elizabeth herself." [2]

In Elizabethan political discussions the correspondences between the human body and the body politic were assumed almost as a form of speech, and they were often worked out in great detail. [3] A curious and extended example of this is

CONCLUDING REMARKS

Edward Forset's *A Comparative Discourse of the Bodies Natural and Politique* (1606), a book in which the "discourse" is pursued almost entirely in terms of these parallels. The powerful familiarity of this analogy may be felt in Sir John Eliot's discussion of the king as a physician, particularly in the fact that Eliot will not allow the comparison to be carried too far:

yett may wee not measure by this office of a Phisitian the authority royall; and argue, that because a King is the phisitian of the Comon wealth, Ergo he may be cast off by his subiects at pleasure, as a Phisitian may be put away of a sick man for noe similies goe vpon fower leggs; but as they doe agree in some things, so also doe they differ in other some, else were they not similia but eadem: not like but the same.[4]

Eliot's "noe similies goe vpon fower leggs" is a warning against the power of analogy, yet it is also a recognition of the deep-rootedness of analogy in the Elizabethan period. It is our age, not the Elizabethan, that is a literal one, so that when we do use symbols, they often have an air of self-consciousness and artifice. They are something too special for us and perhaps not enough a part of the fabric of daily life.

When MacCallum published his excellent study of the Roman plays in 1910, he felt no need at all to deal with imagery or symbolism. He was most interested in two topics: Shakespeare's use of Plutarch and the presentation of character. The genius of the dramatist was clearly seen in his ability to transmute his sources and to create real, believable people. These concerns, so thoroughly explored by critics of the nineteenth and early twentieth centuries, seem very partial and special to us. For one thing, they ignore that large area of symbolic expression that embodies the imaginative life of the play, and for another, they neglect Shakespeare as a man of the theater.

In this study I have tried to move away from the commitment of critics of imagery to lyric poetry. The revival of interest in Donne and the Metaphysical poets in the 1920's brought with it a reawakened sense of the vitality of the metaphoric image. This new emphasis demanded a very close reading of these difficult poets. When the analysis of imagery was applied to the drama, the methods of explication used for the Metaphysicals were taken over bodily. This is in fact the thesis of Elizabeth Holmes' book, *Aspects of Elizabethan Imagery* (1929). The point of view is stated very succinctly by Cleanth Brooks: "our practice in reading Donne — in learning how to thread our way through complex and involved metaphorical statement — may actually enable us to read Shakespeare more richly and may give us special aid in dealing with some of Shakespeare's more difficult tangles of imagery." [5] The statement is undoubtedly true, yet I object to its implication that Shakespeare may be considered another Metaphysical poet. The differences between Shakespeare and Donne seem to me more significant than the similarities; one basic difference is that Shakespeare wrote his plays to be performed in the theater, not as poems to be read in the study. Shakespeare's avowed poems — the Sonnets, *Venus and Adonis, The Rape of Lucrece* — are stylistically quite different from the plays. I would therefore also object to L. C. Knights' comment that in a study of Shakespeare's plays we should "start with so many lines of verse on a printed page which we read as we should any other poem." [6] When Knights said this in 1933, he was attempting to discredit character analysis and to draw our attention back to the poetic substance of Shakespeare. Perhaps we can now assume that this point of view is well established and go on to insist that Shakespeare is a dramatic poet; the poetic character of his imagery should not be separated from its context in the theater. This ought to be our starting-point even if, for readers, it takes a strong effort of the "histrionic sensibility" to place the printed play in this context.

In pursuing my explication of the Roman plays, I have tried to avoid what seem to me two major fallacies among writers on imagery: first, the "inductive fallacy," or the tendency to use images as scientific data from which factual conclusions can be drawn; and second, the "fallacy of autonomy," or the proneness to deal with image patterns as self-contained, autonomous entities within the play. Both of these approaches minimize the symbolic action which the images are created to serve. By ignoring the specific contexts of images, they create a false sense of homogeneity and give criticism a deceptively objective tone.

The inductive fallacy arises from the claim to scientific validity by certain students of imagery, who consider images as data which will yield correct results if only the proper analytic acts be performed. If the researcher is careful enough in his classification, the conclusions to be drawn will be almost self-evident, for the procedure is one approaching laboratory accuracy. One of the most extreme statements of this point of view is that of Miss Ellis-Fermor, who, in 1937, spoke rhapsodically about the possibilities for imagery research:

If we imagine ourselves plotting graphs of each series, for example, we shall have one diagram representing graphically the areas of subject-matter drawn upon by the poet, another representing the themes, and so on. But we ought as the final reward of our investigation to have one diagram in which all these are brought together and in which perhaps some startling relation between the major conclusions themselves is revealed, thus forming a final, significant, geometric design by reference to which alone the ultimate significance of any individual line of enquiry could be revealed.[7]

It is fortunate perhaps that no one has taken up the challenge to make "a final, significant, geometric design" of Shakespeare's imagery, or tried to state the "potential relation . . . of many conclusions not yet reached . . . in general, preferably mathematical, terms." Caroline Spurgeon's influential study, *Shakespeare's Imagery and What it Tells Us* (1935), attempted something along these lines, but Miss Ellis-Fermor seems to consider Miss Spurgeon's work as only a brilliant beginning. It would be more correct to call this quantitative approach an end rather than a beginning, for there would be little profit in pursuing it further.

Even in Miss Spurgeon's book the appearance of objectivity is illusory, for the charts and measurements conceal a strong personal bias: the idolization of Shakespeare the man. From this, it seems to me, all else springs, and even the subject-matter categories by which Shakespeare's imagery was originally classified reflect Miss Spurgeon's own preoccupations. She finds evidence in the imagery, for example, that Shakespeare

was deft and nimble with his hands, and loved using them, particularly in the carpenter's craft, and, contrary to our idea of most poets, he was probably a practical, neat and handy man about the house, as we know that he was a 'Johannes Factotum' about the stage.

She goes on to observe that "that which, next to an orchard

and garden, has registered itself most clearly and continuously upon his mind is the picture of a busy kitchen, and the women's work for ever going on in it. . . ." [8] If we glance now at Chart V, "Showing the Range and Subjects of Shakespeare's Images in their exact proportion," we find that Domestic imagery is the third largest class after Daily Life and Nature. This category includes not only such topics as House, Indoor Games, Textiles, and Light and Fire, but also Human Relations, and Life and Death. We may also note that Miss Spurgeon was not particularly interested in Shakespeare as a man of the theater; her Drama category is therefore incredibly small (about seventy-five examples).

The dangers of the inductive fallacy are also apparent in the scholarly uses of imagery for biography, attribution of authorship, dating, and textual criticism. The tendency here is to assume that a careful researcher can distinguish with certainty an author's characteristic imagery. [9] No one would wish to argue against the presence of the author in some form in his work, but this admission does not necessarily imply that the work is a piece of spiritual autobiography, or that, even if it were, we could determine its exact meaning. Shakespeare's plays are not his artistic diary, but objective and public dramatic fictions, drawing their plots and even some part of their language from other sources and from recognized traditions. For purposes of validation, therefore, one bit of proven external evidence would seem to carry more weight than a great deal of internal evidence from imagery.

The fallacy of autonomy also stems from the feeling that an author's imagery is an expression of objective truths. Once the cautions of fallibility are removed, the sense of scientific accuracy can give the critic a false strength and a kind of interpretive euphoria. As a corrective we need something like Bacon's concept of the idols of the theater, for the critic can sometimes convince himself of the independent reality of his own analytic patterns, "as so many plays brought out and performed, creating fictitious and theatrical worlds" (*Novum Organum* I,44). The word "autonomy" is meant to be contrasted with "relevance," for the one treats images as self-contained and composite pictures, while the other tries to follow the dramatic purposes for which the images seem to be intended.

Of all the modern critics of imagery G. Wilson Knight seems most guilty of the fallacy of autonomy, for his metaphysical, romantic approach often warps the images from any purpose for which they could have been designed. Examples are so apparent in his case that it may be more useful to draw on a subtle instance of autonomy from Caroline Spurgeon. Speaking of Shakespeare the man as presented in his imagery, Miss Spurgeon writes:

What he did like was to watch the deer, unseen by them, in their native forest, and he must often, in the woodlands of the Warwickshire Arden, have seen them 'jouling' horns together, running swiftly 'o'er the land', or grazing on 'sweet bottom grass'.[10]

If we restore these images to their contexts, we find that they have surprisingly little to say about deer. In *All's Well that Ends Well* the Clown is joking about the proverbial horns of the cuckold:

If men could be contented to be what they are, there were no fear in marriage; for young Charbon the Puritan and Old Poysam the Papist, howsome'er their hearts are sever'd in religion, their heads are both one — they may jowl horns together like any deer i' th' herd. (1.3.54–59)

204

Miss Spurgeon was certainly not thinking of this as something Shakespeare watched "unseen" and "often, in the woodlands of the Warwickshire Arden." The image from *Love's Labour's Lost* occurs in a couplet just before the lords arrive disguised as Muscovites:

Boyet. Ladies, withdraw. The gallants are at hand.
Prin. Whip to our tents, as roes run o'er the land. (5.2.308–09)

The deer image here represents victorious female coquetry in the play's war between the sexes. Last, and most char-acteristic of the dangers of autonomy, is the image from *Venus and Adonis*, which occurs in the most sensual part of Venus' amorous plea:

'I'll be a park, and thou shalt be my deer;
Feed where thou wilt, on mountain or in dale;
Graze on my lips; and if those hills be dry,
Stray lower, where the pleasant fountains lie.

'Within this limit is relief enough,
Sweet bottom-grass, and high delightful plain,
Round rising hillocks, brakes obscure and rough,
To shelter thee from tempest and from rain.' (lines 231–38)

It looks as if Shakespeare's bawdy is asserting itself in Miss Spurgeon's book against the author's conscious will; the Shakespeare of these passages is far from "Christ-like." [11]

One of the special concerns of this study has been to call attention to nonverbal, presentational images and to note how these work together with verbal images and help to realize them in dramatic terms. A difficulty inherent in this approach is that Shakespeare's presentational imagery is much less accessible to us than his verbal. In the plays themselves we have only the stage directions of the First Folio (there are no quartos to consider for the Roman plays) and various indications of staging that occur incidentally in the text. I have avoided trying to piece out this evidence with literary and fictional staging not clearly demanded by the play. As Reynolds cautions us, "Just because the text of a play mentions some setting or property does not prove it was actually present, and even directions cannot always be taken literally." [12] It would be much simpler to discuss the presentational imagery of such dramatists as O'Neill or Ibsen, for their stage directions are much fuller than Shakespeare's and the theater for which they wrote much closer to us. But it is just this remoteness of Shakespeare from our modern theater that makes it necessary to insist on his skill in the poetic drama. I have tried to suggest one approach which an imagery study of plays ought to follow, with the understanding that in Shakespeare's Roman plays this approach cannot be demonstrated in great detail. The method, of course, is only one among many and should remain subordinate to the insight it can provoke.

Although critics are said to have a Faustian urge to replace the works they study by their criticism, Shakespeare seems to have successfully withstood them for the past three hundred years — they have not been able to exhaust nor to explain away the fullness of his meaning. This is certainly a tribute to his strength and resilience of imagination. What indeed makes the present study possible is the plenitude of Shakespeare's image-making power, for in this he was a master, and "to be a master of metaphor," as Aristotle tells us in the Poetics, "is by far the greatest thing."

APPENDIX

THE ROMAN PLAYS AS A GROUP

It is an interesting question, though not strictly relevant to this study, whether Shakespeare's Roman plays constitute a well-defined group, as, for example, the "problem" plays or the last plays. I believe there are at least three arguments for the Roman plays as a group: (1) the use of "Roman" costume on the Elizabethan stage; (2) the Roman praise of suicide as an act of moral courage and nobility, an attitude very different from Christian belief; and (3) the common source in North's Plutarch: as in the English history plays, the use of an historical action imposes certain limits on the liberties the author may take. All three of these criteria are external ones, and this perhaps weakens the idea of a group based on intrinsic similarities in tone, style, or the handling of the subject.[1] In these areas the plays are extremely different (see Chapter II), and their themes and purposes are also quite distinct.

In terms of the three criteria mentioned above, neither *Titus Andronicus, Cymbeline,* nor *The Rape of Lucrece* properly belongs in this group, although each of these has Roman elements. Rome in *Titus Andronicus* is only the setting for a revenge play, which is based on such fictional classical themes as the Revenge of Atreus and the Rape of Philomela. The play takes place at some late period of the Roman Empire, but the history in it is incidental and peripheral.[2] Similarly, *Cymbeline* is basically a romantic British play with several subordinate Roman scenes. *The Rape of Lucrece* offers an interesting study of the Roman moral character and suicide and is therefore relevant to our group, but it must be excluded because it is not a play and because it deals with its subject as legend rather than history.

The most striking link between the Roman plays is the use of "Roman" costume, which conveys the sense of the Roman past in strong visual terms. Our best evidence for the existence of a characteristically "Roman" costume is the drawing of *Titus Andronicus*, probably made by Henry Peacham in 1595.[3] It seems very likely that it represents a contemporary performance of the play, and as such it is our fullest graphic record of an Elizabethan production. We are chiefly concerned with the figure of Titus, who is dressed in a sort of Roman toga with a wreath on his head. It is the kind of costume that, in the theater, would give the immediate impression of being "Roman" and would help to create a Roman illusion in the play. The other characters are either wearing Elizabethan dress, or the short, close-fitting tunic that suggests Roman armor. J. Dover Wilson concludes that the lower classes were apparently played in "modern dress," but that "every effort was obviously made, contrary to the assumptions of our theatrical historians, to attain accuracy in the attire worn by patricians."[4] He also thinks that Julius Caesar, Brutus, and Antony were costumed as Romans despite some of the verbal references to "doublet" in *Julius Caesar* — some of these are taken over literally from North's Plutarch. •

It seems most likely that some combination of contemporary and Roman costume was used on the Elizabethan stage. With a painting of Veronese as model, Granville-Barker sees Antony as probably dressed in a "mixture of doublet, breastplate, sandals and hose."[5] This is the way the Romans are pictured in the woodcuts of the first edition of Holinshed's *Chronicles* (1577).[6] They wear breastplate armor over Elizabethan doublets, and their hose are occasionally gartered just below the knee. They also wear Roman helmets and carry battle-axes and swords. There seems to be no attempt at all at historical accuracy in the Roman costume. The "Romaine" on the title page of Speed's *The Theatre of the Empire of Great Britaine* (1614) also displays the same imaginative recreation: a tunic modeled in the shape of armor and an elaborately plumed helmet.[7] All of these costumes resemble the masque designs of Inigo Jones, who more or less established the proper male costume for a Roman for over a century: "the Roman breastplate, shaped to the figure and modelling the torso muscles . . . , the military skirt or kilt, the draped scarf and plumed helmet."[8]

208

APPENDIX

There are a number of allusions in Shakespeare to Roman dress, but they are not extensive enough to form the basis for an argument. Coriolanus wears the traditional "gown of humility" (2.3.43 s.d.) — what he calls contemptuously "this wolvish toge" (2.3.122) — in order to petition the plebeian vote. In *Titus Andronicus*, Titus is offered "This palliament of white and spotless hue" (1.1.182) to be "candidatus" (1.1.185), but he refuses it. And in *Julius Caesar*, Caesar puts on his Roman "robe" (2.2.107) to go to the Capitol. These references, along with the Peacham drawing, give some indication of the use of "Roman" costume on the Elizabethan stage, perhaps in conjunction with contemporary dress, but in some aspects clearly differentiated from it.

The foremost defining element for the Roman character in Shakespeare is the willingness to commit suicide rather than live ignobly or suffer death by another hand.[9] All the suicides in the Roman plays are presented as a proof of virtue. It is interesting to note that they seem to occur in related pairs of major and minor characters: Cassius and Titinius, Brutus and Portia, Antony and Eros, Cleopatra and Charmian. Each of the minor characters affirms the greatness of the major character with whom he is paired. The deaths of Titinius and Charmian, for example, come soon after those of Cassius and Cleopatra, so that the double suicide gives an immediate effect of act and comment. Although Eros' suicide precedes Antony's, it, too, has the same immediate effect.

In each of these cases the suicide is praised as an act of moral courage. The immediate tribute to Cassius is paid with his own life by Titinius:

> Brutus, come apace
> And see how I regarded Caius Cassius.
> By your leave, gods. This is a Roman's part.
> Come, Cassius' sword, and find Titinius' heart. (5.3.87–90)

The act of suicide is specifically set apart, by the leave of the gods, as a "Roman's part." Brutus corroborates this judgment when he comes upon the scene:

> Are yet two Romans living such as these?
> The last of all the Romans, fare thee well!
> It is impossible that ever Rome
> Should breed thy fellow. (5.3.98–101)

209

Brutus' own suicide is presented as a sure demonstration of his Roman virtue. As Strato, who holds the sword for him, tells Messala:

> Brutus only overcame himself,
> And no man else hath honour by his death. (5.5.56-57)

Brutus proves himself "The noblest Roman of them all" (5.5.68) by having the bravery to dispatch himself, the rightness of which is never questioned. None of the other references to suicide in *Julius Caesar* (1.3.89–102, 3.1.20–22, 3.2.50–52) is in any way critical of it as a moral act. The only possible exception is Brutus' speech condemning the Stoic suicide of Cato (5.1.100–07), but it turns out that Brutus "bears too great a mind" to let himself "go bound to Rome" in his enemy's triumph — suicide is preferable to such dishonor.

In *Antony and Cleopatra*, Cleopatra's reported suicide and Eros' actual suicide both prepare us for Antony's in IV,xiv. In terms of structure Antony's death marks a definite rising movement in the action. It is the final proof of his Roman virtue, for, as he tells Cleopatra,

> Not Caesar's valour hath o'erthrown Antony,
> But Antony's hath triumph'd on itself. (4.15.14-15)

And his final words are in the same spirit; he does

> now not basely die,
> Not cowardly put off my helmet to
> My countryman — a Roman by a Roman
> Valiantly vanquish'd. (4.15.55-58)

Cleopatra's own resolution to suicide follows the "high Roman fashion" (4.15.87) set by Antony. This choice of a noble death over the shameful life offered by Caesar's triumph is an important moral decision, and it indicates a final development of her character.

Suicide is not an issue in *Coriolanus*, and we have therefore only one passage of interest to this discussion. During the petition of the family group in V,iii, Volumnia intimates that she will commit suicide if her mission is unsuccessful:

APPENDIX

> For myself, son,
> I purpose not to wait on fortune till
> These wars determine. If I cannot persuade thee
> Rather to show a noble grace to both parts
> Than seek the end of one, thou shalt no sooner
> March to assault thy country than to tread
> (Trust to't, thou shalt not) on thy mother's womb
> That brought thee to this world. (5.3.118–25)

There is further evidence in other plays of Shakespeare for suicide as a characteristically Roman act. Horatio's immediate reaction to Hamlet's mortal wound, for example, is to wish to die with him: "I am more an antique Roman than a Dane./ Here's yet some liquor left" (5.2.352–53). But Hamlet prevents him. Macbeth, on the other hand, defies suicide although he is certain of defeat:

> Why should I play the Roman fool and die
> On mine own sword? Whiles I see lives, the gashes
> Do better upon them. (5.8.1–3)

In a similarly desperate situation Brutus acted in just the opposite manner, and his suicide was a sign of moral courage. Finally, the Jailer in *Cymbeline* makes a curious reference to the Roman readiness for suicide when speaking of Posthumus:

Unless a man would marry a gallows and beget young gibbets, I never saw one so prone. Yet, on my conscience, there are verier knaves desire to live, for all he be a Roman; and there be some of them too that die against their wills. So should I, if I were one. (5.4.206–11)

The Jailer's mother-wit rebels against the idea of self-willed death whether it be Roman or anything else.

There are many references to Roman suicide in Elizabethan literature; [10] Donne's *Biathanatos*, for example, is an elaborate theological discussion of the paradox that "Self-Homicide is not so Naturally Sinne that it may never be otherwise," and it includes many Roman examples. In Webster's play, *Appius and Virginia*, a clear distinction is made between the noble death of suicide and the ignoble desire to live after one has been disgraced. At the end of the play Virginius gives Appius and his accomplice, Clodius, two swords with which to execute judgment on themselves:

APPENDIX

If you be Romans, and retain their spirits,
Redeem a base life with a noble death,
And through your lust-burnt veins confine your breath.[11]

(5.2.120–22)

Roman suicide is offered to both as an honorable way to end their immoral lives, but only the patrician Appius is willing to do the deed, while the plebeian Clodius pleads for life. Icilius sees in their opposing attitudes the obvious

difference 'twixt a noble strain,
And one bred from the rabble: both alike
Dar'd to transgresse, but see their odds in death:
Appius dy'd like a Roman Gentleman,
And a man both wayes knowing; but this slave
Is only sensible of vitious living,
Not apprehensive of a noble death.   (5.2.171–77)

Suicide — "a noble death" — is used to make the same sort of moral distinction here as in *Antony and Cleopatra*, although the elements of the choice are more explicit and less complex in Webster than in Shakespeare. In the "Comparison" following the parallel lives of Antony and Demetrius, Plutarch makes a similar contrast between Antony's suicide "before his bodie came into his enemies hands," and the baseness of Demetrius' desire for life: "For he suffered him selfe to be taken prisoner, and when he was sent away to be kept in a straunge place, he had the hart to live yet three yeare longer, to serve his mouth and bellie, as brute beastes doe." [12]

From a Christian point of view, however, suicide is a sin against the Holy Spirit, for it violates the divine commandment, "Thou shalt not kill." In addition, it is often connected with the sin of despair, which, as in the case of Gloucester in *King Lear*, is the breeding-ground for self-murder. This view is obviously entirely different from the Roman. One way to explain the difference is to say that the Romans are pagans who cannot be held up to the standard of Christian beliefs. But Elizabethan theologians did hold them up to this standard and find them deeply wanting, whereas Shakespeare seems to have separated the Roman from the Christian attitude. As a representative statement of the theological position, Henry Bullinger says quite unequivocally in his *Decades* that it cannot be found in the canonical books of holy scripture, that God did either give leave or commandment to us mortal men to kill ourselves, thereby the sooner to obtain immortality, or to avoid imminent evil. For it must be understood that we are forbidden so to do by the law which saith, "Thou shalt not kill:" namely since he addeth not, "thy neighbour;" as he did in another precept, where he forbiddeth to bear false witness. (For because he nameth not thy neighbour, he doth in that precept include thyself also.) Therefore is the doctrine of Seneca to be utterly condemned, which counselleth men in misery to despatch themselves, that by death their misery may be ended.[13]

Bullinger goes on to support his argument with the authority of Saint Augustine. William Whitaker points to a similar division between the Christian and Roman attitudes, with condemnation of the latter, in his *A Disputation on Holy Scripture Against the Papists* (1588):

The Holy Spirit judges not of valour by the same measures as profane men, who extol Cato to the skies for committing suicide lest he should fall into the power and hands of Caesar: for he either feared, or could not bear to see him, or sought to catch renown by an act of such prodigious horror. Thus he was crushed and extinguished either by despair, or grief, or some other perturbation of mind; any of which motives are foreign from true fortitude. Rightly, therefore, did Augustine deny those books [of Maccabees] to be canonical, in which such a crime is narrated with some commendation by the authors.[14]

Whitaker finds nothing noble in Cato's suicide, and he uses the praise afforded the suicides of Eleasar (I Maccabees 6) and Razis (II Maccabees 14) as sufficient evidence to deny the books of Maccabees a place in the canon: the superficial fortitude of these suicides is foreign to true Christian fortitude.

This doctrine is most clearly echoed in the drama in Massinger's *The Maid of Honour*; at the end of IV,iii Adorni soliloquizes:

> This Roman resolution of selfe-murther,
> Will not hold water, at the high Tribunall,
> When it comes to be argu'd; my good Genius
> Prompts me to this consideration. He
> That kills himselfe, to avoid misery, fears it,
> And at the best shewes but a bastard valour,
> This lifes a fort committed to my trust,
> Which I must not yeeld up, till it be forc'd,
> Nor will I: Hee's not valiant that dares dye
> But he that boldly beares calamitie.[15]

2 I 3

But Shakespeare suspends the workings of the "high Tribunall" for Roman suicides. Outside the Roman plays, however, he appears very explicitly aware of the Christian attitude, as in *Hamlet* 1.2.129–32, *Cymbeline* 3.4.78–90, and *The Rape of Lucrece*, lines 1156–57, 1174–76 (although compare the Roman character of lines 1184–90). Despite this awareness it would be unjust to say categorically that those who commit suicide in Shakespeare's plays are damned. The dramatic context in *Othello*, for example, demands a much more considered response. Like Antony and Demetrius, and Appius and Clodius, Othello is "great of heart" (5.2.361) in his death, while Iago is sullen and obdurate in his desire to live. Shakespeare is definitely not a theologian, and he does not abandon the complexity of his moral attitudes even for his suicides; but in the Roman plays suicide is expected as a proof of virtue.

Aside from the special attitude to suicide in these plays, Shakespeare does not attempt to create a "pagan" setting for them; his aim seems rather to evoke a certain sense of remoteness and difference.[16] The most significant "pagan" detail is the repeated use of "gods" in the plural, a simple and obvious way of calling attention to Roman polytheism. There are twenty-two instances of "gods" in *Julius Caesar*, thirty-six in *Antony and Cleopatra*, and forty-five in *Coriolanus*. In the English history plays, however, we do not find a single reference to "gods," except the remark by the Duke of Norfolk at the beginning of *Henry VIII*:

> To-day the French,
> All clinquant, all in gold, like heathen gods,
> Shone down the English. . . . (1.1.18–20)

The "heathen gods" are obviously quite different from the Christian God who presides over the course of English history. There is another interesting use of these words in *Hamlet*, which has "god" throughout except in the Player's speech about Priam's slaughter (2.2.515, 535, 541). "Gods" here serves to make the transition to Greek antiquity and thereby mark off this "pagan" section from the remainder of the play. "Gods" in the plural also helps to keep us aware of a non-Christian atmosphere in *King Lear*, *Troilus and Cressida*, *Timon of Athens*, *Cymbeline*, *Pericles*, and *The Winter's Tale*. *Titus Andronicus* is the only play in which "god" and "gods" are used inconsistently.

Finally, the most important unifying element in the Roman plays is their common source in Sir Thomas North's translation of Plutarch: *The Lives of The Noble Grecians and Romanes* (1579).[17] Shakespeare seems to have relied very largely on North's Plutarch for his knowledge of Roman history, although there were many intermediate sources available to him, such as translations of classical works, Elizabethan histories of Rome, epitomes of world history, articles in general compendia of learning, and a large number of examples from Roman history in all sorts of other books, especially moral and political treatises.[18] The fact that all three plays are drawn from North's Plutarch acts as a strong factor in their homogeneity, for Shakespeare borrowed quite extensively and literally from this work — the group could as easily be called the "Plutarchan" as the "Roman" plays. Plutarch's popularity in the Elizabethan period is attested by the four folio editions of *The Lives* (1579, 1595, 1603, 1612) as well as by the many laudatory references to him.[19] His *Moralia*, however, in Philemon Holland's translation, was probably even more popular than *The Lives*.[20]

Shakespeare does not use Plutarch so scrupulously as he does Holinshed in regard to actual events, yet he treats both as history, not fiction.[21] This is an important distinction, for the historical pattern of character and events is part of the audience's common, unalterable knowledge: Shakespeare could probably assume that his public would be familiar with the chief events of Roman history, especially those centering about the murder of Julius Caesar and the establishment of the Empire under Augustus. Before the play begins we know that the exiled Coriolanus must threaten destruction to Rome, Brutus die on his own sword, and Antony return to Egypt. These are some of the limits that history imposes on the dramatist, whereas in using a fictional source he need have no such responsibility to the facts of character and event. A good example of the use of history in the Roman plays is the role of Pompey in *Antony and Cleopatra*. We need to know that this is Sextus Pompeius, the son of Pompey the Great. We also need to know that Caesar's defeat of Pompey the Great at Pharsalia was an important step in his rise to power. Further, *Julius Caesar* begins with Caesar's return in triumph from his victory over Pompey's sons in Spain, and there are references to Caesar's former rivalry with Pompey throughout the play. This background is necessary for understanding why Sextus Pompeius in *Antony and Cleopatra* should be continuing the cause of the conspirators against Caesar's avengers; he has his own vengeance to execute for his father. Without some preliminary knowledge, one must find the role of Pompey in *Antony and Cleopatra* confusing. Perhaps it suffers from what Granville-Barker calls the "heroic compression" [22] of Roman politics in this play. If so, the wars of Fulvia and Lucius in Italy are compressed even more heroically. But these are the actual events of Roman history, and, as such, cannot be overlooked.

Our understanding of the historical aspect of Shakespeare's Roman plays may be hindered by our modern desire for history to be an accurate and exact account of the past. Our sense of rightness is jolted by the anachronism of striking clocks in ancient Rome (*Julius Caesar* 2.1.191 s.d.), or by Cleopatra's desire to have her lace cut (1.3.71) or to play billiards (2.5.3). In this respect our attitude may be like Ben Jonson's, who was disturbed by Shakespeare's "Shipwrack in Bohemia, wher ther is no Sea neer by some 100 Miles." We may even be inclined to agree with Jonson "That Shaksperr wanted Arte. . . ." [23] Jonson's *Sejanus* and *Catiline* offer a notable contrast to Shakespeare's Roman plays in the exactness of historical detail. Jonson carefully avoided the factual errors of Shakespeare, but his scrupulousness was perhaps seen as pedantry by some of his contemporaries, as Leonard Digges seems to say in his commendatory verses to Shakespeare's *Poems* (1640):

> So have I seene, when Cesar would appeare,
> And on the Stage at halfe-sword parley were,
> *Brutus* and *Cassius*: oh how the Audience,
> Were ravish'd, with what wonder they went thence,
> When some new day they would not brooke a line,
> Of tedious (though well laboured) *Catilines*;
> *Sejanus* too was irksome. . . . [24]

It almost looks as if Jonson's historical sense, so unusual for his time, hampered his dramatic effectiveness. Shakespeare's anachronisms, after all, would not seem very striking to an audience, but what would make an impression on them would be the re-creation of the Roman past in vividly dramatic terms. In this imaginative presentation of history Shakespeare enjoyed a remarkable success;

APPENDIX

F. P. Wilson puts the matter very well when he says that Shakespeare's

> tact in translating the manners of the ancient world to the modern
> stage is superb. He concentrates on what is permanent in spiritual and
> human values, and if clocks strike and doublets go unbraced, there is
> no offence, for he never sacrifices the dignity of his theme by introduc-
> ing the trivialities of the present or the pedantries of the past.[25]

Roman history was perhaps most important to an Elizabethan audience in its application to the present; they would undoubtedly have seen Shakespeare's Roman plays in terms of an elaborate network of analogies and parallels. We may remember that Ben Jonson was called before the Privy Council for his *Sejanus*, and, as he told Drummond, "accused both of poperie and treason. . . ." [26] This affair suggests that the political ideas in Roman plays were of lively contemporary interest. On this basis we may see some common ground between Shakespeare's English and Roman history plays, for both offer a sort of case-book of illustrations for Elizabethan political theory.[27] This is particularly true of *Julius Caesar* and *Richard II*. One may, in fact, draw a direct comparison between Antony's soliloquy, "Woe to the hand that shed this costly blood!" (*Julius Caesar* 3.1.258ff), and the Bishop of Carlisle's speech, "My Lord of Hereford here, whom you call king . . ." (*Richard II* 4.1.134ff). The prophecy in both speeches is a sinister one: peace can be restored only through bloody civil conflict. There is also a sense in which *Julius Caesar* is one of those "sad stories of the death of kings" that Richard speaks about, with Brutus as an example of the usurpers "haunted by the ghosts they have depos'd" (*Richard II* 3.2.156, 158).

The importance of political ideas in the Roman plays extends into the dramatic action, for each of these plays presents a tragic conflict between the individual and the state, or what Palmer has called "the contrast of the natural man with the public figure." [28] The protagonists — Brutus, Antony, and Coriolanus — are all men of real integrity and worth, but their failure in political action brings on their tragedy. The essence of the tragedy lies in the grinding and pull of public and private motives, choices, and abilities. Brutus, for example, chooses what he conceives to be the good of

Rome over his personal attachment to Caesar, but the course of the action proves him tragically wrong. It is interesting to note that every political decision he makes turns out badly (to spare Antony, to let him speak a funeral oration for Caesar, to fight at Philippi). Not Brutus but Cassius and Antony are the true "political" figures in this play in the sense of their being able to act decisively in public life. But in *Antony and Cleopatra*, Antony sacrifices his public Roman role of "triple pillar of the world" (1.1.12) for Cleopatra and Egypt. It is a significant comment on his defeat at Actium that he asks Caesar "To let him breathe between the heavens and earth,/ A private man in Athens" (3.13.14–15). The political person in this play is clearly Octavius. *Coriolanus* is so thoroughly political that it may be difficult to find any concern for the private man in the play, but I think it lies in Coriolanus' insistence on his own integrity: he cannot dissemble the truth of his nature even if it involves the loss of the consulship and exile from Rome. The political characters in this play are, on one side, Menenius, Cominius, and the Roman Senators, and, on the other, the Tribunes and Aufidius. These political aspects of Shakespeare's Roman plays show how deeply the plays are rooted in the public affairs of Roman history, which, by analogy, could suggest some powerful and perhaps alarming parallels with the politics of Elizabethan England.

NOTES

All references to Shakespeare are to George Lyman Kittredge's *The Complete Works of Shakespeare*, Boston, 1936. Kittredge's single-volume editions have been used for *Julius Caesar* (1939) and *Antony and Cleopatra* (1941). Departures from Kittredge's text are indicated in the footnotes. All references to the First Folio (1623) are to the facsimile edition prepared by Helge Kökeritz (New Haven, 1954), which is indicated simply as "the Folio." "Elizabethan" is used throughout in its literary history sense to cover both the reigns of Elizabeth and James (1558–1625), and "Cambridge" means Cambridge, England. The following short titles replace the full titles of frequently cited works:

Chambers, *Elizabethan Stage*: E. K. Chambers, *The Elizabethan Stage*, 4 vols., Oxford, 1923.

Chambers, *William Shakespeare*: E. K. Chambers, *William Shakespeare: A Study of Facts and Problems*, 2 vols., Oxford, 1930.

Clemen, *Shakespeare's Imagery*: W. H. Clemen, *The Development of Shakespeare's Imagery*, London, 1951.

Granville-Barker, *Prefaces*: Harley Granville-Barker, *Prefaces to Shakespeare*, 2 vols., Princeton, 1946–47.

Knight, *Imperial Theme*: G. Wilson Knight, *The Imperial Theme*, London, 1931.

MacCallum, *Shakespeare's Roman Plays*: M. W. MacCallum, *Shakespeare's Roman Plays and their Background*, London, 1910.

North's Plutarch, Leo reprint: *Four Chapters of North's Plutarch: Containing the Lives of Caius Marcius Coriolanus, Julius Caesar, Marcus Antonius and Marcus Brutus . . .* , photolithographed in the size of the original edition of 1595, ed. F. A. Leo, London, 1878.

Spurgeon, *Shakespeare's Imagery*: Caroline F. E. Spurgeon, *Shakespeare's Imagery and What it Tells Us*, N. Y., 1935.

Variorum Antony and Cleopatra: William Shakespeare, *The Tragedie of Anthonie, and Cleopatra*, ed. Horace Howard Furness, Philadelphia, 1907, a New Variorum edition, Vol. XV.

NOTES TO CHAPTER I

Variorum Coriolanus: William Shakespeare, *The Tragedie of Coriolanus*, ed. Horace Howard Furness, Jr., Philadelphia, 1928, a New Variorum edition, Vol. XX.

Variorum Julius Caesar: William Shakespeare, *The Tragedie of Ivlivs Caesar*, ed. Horace Howard Furness, Jr., Philadelphia, 1913, a New Variorum edition, Vol. XVII.

I. INTRODUCTION

THE FUNCTION OF IMAGERY IN THE DRAMA

1. *The Portable Charles Lamb*, ed. John Mason Brown, N. Y., 1949, pp. 573-74.

2. Norman Holmes Pearson, *"Antony and Cleopatra,"* in *Shakespeare: Of an Age and for All Time*, ed. Charles Tyler Prouty, Hamden, Conn., 1954, p. 128.

3. B. L. Joseph, *Elizabethan Acting*, London, 1951, p. 153. See the objections to Joseph in Marvin Rosenberg, "Elizabethan Actors: Men or Marionettes?" *PMLA*, LXIX (1954), 915-27. In all fairness to Joseph, however, the first chapter of his recent book, *The Tragic Actor* (London, 1959), does try to answer Rosenberg and to develop a theory of creative Elizabethan acting: "In this creative acting, the individual elements of technique which are described in the rhetoric books became transmuted into an embodiment of what those lines are as poetry and character, in terms of the actor's personality, imagination, voice and gesture. It is in this sense that it is valid to say that in the Elizabethan theatre the poet's words were all that counted: they counted in the sense that they were what the player's action embodied" (p. 22).

Although Joseph claims that he was misunderstood in his earlier work, it seems to me that his emphasis here is quite different from what it was in *Elizabethan Acting*. The ever-present analogy with opera is gone, there is a new importance given to the embodiment of character, and the references to Bulwer's very specific rhetorical gestures are omitted. My objection to Joseph's position, therefore, does not apply to his later work.

4. Joseph, *Elizabethan Acting*, p. 60.

5. Quoted from Francis Fergusson, *The Idea of a Theater*, Princeton, 1949, p. 166.

6. Tennessee Williams, "Foreword" to *Camino Real*, Norfolk, Conn., New Directions, 1953, pp. x-xi.

7. R. A. Foakes, "Suggestions for a New Approach to Shake-

speare's Imagery," *Shakespeare Survey* 5, Cambridge, 1952, pp. 85–86.

8. Alan S. Downer, "The Life of Our Design: The Function of Imagery in the Poetic Drama," *Hudson Review*, II (1949), 252. See also W. Moelwyn Merchant, *Shakespeare and the Artist*, London, 1959, chap. i.

9. See Norman Friedman, "Imagery: From Sensation to Symbol," *Journal of Aesthetics and Art Criticism*, XII (1953), 25–37. This article has an extensive bibliography.

10. The use of this word follows Susanne K. Langer, *Philosophy in a New Key*, Cambridge, Mass., 1942, chap. iv: "Discursive and Presentational Forms."

11. Chambers, *Elizabethan Stage*, I, 343. See also I, 342–47; II, 272–92.

12. See Fergusson, *Idea of a Theater*, pp. 236–40.

II. STYLE IN THE ROMAN PLAYS

1. When Caesar goes to the Capitol, however, he changes from gown to robe (2.2.107) to indicate his public role in visual terms. See L. C. Knights, "Shakespeare and Political Wisdom: A Note on the Personalism of *Julius Caesar* and *Coriolanus*," *SR*, LXI (1953), 44 and n. 1.

2. *Julius Caesar* (2,450 lines) has a vocabulary of 2,218 words, while *The Comedy of Errors* (1,753 lines) has 2,037, and *The Two Gentlemen of Verona* (2,193 lines) has 2,153. See Alfred Hart, "Vocabularies of Shakespeare's Plays," *RES*, XIX (1943), 132 (Table I) and 135.

3. See Chambers, *William Shakespeare*, I, 397, 423–24.

4. Hart, "Vocabularies of Shakespeare's Plays," 135.

5. Henry W. Wells, *Poetic Imagery: Illustrated from Elizabethan Literature*, N. Y., 1924, p. 219.

6. Spurgeon, *Shakespeare's Imagery*, Appendix II, pp. 361–62. *Julius Caesar* has 83 images for 2,450 lines of text, while *Antony and Cleopatra* has 266 images for 3,016 lines of text.

7. It is on this basis that one may take issue with the statement of R. A. Foakes: "The imagery of words and action points to the imaginative and dramatic unity of the play as consisting in the completion of the circle of events beginning and ending the rebellion" ("An Approach to *Julius Caesar*," *SQ*, V [1954], 270). The play is clearly an "imaginative and dramatic unity," but this is difficult to demonstrate through its imagery.

8. A. C. Bradley, *Shakespearean Tragedy*, 2 ed., London, 1905, pp. 85–86.

9. *Ibid.*, p. 85, n. 1.

10. J. A. K. Thomson, *Shakespeare and the Classics*, London, 1953, p. 193.

11. Another example of this kind of analogy is Brutus' argument for immediate battle at Philippi: "There is a tide in the affairs of men . . ." (4.3.218ff). The far-fetched "conceits" in the play, such as 3.2.181–86 and 5.1.32–40, also illustrate the analogy form.

12. North's Plutarch, Leo reprint, p. 1002.

13. George Puttenham, *The Arte of English Poesie*, ed. Gladys Doidge Willcock and Alice Walker, Cambridge, 1936, p. 191.

14. *Ibid.*, p. 154. Compare Harry Levin's comment on Marlowe's dramatic use of hyperbole: "The stage becomes a vehicle for hyperbole, not merely by accrediting the incredible or supporting rhetoric with a platform and sounding board, but by taking metaphors literally and acting concepts out. Operating visually as well as vocally, it converts symbols into properties; triumph must ride across in a chariot, hell must flare up in fire works; students, no longer satisfied to read about Helen of Troy, must behold her in her habit as she lived. Whereas poetry is said to transport us to an imaginative level, poetic drama transports that level to us; hyperbolically speaking, it brings the mountain to Mohammed" (*The Overreacher: A Study of Christopher Marlowe*, Cambridge, Mass., 1952, p. 24).

15. *Coleridge's Shakespearean Criticism*, ed. Thomas Middleton Raysor, London, 1930, I, 86.

16. John Marston, Preface to *The Scourge of Villanie* (1599), ed. G. B. Harrison, London, 1925, p. 9. See I. A. Richards' comment on "intrinsicate" in *The Philosophy of Rhetoric*, N. Y., 1936, pp. 64–65.

17. See John Middleton Murry, *Shakespeare*, N. Y., 1936, p. 298. Another example, very obvious and powerful, of this double effect is in Macbeth's harrowing consciousness of guilt:
"Will all great Neptune's ocean wash this blood
Clean from my hand? No. This my hand will rather
The multitudinous seas incarnadine,
Making the green one red." (2.2.60–63)
The simple "green" and "red" restate "multitudinous seas" and "incarnadine" and act as a relief to these learned words. See John

STYLE IN THE ROMAN PLAYS

Crowe Ransom, "On Shakespeare's Language," *SR*, LV (1947), 181–98.
18. See George Rylands, "Shakespeare's Poetic Energy," *Proc. Brit. Acad. 1951*, XXXVII, 101.
19. Peter G. Phialas notes in his New Yale Shakespeare edition (New Haven, 1955, pp. 142–43) that the phrase "infinite varietie" occurs in Florio's Montaigne (Modern Library edition, 1933, p. 108).
20. Helge Kökeritz discusses the possibility of this pun, but regards it as "dubious." It is possible in colloquial speech, but not in the polite speech that Shakespeare uses (*Shakespeare's Pronunciation*, New Haven, 1953, p. 88). E. J. Dobson agrees that "the use of the raised sound was a vulgarism," but notes that it "might occasionally make its way into the speech of higher classes . . ." (*English Pronunciation 1500–1700*, Oxford, 1957, II, 640). Dobson also indicates that "queen" and "quean" appear as homophones on a number of contemporary lists.

Whether or not this pun was actually intended on the Elizabethan stage, it seems to be implied when Antony says, "I must from this enchanting queen break off" (1.2.132), and it is also an innuendo in the exchange between Pompey and Enobarbus in II,vi:
"*Pom.* And I have heard Apollodorus carried —
Eno. No more of that! He did so.
Pom.   What, I pray you?
Eno. A certain queen to Caesar in a mattress." (2.6.69–71)
We can perhaps see an instance here of covert puns setting off meanings already present in our minds. Thomas Heywood very obviously plays on "queen" and "quean" in the card-game of *A Woman Kilde with Kindnesse* (probably performed in 1603 — see Chambers, *Elizabethan Stage*, III, 342):
"*Wend.* I am a Knaue.
Nicke. Ile sweare it.
Anne. I a Queene.
Fr. A quean thou shouldst say: wel the cards are mine,
They are the grosest paire that ere I felt."
(See *The Dramatic Works of Thomas Heywood*, London, J. Pearson, 1874, II, 123.)
21. *Coleridge's Shakespearean Criticism*, I, 86. Compare the "moral realism" of L. C. Knights, "On the Tragedy of Antony and Cleopatra," *Scrutiny*, XVI (1949), 318–23, and D. A. Traversi, *An Approach to Shakespeare*, 2 ed., Garden City, N. Y., 1956, pp. 235–61.

22. *Coleridge's Shakespearean Criticism*, I, 86.

23. Chambers, *William Shakespeare*, I, 479–80. Chambers thinks *Coriolanus* may have been produced early in 1608. The dating of *Antony and Cleopatra* before 1608 partly depends upon the assumption that Daniel made changes in his new edition of *The Tragedie of Cleopatra* in 1607 after he had seen or read Shakespeare's play (see Chambers, I, 477–78). This assumption has been challenged by Ernest Schanzer, who finds evidence that Daniel influenced Shakespeare in some small verbal details. Schanzer would therefore date *Antony and Cleopatra* after the spring of 1608 ("Daniel's Revision of His *Cleopatra*," *RES*, N. S., VIII [1957], 380 and n. 1). The arguments are summarized in Kenneth Muir, *Shakespeare's Sources*, London, 1957, and in Arthur M. Z. Norman, " 'The Tragedie of Cleopatra' and the Date of 'Antony and Cleopatra,' " *MLR*, LIV (1959), 1–9. Norman dates Shakespeare's *Antony and Cleopatra* in 1606–1607.

24. See Traversi, *An Approach to Shakespeare*, pp. 216–34.

25. A. C. Bradley, "Coriolanus," *Proc. Brit. Acad. 1911–1912*, V, 459.

26. D. J. Enright, "*Coriolanus*: Tragedy or Debate?" *Essays in Criticism*, IV (1954), 16–17.

27. See Clemen, *Shakespeare's Imagery*, p. 5. This is one of Clemen's theses about Shakespeare's development.

28. Kittredge, following Tyrwhitt, emends the Folio "Ouerture" to "coverture." Thiselton clarifies the Folio text by regarding "him" as the dative instead of the objective case. Coriolanus would then be making a scornful overture to the parasite to fight in the wars. When the soldier's steel becomes as soft as the parasite's silk, it is time for the parasite to go to the wars and for the soldier to stay at home (*Variorum Coriolanus*, pp. 145–58, esp. p. 157).

29. See Paul A. Jorgensen, *Shakespeare's Military World*, Berkeley, Calif., 1956, chap. v.

30. *Ibid.*, chap. vi.

31. *Johnson on Shakespeare*, ed. Walter Raleigh, London, 1908, p. 179.

32. Morris Le Roy Arnold, *The Soliloquies of Shakespeare*, N. Y., 1911, p. 25. Arnold counts fourteen soliloquies of 291 lines in *Hamlet*.

33. This is the punctuation of the Folio, which Kittredge changes to "*Trumpets, hautboys; drums beat; all together.*" See Granville-Barker, *Prefaces*, II, 270.

34. T. S. Eliot, "Hamlet," in *Selected Essays 1917–1932*, N. Y., 1932, p. 124. See also Eliot's unfinished *Coriolan*, which is based on Shakespeare's play (*The Complete Poems and Plays 1909–1950*, N. Y., 1952, pp. 85–89).

III. THE IMAGERY OF *Julius Caesar*

1. See Chambers, *William Shakespeare*, I, 397, 423–24.
2. See Wolfgang Clemen, *Shakespeares Bilder*, Bonn, 1936, chap. iv. This excellent chapter is omitted from the English translation of 1951.
3. John Earle Uhler, "*Julius Caesar* — a Morality of Respublica," in *Studies in Shakespeare*, ed. Arthur D. Matthews and Clark M. Emery, Coral Gables, Fla., 1953, pp. 96–106.
4. Many allusions to Caesar, Brutus, and the Roman civil wars are collected and discussed in Harry Morgan Ayres, "Shakespeare's *Julius Caesar* in the Light of Some Other Versions," *PMLA*, XXV (1910), 183–227; W. Warde Fowler, "The Tragic Element in Shakespeare's *Julius Caesar*," in *Roman Essays and Interpretations*, Oxford, 1920, pp. 268–87; J. M. Robertson, "The Origination of 'Julius Caesar,'" in *The Shakespeare Canon*, London, 1922, Part I, pp. 66–154; Edward H. Sugden, *A Topographical Dictionary*, Manchester, 1925; James Emerson Phillips, Jr., *The State in Shakespeare's Greek and Roman Plays*, N. Y., 1940; F. S. Boas, "Aspects of Classical Legend and History in Shakespeare," *Proc. Brit. Acad.* 1943, XXIX, 107–32; Alice S. Venezky, *Pageantry on the Shakespearean Stage*, N. Y., 1951, pp. 36–37; D. S. Brewer, "Brutus' Crime: A Footnote to *Julius Caesar*," *RES*, N. S., III (1952), 51–54; Virgil K. Whitaker, *Shakespeare's Use of Learning*, San Marino, Calif., 1953, chap. x; Irving Ribner, "Political Issues in *Julius Caesar*," *JEGP*, LVI (1957), 10–22; T. J. B. Spencer, "Shakespeare and the Elizabethan Romans," *Shakespeare Survey 10*, Cambridge, 1957, 27–38; and J. Leeds Barroll, "Shakespeare and Roman History," *MLR*, LIII (1958), 327–43. For references distinctly favorable to Brutus see the Introduction to John Dover Wilson's New Cambridge edition of *Julius Caesar* (Cambridge, 1949) and S. F. Johnson's long review of T. S. Dorsch's New Arden edition in *SQ*, VIII (1957), 393–94.
5. *Julius Caesar*, ed. S. F. Johnson, Pelican edition, Baltimore, 1960, p. 15.
6. Harold S. Wilson, *On the Design of Shakespearian Tragedy*, Toronto, 1957, p. 87.

NOTES TO CHAPTER III

7. Ernest Schanzer, "The Problem of *Julius Caesar*," *SQ*, VI (1955), 297–308.

8. Both these passages are quoted from W. J. Lawrence, *Pre-Restoration Stage Studies*, Cambridge, Mass., 1927, p. 209.

9. *Ibid.*, p. 263. Lawrence presents his evidence more fully in *The Elizabethan Playhouse and Other Studies*, Second Series, Stratford-upon-Avon, 1913, pp. 17–19. The epilogue to Lovelace's lost play, *The Scholars* (published in 1649), also speaks of "The rosin-lightning flash . . . ," but "monster spire/ Squibs," indicating fireworks, follows immediately (quoted in G. F. Reynolds, *The Staging of Elizabethan Plays*, N. Y., 1940, p. 53). Both Reynolds (pp. 171–72) and Chambers (*Elizabethan Stage*, III, 76, n. 7) give a number of examples of lightning which suggest that fireworks were used. See also C. Walter Hodges, *The Globe Restored*, N. Y., 1954, p. 31.

10. "Calculate" in this context means "prophesy," which was originally done by astrological or mathematical methods. There are several proverbial parallels to this line about the prophesying of fools and children: see T. S. Dorsch's New Arden edition, London, 1955, p. 27, n. 65.

11. See Knight, *Imperial Theme*, pp. 45ff. See also Brents Stirling, " 'Or Else This Were a Savage Spectacle,' " *PMLA*, LXVI (1951), 765–74. This essay, which develops the ritual aspects of blood, is reprinted in somewhat revised form in *Unity in Shakespearian Tragedy*, N. Y., 1956, chap. iv.

12. North's Plutarch, Leo reprint, p. 1062.

13. This is the Folio reading, which there seems no need to emend. It is parallel to the "Let's" in lines 172 and 173. Kittredge reads "Let us."

14. See Lawrence, *Pre-Restoration Stage Studies*, pp. 236–41. See also Leo Kirschbaum, "Shakespeare's Stage Blood and Its Critical Significance," *PMLA*, LXIV (1949), 517–29.

15. See Warren Smith, "Evidence of Scaffolding on Shakespeare's Stage," *RES*, N. S., II (1951), 22–29.

16. Shakespeare's self-consciousness of his own art in these acting images is like Pirandello's; immortality is won in the theater rather than in writing sonnets or in begetting offspring. Compare *Antony and Cleopatra*, where Cleopatra is thinking of her reputation in Rome if she allows herself to be led in Caesar's triumph:

> "The quick comedians
> Extemporally will stage us and present

226

> Our Alexandrian revels. Antony
> Shall be brought drunken forth, and I shall see
> Some squeaking Cleopatra boy my greatness
> I' th' posture of a whore." (5.2.216–21)

The anachronisms of the Elizabethan theater are very obvious here, and the players serve literally as "the abstract and brief chronicles of the time" (*Hamlet* 2.2.547–48).

17. This interpretation was suggested by Capell, who says that "lethe" is a "Term us'd by hunters to signify the blood shed by a deer at its fall, with which it is still a custom to mark those who come in at the death" (*Variorum Julius Caesar*, p. 155). This meaning of "lethe" is not recorded in the OED, but it is approved by Ernest Schanzer in "The Tragedy of Shakespeare's Brutus," *ELH*, XXII (1955), 7, and by Johnson in his Pelican edition, p. 79.

18. North's Plutarch, Leo reprint, p. 1062.

19. "Honour" words are used so frequently by Brutus or in reference to him that they become almost an identifying tag for his character. This is noted by Knight in *Imperial Theme*, pp. 71ff. Of the forty-nine examples of these words, forty-one relate to Brutus, and of the additional eight, there is only one (4.1.19) that is not in any way connected with him. The mass of "honour" words for Brutus seems to exclude these words for others and thus to insist on honor as a tangible aspect of his style of life. The association persists into *Antony and Cleopatra*, where Pompey calls Brutus "the all-honour'd honest Roman . . ." (2.6.16). For the similarity to *1 Henry IV* see Wilson, *On the Design of Shakespearian Tragedy*, p. 241, n. 4.

20. See Schanzer, "The Tragedy of Shakespeare's Brutus," 12–13, and Elias Schwartz, "On the Quarrel Scene in *Julius Caesar*," *CE*, XIX (1958), 168–70.

21. This is the Folio reading, and "fight" makes an assonance with "fiery." The tenses are mixed in this passage — line 23 reads "Horses do neigh" — and most modern editors, including Kittredge, make them consistently past.

22. L. C. Knights, "Shakespeare's Politics: With Some Reflections on the Nature of Tradition," *Proc. Brit. Acad. 1957*, XLIII, 118.

23. Georg Brandes in *Variorum Julius Caesar*, pp. 394–95.

24. Levin L. Schücking, *Character Problems in Shakespeare's Plays*, N. Y., 1922, p. 44. The literal-mindedness of Schücking

NOTES TO CHAPTER III

is justly criticized in J. I. M. Stewart, " 'Julius Caesar' and 'Macbeth'. Two Notes on Shakespearean Technique," *MLR*, XL (1945), 166–73. In German critical studies the glorification of Shakespeare's Caesar runs parallel to the development of Nazism, as we may see in Lorenz Morsbach, *Shakespeares Cäsarbild*, Halle, 1935, and Walter Spiegelberger, "Shakespeares Cäsarbild," *Neuphilologische Monatsschrift*, X (1939), 177–89.

25. Edward Dowden, *Shakspere: A Critical Study of his Mind and Art*, London, 1875, p. 285. The double aspect of Caesar is very interestingly discussed by Knight in *Imperial Theme*, pp. 64ff, and by L. C. Knights in "Shakespeare and Political Wisdom: A Note on the Personalism of *Julius Caesar* and *Coriolanus*," *SR*, LXI (1953), 43–55.

26. Granville-Barker, *Prefaces*, II, 383. See also the comments on names in R. A. Foakes, "An Approach to *Julius Caesar*," *SQ*, V (1954), 264ff.

27. MacCallum, *Shakespeare's Roman Plays*, p. 223.

28. This is the Folio punctuation; Kittredge reads, " 'Tis very like. He hath the falling sickness." S. F. Johnson suggests that the Folio punctuation develops a hint from Plutarch that Caesar's epileptic fit was a piece of acting designed to recapture the sympathy of the mob.

29. See *Variorum Julius Caesar*, p. 47.

30. See the Caesar examples given by Willard Farnham in *The Medieval Heritage of Elizabethan Tragedy*, Berkeley, Calif., 1936, pp. 82, 134, 238, 295, 378, 379. The "Life of Caesar" was one of John Higgins' additions to the 1587 edition of the *Mirror for Magistrates* (in *Parts Added to The Mirror for Magistrates*, ed. Lily B. Campbell, Cambridge, 1946, pp. 290–302). Caesar here speaks of his murder as a just retribution for pride:

"Ere three & twenty wounds had made my hart to quake,
What thousands fell for *Pompeys* pride and mine?"   (p. 302)

31. In the life of Antony we are told: "Thus *Antonius* had the chiefest glory of all this victory, specially because *Caesar* was sicke at that time" (North's Plutarch, Leo reprint, p. 978). This sickness is also mentioned in the life of Brutus (p. 1070). We are informed further that Octavius had himself carried out of his camp to avoid the battle because of the bad dream of one of his friends (p. 1072).

32. MacCallum points out that Shakespeare has transposed this incident from Brutus and Cassius in Plutarch (*Shakespeare's Roman Plays*, p. 298). Plutarch reads: "Then *Brutus* praied *Cassius* he

228

might haue the leading of the right wing, the which men thought was farre meeter for *Cassius*: both because he was the elder man, and also for that he had the better experience. But yet *Cassius* gaue it him . . ." (North's Plutarch, Leo reprint, p. 1072). Shakespeare seems to be deliberately developing Octavius.

IV. THE IMAGERY OF *Antony and Cleopatra*

1. As Robert Kilburn Root observes, classical mythology "suddenly reasserts itself with surprising vigor" in *Antony and Cleopatra*, whose 39 allusions rank third among Shakespeare's plays (*Classical Mythology in Shakespeare*, N. Y., 1903, p. 130). *Troilus and Cressida* is first (56) and *Titus Andronicus* second (53). The large number of allusions in *Antony and Cleopatra* is not simply a matter of its classical subject, since *Coriolanus* has only 26 and *Julius Caesar* 5. A quite unclassical play such as *Love's Labour's Lost* has 38.

2. See Spurgeon, *Shakespeare's Imagery*, pp. 350ff.

3. George R. Kernodle, "The Open Stage: Elizabethan or Existentialist?" *Shakespeare Survey* 12, Cambridge, 1959, p. 4. See also Kernodle's much more extensive treatment of this theme in *From Art to Theatre*, Chicago, 1944.

4. C. Walter Hodges, *The Globe Restored*, N. Y., 1954, p. 44. The contract is reprinted in Appendix F.

5. The phrase is Richard Southern's, who discusses the bearing of the Elizabethan stage on our modern practice in *The Open Stage*, London, 1953.

6. "World" is Hanmer's emendation for the Folio "would." The line reads: "Then would thou hadst a paire of chaps no more. . . ."

7. The name is given as "Thidias" in the Folio. Most editors, including Kittredge, follow Theobald in changing this to "Thyreus" on the authority of North's Plutarch (see *Variorum Antony and Cleopatra*, p. 232). "Thidias" is approved by Granville-Barker (*Prefaces*, I, 389, n. 16) and adopted by J. Dover Wilson in his New Cambridge edition (Cambridge, 1950).

8. Paul Stapfer in *Variorum Antony and Cleopatra*, p. 506.

9. See J. Leeds Barroll, "Shakespeare and Roman History," MLR, LIII (1958), 327–43, and James Emerson Phillips, Jr., *The State in Shakespeare's Greek and Roman Plays*, N. Y., 1940, pp. 198ff.

10. Harold S. Wilson, *On the Design of Shakespearian Tragedy*, Toronto, 1957, p. 161.

11. When Mardian reports Cleopatra's supposed death to Antony, he has her die in the middle of a word:

"Then in the midst a tearing groan did break
The name of Antony; it was divided
Between her heart and lips." (4.14.31–33)

Mardian is obviously wording it "piteously" (4.13.9) according to his mistress' instructions, but he goes beyond these to make his one great occasion in the play memorable. Hotspur also dies in the middle of a sentence (*1 Henry IV* 5.4.86), which is completed by Prince Hal. These deaths are ridiculed in Sheridan's *The Critic* (see the note in M. R. Ridley's New Arden edition of *Antony and Cleopatra*, London, 1954, p. 187).

12. Kittredge retains the Folio reading "wilde," but Capell's emendation, "vile," seems more appropriate in context; it is part of the devaluation-of-the-world theme. If "wild" is correct, it is the only occurrence of "wild world" in Shakespeare, whereas "vile world" appears in both *2 Henry VI* 5.2.40 and Sonnet LXXI, and the two words are closely associated in *The Merry Wives of Windsor* 3.4.32. We should also note "Vile earth" in *Romeo and Juliet* 3.2.59 and "vilest earth" in *1 Henry IV* 5.4.91. In addition, "vile" is twice used for Cleopatra (2.2.243–44 and 4.14.22). There is further support for "vile" in the common Elizabethan confusion between "wilde" and "vilde" (a form of "vile") — see *Variorum Antony and Cleopatra*, pp. 369–70. In many Elizabethan hands it is very easy to confuse "v" with "w."

13. See John F. Danby, "The Shakespearean Dialectic: An Aspect of 'Antony & Cleopatra,' " *Scrutiny*, XVI (1949), 196–213, and S. L. Bethell, *Shakespeare & The Popular Dramatic Tradition*, London, 1944, pp. 116–31.

14. It is interesting to note that Henry James, in *The Ambassadors*, conceives his European heroine, Madame de Vionnet, in the image of Cleopatra: "Her head, extremely fair and exquisitely festal, was like a happy fancy, a notion of the antique, on an old precious medal, some silver coin of the Renaissance; while her slim lightness and brightness, her gaiety, her expression, her decision, contributed to an effect that might have been felt by a poet as half mythological and half conventional. He could have compared her to a goddess still partly engaged in a morning cloud, or to a sea-nymph waist-high in the summer surge. Above all she suggested to him the reflection that the *femme du monde* — in these finest developments of the type — was, like Cleopatra in the

play, indeed various and multifold. She had aspects, characters, days, nights — or had them at least, showed them by a mysterious law of her own, when in addition to everything she happened also to be a woman of genius. She was an obscure person, a muffled person one day, and a showy person, an uncovered person the next" (New York edition, 1909, I, 270–71).

15. So notable a scholar of the Elizabethan stage as E. K. Chambers seems to be burdened with a modern idea of "place" and "locality," as in the following passage: "Quite a late play, *Antony and Cleopatra*, might almost be regarded as a challenge to classicists. Rome, Misenum, Athens, Actium, Syria, Egypt are the localities, with much further subdivision in the Egyptian scenes. The second act has four changes of locality, the third no less than eight, and it is noteworthy that these changes are often for quite short bits of dialogue, which no modern manager would regard as justifying a resetting of the stage. Shakespeare must surely have been in some danger, in this case, of outrunning the apprehension of his auditory . . ." (*Elizabethan Stage*, III, 124).

These arguments are answered by Granville-Barker in his essay on the play and, more specifically, in his article, "A Note upon Chapters XX. and XXI. of *The Elizabethan Stage*," *RES*, I (1925), esp. 66–68. See also Arthur Sewell, "Place and Time in Shakespeare's Plays," *SP*, XLII (1945), 205–25, and Southern, *The Open Stage*, chap. iv: "Stage Scenery and 'Placelessness.' "

16. Chambers notes some of Henslowe's expenses for apparel, which ran as high as £19 for "a rich cloak bought of Langley" (*Elizabethan Stage*, II, 185; see also 184, 228). The sumptuous dress of the players often drew contemporary comment and criticism. Thomas Platter wrote of his visit to England in 1599: "The comedians are most expensively and elegantly apparelled" (*ibid.*, II, 365). But an anonymous Puritan communication to Sir Francis Walsingham in 1587 complained: "Yt is a wofull sight to see two hundred proude players jett in their silkes, wheare five hundred pore people sterve in the streets" (*ibid.*, IV, 304; see also 199). A good idea of the impressiveness and variety of Elizabethan stage costume may be gained from Reynolds' list of costume directions in the Red Bull plays (*The Staging of Elizabethan Plays*, N. Y., 1940, pp. 173–75). See also M. Channing Linthicum, *Costume in the Drama of Shakespeare and his Contemporaries*, Oxford, 1936.

17. Robert Ralston Cawley, *The Voyagers and Elizabethan Drama*, Boston, 1938, p. 19.

18. See Edward H. Sugden, *A Topographical Dictionary*, Manchester, 1925, pp. 166–69 ("Egypt"); Cawley, *The Voyagers and Elizabethan Drama*, "Book One: The South" (esp. pp. 7–66); Edgar I. Fripp, *Shakespeare: Man and Artist*, London, 1938, II, 678–80; and Danby, "The Shakespearean Dialectic."

19. Sugden, *Topographical Dictionary*, p. 169.

20. See J. Dover Wilson's edition, p. 176.

21. Clemen, *Shakespeare's Imagery*, p. 161.

22. Compare a matrimonial theme in Cleopatra's "Husband, I come!/ Now to that name my courage prove my title!" (5.2.290–91). Her "courage" in following Antony's Roman example of suicide will prove her title to be called his wife, not his whore or mistress. She had earlier referred scornfully to Fulvia as "the married woman" (1.3.20).

23. There is a similar use of food imagery in *Troilus and Cressida* and *Hamlet*. See Spurgeon, *Shakespeare's Imagery*, pp. 320ff and Chart VII.

24. J. Leeds Barroll, "Antony and Pleasure," *JEGP*, LVII (1958), 708–20.

25. This is the Folio reading. Kittredge, following later Folios, reads "browsed'st," which is grammatically more correct, but also more unpronounceable.

26. The Folio spelling, "Spleet's," suggests a more dramatically appropriate form of the word.

27. See Franklin M. Dickey, *Not Wisely But Too Well*, San Marino, Calif., 1957, p. 180.

28. This is the Folio reading, which makes quite good sense and good meter without the "me" usually added after "Unarm" (Kittredge follows Rowe in reading "Unarm me").

29. North's Plutarch, Leo reprint, p. 979.

30. Dickey, *Not Wisely But Too Well*, p. 175. See also Daniel Stempel, "The Transmigration of the Crocodile," *SQ*, VII (1956), 59–72, and Barroll, "Antony and Pleasure."

31. Dickey, *Not Wisely But Too Well*, pp. 158–59.

32. Knight, *Imperial Theme*, p. 264.

33. *Ibid.*, p. 297.

34. Levin L. Schücking, *Character Problems in Shakespeare's Plays*, N. Y., 1922, pp. 119–44. There has been strong objection to Schücking's thesis; see, for example, E. E. Stoll, "Cleopatra," *MLR*, XXIII (1928), 145–63; Leo Kirschbaum, "Shakspere's Cleopatra," *SAB*, XIX (1944), 161–71; and J. I. M. Stewart, "Profes-

sor Schücking's Fatal Cleopatra," in *Character and Motive in Shakespeare*, London, 1949, pp. 59–78.

35. See F. R. Leavis, " 'Antony and Cleopatra' and 'All for Love,' " *Scrutiny*, V (1936), 158–69.

36. John Dryden, "Preface" to *Troilus and Cressida*, in *Works*, ed. Sir Walter Scott, rev. George Saintsbury, Edinburgh, 1883, VI, 255. This play was published in 1679, one year after *All for Love*.

37. See Benjamin T. Spencer, "*Antony and Cleopatra* and the Paradoxical Metaphor," *SQ*, IX (1958), 373–78. See also L. C. Knights, "On the Tragedy of Antony and Cleopatra," *Scrutiny*, XVI (1949), 322, n. 3.

38. This is the word Knights uses in the article cited above, p. 322. There is a similar interpretation of the play in D. A. Traversi, *An Approach to Shakespeare*, 2 ed., Garden City, N. Y., 1956, pp. 235–61.

39. Dickey, *Not Wisely But Too Well*, p. 187.

40. Suggested by Ridley, New Arden edition, p. 257.

41. This is the Folio reading, which Kittredge changes to "Where is."

42. This statement is on the authority of Bartlett's *Concordance*. The word is an interesting example of a small but crucial change from Plutarch, who reads: "and her [Cleopatra's] other woman called *Charmion* halfe dead, and trembling, trimming the Diademe which Cleopatra ware vpon her head" (North's Plutarch, Leo reprint, p. 1008). Pope uses "tremblingly" in "An Essay on Man" (which appeared in 1733–34, eight years after his edition of Shakespeare): "Or touch, if tremblingly alive all o'er/ To smart and agonize at ev'ry pore?" (Twickenham edition, ed. Maynard Mack, London, 1950, pp. 39–40).

43. Geoffrey Bush, *Shakespeare and the Natural Condition*, Cambridge, Mass., 1956, p. 130.

44. As Ridley points out in his New Arden edition, the Folio has "Decretas" six times and "Dercetus" only once (pp. 203–04). The latter is a variant of Plutarch's "Dercetaeus." Kittredge gives the name as "Dercetas."

45. See *Variorum Antony and Cleopatra*, p. 131. For the similarity with Book V of the *Faerie Queene* see Dickey, *Not Wisely But Too Well*, p. 157; see also Sidney's *Defense of Poesy*, ed. Albert S. Cook, Boston, 1898, p. 51. Compare Strindberg's powerful use of Omphale in *The Father*. The identification between

Antony and Hercules is developed in some detail in Plutarch (for example, Leo reprint, p. 970).

46. North's Plutarch, The Tudor Translations, ed. W. E. Henley, London, 1896, VI, 91.

47. According to the Folio, Cleopatra enters (1.2.82), and then Enobarbus makes his deliberately ironic comment. Kittredge shifts Cleopatra's entrance to the end of this line (1.2.83), making Enobarbus' remark a casual oversight. See Elkin Calhoun Wilson, "Shakespeare's Enobarbus," in *Joseph Quincy Adams Memorial Studies*, ed. James G. McManaway *et al.*, Washington, 1948, p. 392, n. 3.

48. See Paul A. Jorgensen, "Vertical Patterns in *Richard II*," *SAB*, XXIII (1948), 119–34, and Arthur Suzman, "Imagery and Symbolism in *Richard II*," *SQ*, VII (1956), 355–70.

49. North's Plutarch, Leo reprint, p. 1004.

50. Both Reynolds (*The Staging of Elizabethan Plays*, p. 105) and Lawrence (*The Physical Conditions of the Elizabethan Public Playhouse*, Cambridge, Mass., 1927, p. 76, n. 2, and p. 77) mention twelve feet as the height of the upper stage, and both give examples of actors' jumping from there to the main stage. See also Richard Hosley, "Shakespeare's Use of a Gallery over the Stage," *Shakespeare Survey 10*, Cambridge, 1957, pp. 86–87, n. 10.

But Granville-Barker thinks the twelve-foot height "impracticable," and that "8 or 9 foot from upper to lower stage is drop enough for boy or man, and height enough for scaling ladders that can be carried quickly through doors, height enough too for the hoisting of the dying Antony and the like." He would explain this lower height by the fact that the main stage may well have been three feet above the ground level of the lowest gallery (in review of Lawrence, *Physical Conditions*, and *Pre-Restoration Stage Studies*, in *RES*, IV [1928], 232).

51. See Hodges, *The Globe Restored*, pp. 58–61, with sketch of the suggested staging on p. 59. See also A. M. Nagler, *Shakespeare's Stage*, tr. Ralph Manheim, New Haven, 1958, pp. 61–62. Hodges' theory would seem to be supported by the discovery of a drawing from van de Venne's *Tafereel* (1635), which shows a projecting inner stage like a player's booth at a fair (see Richard Southern, "A 17th-Century Indoor Stage," *Theatre Notebook*, IX [1954], 5–11). J. Dover Wilson has also proposed a property monument, "a square painted wooden structure, with a barred gate in front . . . and a flat roof" (New Cambridge edition, p.

230). But his insistence that this be erected by servitors at the end of IV, xiv has been strongly attacked by Ridley as impracticable in a theater (New Arden edition, p. 247). The "mansion" staging of Leslie Hotson also has some resemblances to these theories ("Shakespeare's Arena," SR, LXI [1953], 347–61).

For other suggestions on the staging of this scene see John Cranford Adams, The Globe Playhouse, Cambridge, Mass., 1942, pp. 346–49, and Irwin Smith, Shakespeare's Globe Playhouse, N. Y., 1956, pp. 150–51 — both of these studies offer similar proposals; Bernard Jenkin, "Antony and Cleopatra: Some Suggestions on the Monument Scenes," RES, XXI (1945), 1–14; Warren Smith, "Evidence of Scaffolding on Shakespeare's Stage," RES, N. S., II (1951), 27–29; Joan Rees, "An Elizabethan Eyewitness of Antony and Cleopatra?" Shakespeare Survey 6, Cambridge, 1953, pp. 91–93; and J. W. Saunders, "Vaulting the Rails," Shakespeare Survey 7, Cambridge, 1954, pp. 72–74.

52. North's Plutarch, Leo reprint, p. 1004.

53. Compare the awesome effect of the Ghost of Hamlet's Father, who "cries under the stage" (1.5.148 s.d.). Hamlet begins with the abrupt, anxious talk of the changing of the guard that resembles the conversation of the soldiers in Antony and Cleopatra IV,iii (see Cumberland Clark, Shakespeare and the Supernatural, London, 1931, p. 150). Macbeth, too, makes portentous use of "hautboys," which play as the Witches' cauldron sinks (4.1.106 s.d.).

54. This is an emendation suggested by Thirlby for the Folio "discandering."

V. THE IMAGERY OF Coriolanus

1. Oscar James Campbell, Shakespeare's Satire, N. Y., 1943, pp. 200 and 208.

2. See Willard Farnham, Shakespeare's Tragic Frontier, Berkeley, Calif., 1950, chap. v. Coriolanus offers one of the best examples for Farnham's thesis, while Antony and Cleopatra seems somewhat constrained by it. See also D. J. Enright, "Coriolanus: Tragedy or Debate?" Essays in Criticism, IV (1954), 1–19.

3. Plutarch speaks of the rebellion against "the sore oppression of vsurers" as if it were justified (Leo reprint, p. 237). The later corn insurrection, however, was stirred up by the flatterers of the people "without any new occasion, or iust matter offered of complaint" (p. 241). Shakespeare completely recasts the sequence and import of these events in Plutarch.

4. See Sidney Shanker, "Some Clues for *Coriolanus*," *SAB*, XXIV (1949), 209–13; Brents Stirling, *The Populace in Shakespeare*, N. Y., 1949, pp. 42, 126, 127; and E. C. Pettet, "*Coriolanus* and the Midlands Insurrection of 1607," *Shakespeare Survey* 3, Cambridge, 1950, pp. 34–42.

5. See Frederick Tupper, Jr., "The Shaksperean Mob," *PMLA*, XXVII (1912), 486–523; Frederick T. Wood, "Shakespeare and the Plebs," *Essays and Studies by Members of the English Association*, XVIII (1932), 53–73; and Stirling, *The Populace in Shakespeare*.

6. See James Emerson Phillips, Jr., *The State in Shakespeare's Greek and Roman Plays*, N. Y., 1940, chap. viii and pp. 6–10. See also the analogues noted by Kenneth Muir in "Menenius's Fable," *Notes and Queries*, CXCVIII (1953), 240–42.

7. "Awe" is a favorite word of Hobbes for the attitude the sovereign authority in his state should inspire in his subjects, as in the following passage: "men have no pleasure, but on the contrary, a great deal of grief, in keeping company, where there is no power able to over-awe them all" (*Leviathan*, ed. Michael Oakeshott, Oxford, 1946, p. 81); or in the passage where he speaks of war as "necessarily consequent . . . to the natural passions of men, when there is no visible power to keep them in awe . . ." (p. 109).

To pursue this doctrine further: R. W. Chambers sees a similarity in point of view between *Coriolanus* and the 147 lines of *Sir Thomas More* that seem to be in Shakespeare's hand, especially the passage describing the anarchy of rebellion: "men lyke rauenous fishes/ Woold feed on on another" ("The Expression of Ideas — Particularly Political Ideas — in the Three Pages, and in Shakespeare," in *Shakespeare's Hand in the Play of Sir Thomas More*, Cambridge, 1923, pp. 142–87). But this animal image was also a commonplace at the time — see the examples given in F. P. Wilson, "Shakespeare's Reading," *Shakespeare Survey* 3, Cambridge, 1950, pp. 19–20.

8. Kittredge's "beesom multitude" follows an emendation first proposed as "bisson multitude" by Collier. The Folio reading makes good sense if interpreted metaphorically. A. E. Brae notes that the image behind this passage is that of the body politic, which the belly-members fable has established as a "prevailing metaphor." "Digest" completes the metaphor of food and eating in "bosom-multiplied" as well as the metaphor of "nourish'd" and "fed" above (3.1.117 — see *Variorum Coriolanus*, pp. 300–04, esp. p. 301).

9. The Folio reads "boyld," which Kittredge, following Pope, changes to "broil'd" for the sake of consistency with "carbonado." But these two speeches need have no logical connection.

10. See Kenneth Muir, "The Background of *Coriolanus*," *SQ*, X (1959), 141–44.

11. See Spurgeon, *Shakespeare's Imagery*, pp. 316ff (*Hamlet*), p. 320 (*Troilus and Cressida*), and Chart VII. After *Hamlet*, *Coriolanus* has the largest number of disease images in Shakespeare. See also Knight, *Imperial Theme*, pp. 176ff.

12. L. C. Knights, "Shakespeare and Political Wisdom: A Note on the Personalism of *Julius Caesar* and *Coriolanus*," *SR*, LXI (1953), 52.

13. See J. C. Maxwell, "Animal Imagery in 'Coriolanus,' " *MLR*, XLII (1947), 417–21. This study is a model of how a detail of imagery can illuminate the general character of a play. See also Knight, *Imperial Theme*, pp. 163ff. Audrey Yoder finds 105 animal references in *Coriolanus* (*Animal Analogy in Shakespeare's Character Portrayal*, N. Y., 1947, p. 65).

14. See Leonard F. Dean, "Voice and Deed in *Coriolanus*," *UKCR*, XXI (1955), 177–84.

15. See E. M. W. Tillyard, *The Elizabethan World Picture*, N. Y., n. d., Modern Library Paperbacks, p. 35.

16. See Granville-Barker, "Othello," *Prefaces*, II, 104ff. See also E. K. Chambers, "William Shakespeare: An Epilogue," in *Shakespearean Gleanings*, London, 1944, pp. 41–51, and Dean, "Voice and Deed in *Coriolanus*."

17. Quoted in Bertram Joseph, *The Tragic Actor*, London, 1959, p. 5.

18. This is the Folio reading, which makes a clear distinction between the gesture and the speaking part. Kittredge, following Hanmer, omits "or."

19. *Coriolanus*, ed. Harry Levin, Pelican edition, Baltimore, 1956, p. 24.

20. North's Plutarch, Leo reprint, p. 243.

21. See J. L. Styan, "The Actor at the Foot of Shakespeare's Platform," *Shakespeare Survey* 12, Cambridge, 1959, pp. 56–63.

22. MacCallum notes a significant change from Plutarch here, who says that Marcius "entred the cittie with very fewe men to helpe him . . ." (*Shakespeare's Roman Plays*, p. 572).

23. Reynolds says of Heywood's *II Iron Age* that "the gate to the

city seems one of the side doors" (*The Staging of Elizabethan Plays*, N. Y., 1940, p. 129). See also Richard Hosley, "The Gallery over the Stage in the Public Playhouses of Shakespeare's Time," *SQ*, VIII (1957), 18. For gates as removable properties on the Elizabethan stage, see Chambers, *Elizabethan Stage*, III, 83; Granville-Barker, *Prefaces*, II, 194, n. 13; Irwin Smith, " 'Gates' on Shakespeare's Stage," *SQ*, VII (1956), 159–76; and A. M. Nagler, *Shakespeare's Stage*, tr. Ralph Manheim, New Haven, 1958, pp. 63–64. Lawrence has an overly ingenious theory that the gates were permanently set in the rear stage with a door in them for ordinary business (*The Physical Conditions of the Elizabethan Public Playhouse*, Cambridge, Mass., 1927, p. 61).

24. The fact that Coriolanus appears on stage "mask'd" in Volscian blood is an important visual sign of his victory at Corioles. This bloody appearance is made particular point of in I,vi, where Marcius "does appear as he were flay'd" (22), but he is "mantled" (29) in the blood of the enemy, not his own. At the end of the scene Marcius uses this blood to appeal for fighters who "love this painting/ Wherein you see me smear'd . . ." (68–69). This is the same blood that Marcius "will go wash" (1.9.67) and of which Cominius says: "The blood upon your visage dries; 'tis time/ It should be look'd to" (1.9.92–93). And in his speech before the Senate Cominius says of Marcius: "From face to foot/ He was a thing of blood . . ." (2.2.112–13). Compare the use of blood imagery in *Julius Caesar*.

25. D. A. Traversi, *An Approach to Shakespeare*, 2 ed., Garden City, N. Y., 1956, pp. 226–27.

26. Granville-Barker suggests that Coriolanus' Roman dress calls attention to his being an alien among the Volscians: "quitting the 'mean apparel' in which he went to encounter Aufidius, he would reappear as a Roman general, the dramatic effect being worth more than any logic" (*Prefaces*, II, 155, n. 3). The suggestion cannot be demonstrated, but it makes for a good stage effect, and "the graphic discord vivifies the play's ending" (p. 155).

27. The Folio reading is "Wooluish tongue," which Kittredge, following Steevens, emends to "wolvish toge." It is not hard to see how "togue" and "tongue" could be confused by a compositor working from a manuscript, since the letter "n" was often represented in Elizabethan script by a mark placed over the "o." In *Othello*, for example, Iago's "toged consuls" (1.1.25), the reading of the First Quarto and the one adopted by most modern editors, appears

as "tongued consuls" in the Folios and in the later Quartos (see *Variorum Coriolanus*, pp. 256–64).

28. See Morris Palmer Tilley, *A Dictionary of the Proverbs in England in the Sixteenth and Seventeenth Centuries*, Ann Arbor, Mich., 1950, numbers W 614 and S 300; also D 146; L 339; S 301, 303, 306; W 602, 604, 612, 619.

29. To try to reconstruct these "missing" steps, as Bradley does ("Coriolanus," *Proc. Brit. Acad. 1911–1912*, V, 466), seems to me to misconstrue the art of the theater. MacCallum follows Bradley here (*Shakespeare's Roman Plays*, pp. 611–16).

30. See C. Walter Hodges, *The Globe Restored*, N. Y., 1954, p. 82.

31. See F. N. Lees, "*Coriolanus*, Aristotle, and Bacon," *RES*, N. S., I (1950), 117. This quotation is the epigraph to Delmore Schwartz's verse commentary on *Coriolanus*: "Coriolanus and His Mother: The Dream of One Performance" (in *In Dreams Begin Responsibilities*, Norfolk, Conn., New Directions, 1938).

32. At the beginning of his life of Coriolanus, Plutarch stresses the fact that "orphanage bringeth many discommodities to a childe . . ." (Leo reprint, p. 235). Many of Coriolanus' characteristic defects arise from his having been raised by his mother alone. The place of the missing father is to some extent filled by Menenius, although he is perhaps more avuncular than fatherly. In V,ii, however, the paternal theme is very specifically developed in Menenius' appeal: "The glorious gods sit in hourly synod about thy particular prosperity and love thee no worse than thy old father Menenius does! O my son, my son! Thou art preparing fire for us. Look thee, here's water to quench it" (73–77).

33. But Volumnia through most of the play seems to reject the maternal role in a manner similar to Lady Macbeth. She tells her son, "Thy valiantness was mine, thou suck'st it from me" (3.2.129), and in I,iii she is scornful of Virgilia's tenderness for her husband, who has just gone off to war:

> "Away, you fool! It [blood] more becomes a man
> Than gilt his trophy. The breasts of Hecuba
> When she did suckle Hector, look'd not lovelier
> Than Hector's forehead when it spit forth blood
> At Grecian sword." (1.3.42–46)

(In the last line I follow the Folio reading: "At Grecian sword. *Contenning*, tell Valeria. . . ." As Miss C. Porter points out, "*Contenning*" may be a slightly misprinted name for a servant

[*Variorum Coriolanus*, p. 92]. This name seems to refer to the Gentlewoman who exits at 1.3.47 and returns with Valeria three lines further. Kittredge reads: "At Grecian sword, contemning. Tell Valeria. . . .")

34. Kittredge, following Collier, adds an apparently unnecessary "He" at the beginning of this stage direction.

35. There are perhaps two additional examples of "physical contact" in the play: Coriolanus seems to embrace Cominius at 1.6.30, and Aufidius seems to embrace Coriolanus at 4.5.115.

VI. CONCLUDING REMARKS

1. See E. M. W. Tillyard, *The Elizabethan World Picture*, N. Y., n. d., Modern Library Paperbacks, and Theodore Spencer, *Shakespeare and the Nature of Man*, 2 ed., N. Y., 1949, chaps. i and ii. The basis for both of these works was laid by Arthur O. Lovejoy, *The Great Chain of Being*, Cambridge, Mass., 1936. Recently, Geoffrey Bush has questioned the orthodox version of the Elizabethan idea of order in *Shakespeare and the Natural Condition*, Cambridge, Mass., 1956.

2. Chambers, *William Shakespeare*, I, 353.

3. See James Emerson Phillips, Jr., *The State in Shakespeare's Greek and Roman Plays*, N. Y., 1940, esp. chap. iv: "The Significance of Analogical Argument."

4. Sir John Eliot, *De Jure Maiestatis or Political Treatise of Government* (1628–30), ed. Alexander B. Grosart, [London], 1882, I, 174–75.

5. Cleanth Brooks, "Shakespeare as a Symbolist Poet," *Yale Review*, XXXIV (1945), 642.

6. L. C. Knights, "How Many Children had Lady Macbeth?" in *Explorations*, London, 1946, p. 16.

7. Una Ellis-Fermor, "Some Recent Research in Shakespeare's Imagery," London, The Shakespeare Association, 1937, pp. 12–13.

8. Spurgeon, *Shakespeare's Imagery*, p. 205.

9. For one example among many see K. Wentersdorf, "The Authenticity of *The Taming of the Shrew*," SQ, V (1954), 11–32. Moody E. Prior raises strong objections to this study in "Imagery as a Test of Authorship," SQ, VI (1955), 381–86.

10. Spurgeon, *Shakespeare's Imagery*, p. 102.

11. *Ibid.*, p. 207.

12. George F. Reynolds, "*Troilus and Cressida* on the Eliza-

bethan Stage," in *Joseph Quincy Adams Memorial Studies*, ed. James G. McManaway *et al.*, Washington, 1948, p. 229.

APPENDIX

THE ROMAN PLAYS AS A GROUP

1. We should be wary of the relative ease with which we can find verbal parallels in the three plays; these in themselves do not constitute an argument for a Roman group. Consider, for example, the following seven parallels between *Antony and Cleopatra* and *Coriolanus* (given in abridged form):

Antony and Cleopatra	*Coriolanus*
a. "From my cold heart let heaven engender hail" (3.13.159)	a. "hailstone in the sun" (1.1.178)
b. "half to half the world" (3.13.9)	b. "half to half the world" (1.1.237)
c. "The sevenfold shield of Ajax cannot keep/ The battery from my heart" (4.14.38–39)	c. "shields before your hearts" (1.4.24)
d. "very heart of loss" (4.12.29)	d. "very heart of hope" (1.6.55)
e. "Phoebus' amorous pinches" (1.5.28)	e. "Phoebus' burning kisses" (2.1.234)
f. "palates" (5.2.7)	f. "palates" (3.1.104)

These two, with "palating" in *Troilus and Cressida* 4.1.59, are the only uses of this word as a verb in Shakespeare.

g. "unparallel'd" (5.2.319) g. "unparallel'd" (5.2.16)

The only other example of this word in Shakespeare is in *The Winter's Tale* 5.1.16.

Many additional verbal parallels between these two plays are pointed out in the notes to the Arden edition of *Coriolanus*, ed. W. J. Craig and R. H. Case, London, 1922.

2. T. J. B. Spencer makes a strong argument for *Titus Andronicus* as a more typical Roman history play than those based on North's Plutarch ("Shakespeare and the Elizabethan Romans," *Shakespeare Survey 10*, Cambridge, 1957, p. 32).

3. The drawing is reproduced with the text that accompanies it in *Shakespeare Survey 1*, Cambridge, 1948, facing p. 32. It may also be found (without the text) in Chambers, *William Shakespeare*,

I, facing p. 312, and in C. Walter Hodges, *The Globe Restored*, N. Y., 1954, p. 151.

4. J. Dover Wilson, " 'Titus Andronicus' on the Stage in 1595," *Shakespeare Survey 1*, Cambridge, 1948, p. 21.

5. Granville-Barker, *Prefaces*, I, 408; see also II, 407–09. This conception of Roman costume has been fairly influential in modern productions: see W. M. Merchant, "Classical Costume in Shakespearian Productions," *Shakespeare Survey 10*, Cambridge, 1957, p. 75.

6. Pointed out by M. St. Clare Byrne in *A Companion to Shakespeare Studies*, ed. H. Granville-Barker and G. B. Harrison, N. Y., 1934, p. 194, n. 1. I have consulted the copy of Holinshed in the Berg Collection, New York Public Library.

7. See Hodges, *The Globe Restored*, Plate 42, p. 152; see also Plates 26 and 41.

8. Merchant, "Classical Costume in Shakespearian Productions," p. 71.

9. See James Holly Hanford, "Suicide in the Plays of Shakespeare," *PMLA*, XXVII (1912), 280–97, and Theodore Spencer, *Death and Elizabethan Tragedy*, Cambridge, Mass., 1936, pp. 158–79.

10. See Edward H. Sugden, *A Topographical Dictionary*, Manchester, 1925, pp. 436–37, for an interesting collection of quotations about Roman suicide from the Elizabethan drama.

11. *The Complete Works of John Webster*, ed. F. L. Lucas, London, 1927, III, 222.

12. North's Plutarch, "The Comparison of Demetrius with Antonius," The Tudor Translations, ed. W. E. Henley, London, 1896, VI, 93.

13. Henry Bullinger, *The Decades*, tr. "H. I." (1577), ed. Thomas Harding, The Parker Society, Cambridge, 1850, II, 414–15.

14. William Whitaker, *A Disputation on Holy Scripture Against the Papists* (1588), tr. and ed. William Fitzgerald, The Parker Society, Cambridge, 1849, p. 95.

15. Massinger, *The Maid of Honour*, ed. Eva A. W. Bryne, London, 1927, p. 59.

16. See Introduction to Harold S. Wilson, *On the Design of Shakespearian Tragedy*, Toronto, 1957.

17. Shakespeare could have used either the 1579 edition of North's Plutarch or the one printed in 1595; the 1603 edition is unlikely since *Julius Caesar* had already been written. See Robert

Adgar Law, "The Text of 'Shakespeare's Plutarch,'" *HLQ*, VI (1943), 197–203.

18. See the full discussion of these sources in J. Leeds Barroll, "Shakespeare and Roman History," *MLR*, LIII (1958), 327–43. See also Louis B. Wright, *Middle-Class Culture in Elizabethan England*, Chapel Hill, N. C., 1935, pp. 322–23 (and n. 40), and p. 336; and Martha Hale Shackford, *Plutarch in Renaissance England*, Wellesley, Mass., 1929, esp. chap. iv.

19. See Shackford, *Plutarch in Renaissance England*.

20. See Spencer, "Shakespeare and the Elizabethan Romans," p. 33.

21. See MacCallum, *Shakespeare's Roman Plays*, esp. chap. ii: "Shakespeare's Treatment of History." A. C. Bradley, too, makes an important point of the Roman plays as "tragic histories or historical tragedies" (*Shakespearean Tragedy*, 2 ed., London, 1905, p. 3) rather than pure tragedies such as *Hamlet, Othello, Macbeth*, and *King Lear*. But Bradley goes much too far in stressing "the intractable nature of the historical material" (p. 53), as if this were the source of most of the defects in these plays (see pp. 3–4, 53, 71–72, 85, 260).

22. Granville-Barker, *Prefaces*, I, 377.

23. From Jonson's *Conversations with William Drummond*, quoted in Chambers, *William Shakespeare*, II, 207. There is an interesting conversation reprinted by Chambers from Rowe's "Life of Shakespeare" (1709), in which Ben Jonson is reported as "frequently reproaching him [Shakespeare] with the want of Learning, and Ignorance of the Antients . . ." (p. 211).

24. Quoted in Chambers, *William Shakespeare*, II, 233.

25. F. P. Wilson, "Shakespeare and the Diction of Common Life," *Proc. Brit. Acad. 1941*, XXVII, 189.

26. Quoted in Chambers, *Elizabethan Stage*, III, 367.

27. See Sir Mark Hunter, "Politics and Character in Shakespeare's 'Julius Caesar,'" *Transactions of the Royal Society of Literature*, N. S., X (1931), 109–11, and James Emerson Phillips, Jr., *The State in Shakespeare's Greek and Roman Plays*, N. Y., 1940.

28. John Palmer, *Political Characters of Shakespeare*, London, 1945, p. 39. See also L. C. Knights, "Shakespeare and Political Wisdom: A Note on the Personalism of *Julius Caesar* and *Coriolanus*," *SR*, LXI (1953), 43–55, and "Shakespeare's Politics: With Some Reflections on the Nature of Tradition," *Proc. Brit. Acad. 1957*, XLIII, 115–32.

INDEX

INDEX